SEARCHING FOR
NOVAK

SEARCHING FOR
NOVAK

THE MAN BEHIND
THE ENIGMA

MARK HODGKINSON

First published in Great Britain in 2024 by Cassell,
an imprint of Octopus Publishing Group Ltd
Carmelite House
50 Victoria Embankment
London EC4Y 0DZ
www.octopusbooks.co.uk

An Hachette UK Company
www.hachette.co.uk

ISBN: 978-1-78840-516-4

A CIP catalogue record for this book is available from the British Library.

Printed and bound in Canada.

1 3 5 7 9 10 8 6 4 2

MIX
Paper | Supporting
responsible forestry
FSC
www.fsc.org
FSC® C016245

In memory of Mum.

CONTENTS

INTRODUCTION

It's not subtle, but no one ever booked a table at the Novak Restaurant expecting – or wanting – subtle. In an endless, glorious loop of tennis nostalgia – Novak-stalgia, if you must – wall-mounted televisions with the sound turned down low forever replay old matches, including his best bits from down the years. Novak Djokovic has, of course, recommended that you don't watch TV while eating as that can expose your food to bad emotions, but he has made an exception for his own restaurant in Belgrade: there are only good vibes here.

Walking in, you pass the Djokovic water feature and, at the top of the stairs, you're welcomed first by an outsize, terracotta warrior-style statue of the tennis player – impassive and somehow also knowing and unflappable – and then, secondly, by the maître d'. Much here is on a mega scale – because why not? – with gigantic glass cabinets showcasing some of Djokovic's trophies. On the way to your table, you're drawn to a framed motivational quote – 'Make it Happen' – surrounded by lit candles, giving those words the look of a piece of religious scripture. There's also what appears to be a metal, three-dimensional sculpture of his logo. Almost every bit of wall space that isn't taken up with televisions is filled with photographs of Djokovic hitting tennis balls and hoisting trophies.

A pillar is filled with hundreds of old tennis balls, perhaps even ones he once hit – almost as if all the toil and sweat from the practice court is propping this restaurant up. There's even a bright, almost psychedelic piece of artwork of Djokovic as a small child swinging a racquet, a reminder of how this all began. Just in case you haven't realized it yet, you're lost in Novak Djokovic's world (where gluten-free options are available).

If you've just landed in Belgrade and you're searching for Djokovic – if you're looking for a greater understanding of who he is and how he thinks – the Novak Restaurant is about as good a place as any to start. Fresh off the plane, you're psychoanalysing a menu decorated with tennis balls. What does success taste like? That's the question this restaurant is trying to answer. But, sitting here, eating your mushroom risotto, your tomato side salad and your Novak Tart and surrounded by the still and moving images of the player, you do start to wonder: who is getting into whose head here? It's hard to think of another restaurant anywhere in the world that celebrates a public figure in this full-spectrum, multi-media way; harder still to bring to mind a restaurant like this which is owned by the star athlete and their family. None of this is meant to sound snide or snarky. It's a fun, joyous space, the food's good, and if you're ever in Belgrade, you should go. The Novak Restaurant's also – in a good way – quite overwhelming. It's much more – so much more – than you had possibly imagined. But that's also true of almost every element of Djokovic's story.

Djokovic is the most successful tennis player in history. He's the GOAT, the Greatest of All Time. That's interesting in itself. Even more compelling is the way he has achieved that greatness: the bombs and the hardships in his backstory and his more recent experiences in a Melbourne 'prison', plus all the other psychological struggles that come with trying to win big. Plus, Djokovic is the most curious, unconventional and progressive of tennis players. Yes, Djokovic can slide and do the splits with more flexibility and panache than anyone else in tennis. There's also no more accomplished returner of serve, thanks, in part to the Beatles' back catalogue (more on that later). And yet the most fascinating thing about him isn't how he moves or how he strikes the ball, but how he thinks. He has the most original mind in tennis, perhaps across all sports.

Maybe you already love Djokovic. You're part of the #NoleFam. Or you're not, but you're intrigued by him all the same. Whatever your starting point, if you want to truly appreciate and understand modern tennis – and all its psychodrama – you're going to need to poke around in Djokovic's head. Searching for Novak means journeying, as deep as you can, inside his psyche.

GOLDEN CHILD

Going deep inside Novak Djokovic's basement bomb shelter – into the space where he spent many nights during the NATO bombings in 1999 – is to feel as though you're dipping yourself in Yugoslav concrete. Low concrete ceilings. Concrete walls, blotted with damp, that seem as though they're crowding in on you. Concrete floors. The air – and there isn't too much of that down here – even smells faintly of concrete. People talk about the Belgrade greyscape, and about the concrete overload in some parts of the city. But nothing quite prepares you for the greyness and the starkness of this bunker beneath a Brutalist apartment block in the Banjica neighbourhood, a few miles south of downtown Belgrade.

It's not just the concrete, all cold, rough and unforgiving, that unsettles you. It's imagining how Djokovic and others would have felt inside this bunker; there's a sense that this is somehow still a place of fear and confusion and gathering rage, almost as if the concrete all around you absorbed some of those emotions and now it's radiating them back at you.

For Djokovic, who was 11 years old when NATO planes started pounding Serbia, this is where he felt fear and horror, where he was 'disturbed emotionally', not knowing what the next moment would bring for him, his two younger brothers Marko and Djordje and his parents Srdjan and Dijana. This was the safest spot around, originally built as an atomic shelter in case of nuclear war. To get into the heart of the bunker, you must pass through a metal door the colour of freshly oxygenated blood, head down concrete steps and then open up two steel doors, the heftiest of which must be 30cm (12in) thick, like something you might imagine in a bank vault or a submarine. Residents would close and seal those doors behind them, spinning the giant locks, to protect themselves from any explosions or fires.

But even inside here, supposedly bomb-proof and fire-proof, they understood that nowhere could be completely safe, that even an atomic bunker couldn't save you from a direct hit. In the near-darkness, Djokovic would stare at his mother's face to understand how he should be feeling – if she looked scared, and she mostly did, then he knew he should be terrified too.

Hidden away, immortalized in concrete, the basement is still pretty much as it was in the 1990s, as close as you're going to get to a time capsule taking you back to when Djokovic was a scared, confused child, amid so many other frightened and disorientated children, and adults too. Back to when he would listen to the low-flying jets, which sounded as though they were ripping holes in the Belgrade night sky, and then to the devastating, endless thunder of the bombs and the rockets (while muffled by the concrete, that didn't reduce the fear that the bunker's inhabitants felt during those long, terrible nights).

On some level, and maybe you have to physically be here too to fully make sense of this, stepping inside this bunker almost feels as though you're also going inside and reaching some part of Djokovic's mind. It's a series of small rooms and darkened corners and, as you walk around and kung-fu the cobwebs, you appreciate that this isn't somewhere that Djokovic's old neighbours, and any new residents, like to revisit too often. Just a handful of times, Djokovic has gone back to remind himself exactly what the bunker looks like; what he won't forget is the intensity of the emotions, and how he felt when he was inside.

Old armchairs and some wicker seats are scattered around; this is possibly the same furniture that would have been there in 1999. The rubbish on the tables and the floor could also be vintage, a quarter of a century old. Light fittings dangle from the ceilings, bare and without lamps, and emitting a weak, chemical-yellow glow that barely punches through the darkness. One difference between now and then, according to a neighbour who had found a key and unlocked the basement, was that they would have had mattresses on the floor in 1999. That is where Djokovic shivered under a blanket as Belgrade achieved an unwelcome first: the first European capital to come under NATO bombardment, which was designed to force the Serbian military's withdrawal from Kosovo.

In his chilling phrase, Djokovic was 'surrounded by death'. Outside that bunker, he has recalled, Belgrade was glowing like a ripe tangerine. The city was either in black-out or lit up by NATO jets, and nothing in between. For 78 consecutive nights, the planes came, scattering their bombs. When the sirens started, the Djokovic family would scramble to get inside the bunker, which was in the basement of his grandfather Vladimir's apartment building. At the start of the bombing campaign, Djokovic and his brothers and parents had been living around 200m (650ft) away, in a building that didn't have its own shelter. They had to make their way there through the darkness and the chaos and the noise.

As Srdjan Djokovic saw it, there was trauma in the spring of 1999 that would last a lifetime. Novak's most distressing memory is of one night during the first week of the bombings when, around three in the morning, the sound of explosions near to the apartment, and of breaking glass, woke and startled the family. Quickly getting to her feet, Novak's mother bashed her head against a radiator and knocked herself out. For what seemed like an age, but might have been only a few seconds, she was out cold on the floor. All three Djokovic brothers were crying. When Dijana came to, the family tried to find their way to the shelter but they could hardly see – there was no lighting and the streets were filled with smoke. And with the sound of the planes and the explosions, it was so loud they couldn't hear each other, even when they were only centimetres apart and screaming in each other's ears.

Overwhelmed and panicking, Novak slipped on a stone and, as he scraped his hands and knees and fell to the ground, he looked up and saw a grey steel triangle, which he later realized was a F-117 stealth bomber, 'tearing across the sky'. It's an image that has always stayed with him; the deathly triangle coming from nowhere and unleashing rockets at a hospital just a couple of blocks away. With its horizontal design, the hospital had become 'a giant club sandwich stuffed with fire'. Djokovic thought he was going to die. A moment later, the jet was gone, and the Djokovic family continued to the shelter. As much as Djokovic now craves the rush of sound from a cheering crowd after winning a big point, he is still afraid of sudden, loud noises. If a fire alarm goes off, it can make him jump.

To be closer to the bunker, the family of five moved into the first-floor, two-bedroom apartment that belonged to Djokovic's grandfather, which for security had a metal gate as well as a regular front door. Outside the bunker, the streets were thrumming with explosions; inside, children were trembling and shaking with fear.

For the first few nights, at least. Something shifted after that. The families in the bunker had come to accept that this was their new reality, and since they were going to be down there, they might as well try to distract themselves. Packed closely together – Djokovic has estimated that there were 50 apartments in the building, and every part of the concrete floor was occupied – the residents played some cards, they sang and they played Monopoly, Risk and other board games. But that normality was just surface deep. Strong, lifelong bonds were formed inside that place of huge physical and emotional discomfort – it was around that time that Djokovic met a boy of his own age, Neven Markovic, who also lived on the first floor of that building. Markovic, a former professional footballer who was Djokovic's best man at his wedding to Jelena Ristic, remains one of the tennis player's closest friends.

Spend just a few minutes inside the basement and you start to crave air and natural light (it's troubling to imagine returning to that bunker night after night). Outside, murals of Djokovic break up the greyness. Beneath Djokovic's old home is an image of him with his grandfather on one side and his first coach, Jelena Gencic, on the other. Go past the concrete playground – where Djokovic used to hit tennis balls around as a child – and you will find another painting of him, which says in Serbian: 'In god we trust.' As one neighbour pointed out, there's an unforced error in the mural, as it shows Djokovic hitting a backhand left-handed, but that hardly takes away from the power of the image and what the athlete signifies to the people of Banjica: how one of their own made something of himself on the world stage.

A group of teenagers hanging around near Djokovic's old apartment block spoke fondly of him, and not so much about his tennis (their grandmothers always let them know when his matches are on television and encourage them to watch too), but about his generosity. About the money he has donated to the local school to buy essentials and how, if he has been in the city, he has found the time to present the trophies to the winner of a football tournament played on the concrete pitch. For all the horror that Djokovic experienced in Banjica, it's also somewhere that brings back fond memories, of the times when he was outside playing games with his friends (though he shredded his knees so often on the concrete playground that he's not quite sure how they are still healthy, and there were times when he accidentally smashed the windows of a neighbour's ground-floor apartment with a ball and had to run for it).

This is indelible trauma. On the drive back into the centre of Belgrade, you pass an old military building that was bombed in 1999 and never repaired; this is a city where you don't have to look too hard to see the scars of war, but where most, Djokovic included, want to move on from the past.

For many years, anger was eating up Djokovic from the inside. He regarded the 1999 bombings as the 'ultimate cruelty' and, like many other Serbians, he was raging, even vengeful. From childhood into adulthood, he felt that inner rage. Djokovic couldn't understand why the nations that made up NATO had joined together in bombarding a small country, dropping bombs on what he described as the helpless people on the street. 'The scars of this emotion, of this anger, are still today present in everybody,' Djokovic has said. In the early stages of his career, he used that rage as fuel, propelling him to some success on tour. If Djokovic was 'stuck', as he put it, in hatred and anger, it felt as though he had at least turned that to his advantage. Djokovic was playing angry and that anger was taking him places.

And yet, in time, Djokovic came to see that carrying feelings of 'hatred, revenge and betrayal' can weigh you down and hold you back, both professionally and personally. Djokovic no longer wanted to feel that way. There's a parable about a snake and a carpenter's saw that Djokovic has felt fits with his realization that staying angry was only going to hurt himself. When the snake accidently cuts itself on a saw, it believes the tool has attacked it and, upset and wanting revenge, envelops the saw. The snake bleeds to death.

As Djokovic has acknowledged, there are different levels of suffering and trauma among the Serbian people. Djokovic's family was fortunate in the sense that they didn't lose their home or anyone close, though when the newspapers printed the names of the dead, his parents recognized some of them – he has struggled to imagine the pain that some Serbs would have felt when their relatives or friends were killed. While Djokovic will never forget the NATO bombings and the death and devastation that they brought to his country, and he would have seen the 'fuck NATO' graffiti in Belgrade, he chose to forgive. It was a conscious decision, to work on himself and his emotions and to deal with that inner rage. Djokovic no longer wanted to be fuelled by anger, but by love and 'love is forgiveness'.

That wasn't easy but Djokovic had an open mind – which we will explore in greater depth later in the book – and he has also said he was opening his heart. 'Novak probably reached that place of forgiveness, and came to that realization, sooner than someone else might have done,' said Dusan Vemic, who first met Djokovic when the future great was six or seven years old, and who then went on to coach him on the ATP Tour. 'As a human, Novak is always growing and learning. He has a growth mindset and he's a never-ending student of life. He came to that place in life where he tried to understand people's decision-making and to put himself in their shoes and trying to be as rational as he can be.'

Moving on from that anger would have helped Djokovic to become a stronger person, according to Jelena Jankovic, a Serb who was the world number one for women's singles. 'As a nation, you're going to be angry when someone is bombing you. That's a scary situation. But us normal people, we couldn't do anything about that,' she reflected. 'But once you overcome that, it makes you stronger as a person, and you try to do the best that you can to make a living for yourself and to make a name for yourself.'

Djokovic's faith, as an Orthodox Christian, allowed him to forgive, said his boyhood coach Bogdan Obradovic, who has known him since he was ten years old. 'That is Novak's philosophy and generally people in Serbia have that Orthodox approach,' said Obradovic. 'We are able to forgive.' Djokovic was able to move on, to unstick himself.

'If you're stuck in [anger],' Djokovic has said, 'what are you going to make out of your life?'

*

Djokovic liked, if possible, to be one day behind the bombers. After dressing for practice and packing his racquet bag with the care you might take before going to a country club, he would leave the apartment at dawn and go out to chase the destruction around Belgrade. He was looking for newly blackened grass, just-formed craters, and steel and concrete that was freshly disfigured. For the places that were still rattling and burning from the day before.

As perverse or as ghastly as it might seem now, there was a logic to Djokovic and his family listening to the news on the radio about where the bombs had been dropped the night before and then seeking out courts in areas of the city that had just been hit: the NATO bombing command were unlikely to target the same spots again so soon. Djokovic also had to keep an eye on the time: to be an aspiring young tennis player in Belgrade in the spring of 1999 was to be an amateur analyst of NATO's bombing patterns. You had to learn – and sometimes, despite all the horror, this almost felt like a game to him – when was the safest time of day to be on court. Often dawn was the quietest part of the day; sometimes it was lunch.

When Djokovic is in Belgrade these days, he tends to train elsewhere, at a smarter, slicker facility, where there's a bit of a scene, with expensive-looking men and women sipping espressos on the terrace above the outside courts (there are also indoor courts). But as a boy he often played at the Partizan Tennis Club. Scruffy around the edges, with graffiti on the outside walls and green paint flaking off inside, it's hardly the most Instagrammable of locations; it's a tennis club with a friendly, understated, unassuming vibe that doesn't make too much of its Djokovic connection. While there are posters of Djokovic inside the entrance, they are fading and yellowed – from years back when he used to endorse Adidas – and he gets equal billing with Ana Ivanovic, a winner of one Grand Slam title, with images of her all over the other side. A few old photographs of Djokovic – including some showing him in the club's black and white striped kit – hang from the walls. But there isn't a statue or anything official celebrating how the most successful tennis player in history used to train here; while there is a bust, it's of a former general who was part of the club's earlier history.

Even at a time when almost every choice you made came with substantial risk, playing at the Partizan Tennis Club could have been a particularly dangerous move: it was close to Banjica, but it was also near a military school, which often drew the bombers to the area. His mother was on edge; what if NATO dropped a bomb on her son's practice court?

A few weeks into NATO's bombing campaign, something surprising had happened: many people in Belgrade had decided they were going to stop being afraid. 'After so much death, so much destruction, we simply stopped hiding,' Djokovic wrote in *Serve to Win*. There was a freedom, Djokovic has observed, in recognizing that you were powerless in the face of NATO's firepower, and to accept your fate. Djokovic and his family had been part of that shift in mindset around the city. They had stopped going to the bunker every night. Djokovic's mother became fatalistic about the prospect of death, telling her family and others in the basement that she would go crazy if she spent another night there. She would be taking her family back home to their apartment and if NATO dropped a bomb on their building, that was their destiny. Djokovic, no doubt influenced by what his parents were saying, was thinking along the same lines: 'If we're hit, we're hit, what can we do?'

The war brought the Djokovic family together. Physically – as the five of them slept in the same bed, with blankets covering the windows to stop shattered glass – and emotionally too. One of Djokovic's strongest memories from the bombing campaign – this was a powerful and unifying moment, but also a subversive one – was when thousands of people gathered on one of Belgrade's bridges, all wearing T-shirts with targets on the front. They even had targets painted on top of their heads and they were singing; they were mocking NATO's pilots. If Djokovic's family and nation could survive this, he thought, then there wasn't much that could break them down, and he could do anything he wanted with the rest of his life. After this, everything else, tennis included, would seem easy by comparison.

In the middle of a bombing campaign, Djokovic had also carried on playing tennis. Djokovic's desire to keep on training, amid the hellish circumstances, meant that his tennis education didn't slip at a time of war (there was only a short loss of focus in the first few days of the bombings). In fact, with the schools closed, his training intensified. Even more importantly, the focus on Novak's training – up to four or five hours – also helped to keep his family going during those times, providing some sense of normality and routine (even if he was hopping around the city looking for somewhere to play).

Djokovic's mother was adamant – the family weren't going to sit around all day at home crying. If you did that, she has said, you would have gone mad with worry about whether your apartment was about to be bombed. Djokovic's love for tennis – he had been fascinated by the sport since he saw a tennis court for the first time at the age of three – gave them a reason to get out of the apartment each day, to continue living. Often there wasn't a net on the court that Djokovic found, or the surface was cracked and broken, with Belgrade's tennis facilities among the collateral damage of war. But that never mattered. And while it was dangerous to be on a tennis court in Belgrade, it was often no more dangerous than anywhere else in the city; Djokovic's coach at the time, Jelena Gencic, had lost her sister who was killed during a bombing raid. By seven o'clock in the evening, the Djokovics would be home with the curtains closed, just as they were supposed to be. Sometimes, Djokovic's need for normality collided with the ongoing reality of living in a city under bombardment. Sirens going off during practice along with jets slicing up the sky. When Djokovic celebrated turning 12 at the Partizan Tennis Club, his family were singing happy birthday to him when a plane suddenly rushed over them, drowning them out.

Coming through – as he described – 'horrifying' moments such as those, when he felt completely helpless, gave Djokovic an inner strength and resilience that has stayed with him throughout his career; it also made him hungrier, even more ambitious to succeed as a tennis player. He wanted to show how a young boy who had survived the horrors of war could become the best in tennis, a global sport played by athletes from far wealthier nations that also weren't being bombarded.

Destroyed but still alive. That was Djokovic during the war, according to Bogdan Obradovic. In his view, Djokovic's early experiences in life gave him extra energy and lasting strength and resilience. 'The people who suffered so much during the terrible war, it couldn't keep on getting worse. It had to stop at some point. You're going to hit the ground. After that, it's either going to be bad or you're going to climb up again. There are no other options. When you have some evil that attacks you, you get used to it. You get to know exactly who you're fighting against and you see that even the evil doesn't even enjoy it that much. You're destroyed but you're still alive,' Obradovic said. 'After that, you come with some sort of unexplainable energy. All these things, they're either going to destroy you or they're going to make you stronger. That's what happened with Novak – he became a stronger person.'

Even before the bombing had started, life had been extraordinarily hard in Belgrade under an international trade embargo – Djokovic has recalled queuing at 5.45am for bread to share with his family. 'A boy like me, growing up in Serbia, becoming a tennis champion? It was unlikely in even the best of circumstances. And it became ever more unlikely when the bombs started dropping,' Djokovic once wrote. But is it possible that the opposite is true? That the bombing campaign actually increased Djokovic's chances of making it to the tennis tour? Just as there are ups and downs in life, Obradovic said, you get the same wild ride on a tennis court; Djokovic wouldn't have realized it at the time but being brutalized by war, including spending night after night in a bomb shelter, would have given him even more inner strength.

War also appeared to have hardened Djokovic's friend Ivanovic, who as a girl sometimes used to practise at the bottom of an empty swimming pool, and who would go on to become the women's world number one. With Jankovic, another Serb who would top the world rankings, this was a golden generation of three future world number ones. 'We were hungry because nothing was ever given to us,' Jankovic said. 'Everything we had, we had to earn, and we had to work harder than everybody else from other countries just to prove ourselves. While we came from a country that wasn't very wealthy and didn't have any great facilities or any tennis tradition, and at times it felt like a mission impossible, what we did have was a strong will. As a nation, we don't accept second place. We had to be number one, there was no other option. Either you're the best or you're nothing. That's the mentality we have.'

They say there's no direct translation into English of the Serbian word 'inat'. It's kind of a mix of defiance, spite, stubbornness and f-you bloody-mindedness, with perhaps a little snark and acid wit blended in; some would say that Djokovic has had that since his early days in tennis, and that it still pushes him today. 'Inat is when you're angry and you have this really strong motivation to prove people wrong. You want to do really well. I think Novak has had that feeling his whole career,' said Jankovic. 'I also had that. As a nation we all have that in our nature. We want to be the best. We're going to succeed even though we come from a small country that isn't the wealthiest and doesn't have the greatest facilities. But we have what other athletes don't have. We have inat. And we're going to prove you wrong.'

The 1999 bombings continue to shape Djokovic's thinking on court. 'Novak's background, with the war and bombs going off all around him, has made him fearless,' observed Chris Evert, a former world number one and a winner of 18 Grand Slam women's singles titles. 'When you've been through a childhood like that, those kind of PTSD experiences, you lose all fears. If that doesn't mould you into a certain type of person, having those experiences at such a young age, I don't know what would. Novak uses all the negative times in his life, such as his country going to war, to give himself strength in his matches. He's saying to himself: "OK, it's five-all in the fifth set, Novak, but you've been through a lot worse than this." The war has taken away the fear factor in his tennis and in his life. It's made him stronger and more resilient as a result. There's a depth of strength to him.'

Some close to Djokovic would suggest that the war's impact on his route to greatness shouldn't be overstated. While it has helped galvanize him, it's possible that, if he had grown up in more peaceful and prosperous times, he would still have been so successful. 'It's true that this part of Novak's story is extreme,' said Janko Tipsarevic, who grew up in Belgrade before becoming a top-ten player and is one of Djokovic's closest friends (they have been on holiday together with their families a few times).

'Lots of athletes come from poverty or from single-parent homes or areas with gun violence – look at the NBA or the NFL in America. But this was so remarkable because these were life-threatening moments, night after night. For two and a half months, for us it was normal that they were going to bomb us in the evening so we went into the shelter and during the day we would play tennis. I'm sure that these moments made Novak even more resilient in the end and helped him achieve his goals. But it helped by 5 or 10 per cent, and nothing more than that. I have such a big belief in his mental ability, in his mental greatness, that even if his father had been Jeff Bezos, and he had grown up in a rich country, he still would have become what he was destined to be, the greatest.'

From her perspective as a tennis psychologist – for the past few years she has travelled on the tour with the Polish Grand Slam winner Iga Swiatek – Daria Abramowicz has sensed that Djokovic's early life experiences, and the story he tells himself and others, appear to have made him extraordinarily resilient. 'Novak identifies as a proud Serbian. He's strongly connected to his country. When your country has this kind of history and you're then able to go on to build a happy life, and a successful career, it may give you an enormous strength and a resilience that is beyond measure. Sometimes also it might be a burden, and it might be both in some situations. It's extremely individual, that's for sure,' Abramowicz said. 'My take, and you can see this on so many levels, is that Novak has become incredibly strong and resilient.'

Inside Djokovic's head there are other lasting effects of the bombings. Having survived the horror and the hardships, he is always appreciative of what he has in his life. And, strange as it might sound, Djokovic came through 1999 with something even more powerful: hope.

*

To say that Djokovic came from nowhere isn't hyperbole. He was born into a country – Yugoslavia – that no longer exists and a place where there was next to no tennis culture.

As Djokovic has acknowledged, tennis used to be about as popular in Belgrade as fencing. At that time, 'tennis was nowhere – it was almost dead', according to Bogdan Obradovic, who, as well as coaching Djokovic on and off from the age of ten to sixteen, also later captained him to the Davis Cup title. Aside from all the concrete, one of the legacies of communism was that tennis was still regarded as an aristocratic sport in Yugoslavia and then Serbia. One club in Belgrade was purely for ambassadors and diplomats and for years Serbian television only broadcast one professional tennis match a year, the Wimbledon men's singles final; images from Centre Court, where the players were dressed all in white, would hardly have persuaded viewers in Belgrade that it was a game for the workers. 'It was a sport for aristocrats,' Obradovic recalled. 'Everyone was a bit scared of tennis.'

If the Serbian government had any money to invest in sport, it was directed at team sports such as football, basketball and handball, as well as volleyball and water polo. Why take the risk of investing in an individual who had big dreams in, of all things, an aristocratic pursuit?

Once a place of 'serenity' – Djokovic's word – where he would see rabbits running through the trees, the area around Kopaonik in the Serbian mountains had been covered in cluster-bombs in 1999. For years afterwards, the danger of unexploded ordnance in those mountains meant it wasn't safe for Djokovic to return to what he has called 'the most beautiful tennis club in the world'. It was there, aged four, on three clay courts near his parents' Red Bull pizzeria, that he had first played tennis. Almost 20 years after the war, by which time the bombs had been deactivated, Djokovic was able to go back. The club was abandoned, ruined, and had been absorbed by the forest. But, for Djokovic, it was still a place loaded with meaning and significance. One of the stone buildings was in ruins, half of a wooden structure was flattened and the tennis wall – where he had spent so many happy hours and days as a child practising his technique – was pocked with holes from bomb damage.

But at least the wall was somehow still standing, that it had, as Djokovic put it, 'endured', as had his emotional connection with that spot of land. Djokovic's affection for those courts – which were covered in vegetation when he returned in the late 2010s – is partly because of the nature around there. But also because of how that place changed his life.

No one in Djokovic's family had ever played tennis before. It was just pure luck, an outrageous piece of good fortune – or as Djokovic would say, 'destiny' – that someone had decided to construct some courts right there in front of the restaurant. If those tennis courts hadn't been built right there, it's possible that he might have never been exposed to the sport at a young age, or perhaps not at all. Did Djokovic even get to choose the 'journey' – as he described it – that he was on? He believes that his soul – just like everyone else's – had some predetermined goals and missions. He just had to find out what they were.

Djokovic also believes his soul chose his parents. He was born into a skiing family – his father, uncle and aunt were skiers and they all idolized Italian ski racer Alberto Tomba. Djokovic's parents even met on a ski slope – his mother had fallen over in the snow when his father, a ski instructor, appeared and asked her whether she needed any help. Djokovic doesn't think it was surprising that he got into sport; it was just unexpected that he chose tennis, a decision that would mean his parents would be out of their comfort zones. It wasn't a world they knew and, not for the last time, the Djokovics would have to open their minds. Srdjan and Dijana couldn't be completely certain what they were signing up for.

From the moment he saw tennis, Djokovic adored the sport. Djokovic's love for tennis didn't start in 1991 when he had his first racquet. You can spool even further back in time, to when he was just three and he would take food and drinks out to the men who were constructing the tennis courts in front of his family's restaurant. In those moments, Djokovic's father noticed how his son looked at the courts. Srdjan bought 'Nole' (Djokovic's nickname) a neon pink racquet and a foam ball. Djokovic didn't care what colour it was, only that it was his. When Djokovic wasn't taking big swings with that racquet – a video has survived of him on court wearing a green tracksuit, a baseball cap and a look of total concentration – he carried it around all day, not ever wanting to put it down.

There was a second piece of luck. Jelena Gencic, who had previously mentored Monica Seles and Djokovic's future coach Goran Ivanisevic, started running sessions for children on those courts. Djokovic was five years old when he first joined in. He was no ordinary five-year-old, as Gencic discovered. Before that first session, Djokovic was half an hour early and had brought with him a large tennis bag containing his racquet, a towel, a bottle of water, a banana and some wristbands. Gencic was astounded: 'Who packed your bag, your mother?' To which Djokovic replied: 'No, I packed it.' She asked him how he had known what he would need. From watching tennis on television, he said. Djokovic's perfectionism, so obvious to everyone now, was there from the start.

Just days later, Gencic would tell Djokovic's parents that their boy, about the same height as a net post, was special, that he was a 'zlatno dete', a golden child. Golden because, as well as talent, he had a focus that suggested he had a big future in professional tennis. That resonated with Dijana, who saw Novak as 'a child of god'. 'Jelena gave Novak and his family hope that he could make it as a tennis player,' said Jankovic. 'Nobody believed that was possible until Jelena supported him.'

Djokovic's dreams in tennis started with the conversations he had with Gencic. 'Jelena triggered a dream in Novak and that's what he has been following all of his life,' said Obradovic. 'Jelena passed Novak the love and passion for tennis. It was big for Novak, and for the family too, to have somebody supporting him and saying good things about him that he was very talented and that one day he could be number one. She loved tennis and she loved hard work. She was very disciplined. She was like an officer in the army, very tough. But she did it all with a big smile on her face. Jelena was very positive.'

You don't need to be a psychologist to recognize that there are few more contrasting tennis personalities than Pete Sampras and Djokovic. Every so often in the 1990s, Sampras would leap high off the Wimbledon grass, hanging in the air like he was a basketball player in the NBA, and hit a slam-dunk smash. But, that aside, the Californian was all tennis and never showbusiness. And yet it was Sampras, the quiet and reserved alpha of the All England Club, who would inspire a young Serbian boy, who would become one of the great extroverts of the sport, to think he was destined to win Wimbledon too. Djokovic's first memory of watching the Championships on television – he was six years old at the time – was seeing Sampras win the title in 1993. Looking back, Djokovic can appreciate that he and Sampras are very different people, but what he liked about his idol was how he coped with the pressure and always seemed to serve well on the biggest points. Mentally, Djokovic had never seen anyone as robust as Sampras inside the white heat of Wimbledon's Centre Court.

Using pieces of plastic and scraps of paper, Djokovic made himself a pretend Wimbledon trophy. He wouldn't have known it at the time, but the young Novak was using a mental approach that he would often rely on as an adult: visualization. 'Hello,' he would say, holding up his plastic trophy and talking to himself in the mirror, 'my name is Novak Djokovic and I'm the Wimbledon champion.' Years later, when Djokovic won

Wimbledon for the first time in 2011 – and he hoisted the actual golden, pineapple-topped trophy – his mind flashed back to his childhood, to the moments when he had dreamed of that very moment. Until he was seven, tennis was all about fun. But then it got serious. That was Djokovic's age when he made an appearance on Serbian national television, informing viewers that, 'tennis is my job' and articulating his vision for the future: he was going to become the world number one.

It was around that time that Dusan Vemic, who is 11 years Djokovic's senior, met a young Novak at the Partizan Tennis Club. Vemic was astounded by the way the young boy spoke. 'The racquet bag was almost as big as him, almost down to his knees. In the beginning, I thought he was just a cute little kid and then after speaking to him – and he would have been just six or seven years old at the time – I realized that I could have had an adult conversation with him. He was one of those prodigy kids,' recalled Vemic, who years later would become part of Djokovic's coaching team.

'Novak's mind is brilliant in so many ways. He acts and thinks and speaks probably 20 years older than he is. He can surprise you with some of the things that he can grasp. That was true when he was a boy. I immediately realized that he was a deep thinker and that he was clear about what he was doing, such as working on his technique and his footwork. You understood that he meant what he was saying. It was amazing to see someone that young who was thinking of tennis in that way, and who wasn't just playing around. I couldn't have imagined then that Novak would become who he is today. But I did think, from that very first conversation, that there was something special about that kid's mind.'

Djokovic's mind, rather than his game, was the first indication that he had greatness ahead.

As a child, he had a focus, even during the less exciting moments of matches, that was beyond some adult athletes. 'Sometimes tennis can be a bit boring as it's not like every second, and every point, feels as though it should be on a highlights reel,' said Vemic. 'That's where you need focus. Maturity usually comes with many years of high-level tennis. He played that way from the get-go, since he was a child. He prepared for every single match to the best of his abilities and he was focused on every point. He respected every single point.'

Fortunately for Djokovic, he had Gencic, his 'second mother'. She was so much more than a tennis coach to him. Learning how to hit a tennis ball was just one element of the education that Djokovic got with Gencic. From a young age, Djokovic knew about the importance of nutrition, with Gencic telling him how Seles didn't drink Coca-Cola or eat cheeseburgers, or about how Seles valued sleep. Every day, it felt to Djokovic as though Seles was in his head. He grew to admire and love the nine-time Grand Slam champion (and as an adult, he has wondered how many more majors she would have won if she hadn't been stabbed in the back while on court in Hamburg in 1993). Listening to classical music was one key module. Gencic introduced him to Tchaikovsky's *1812 Overture* and asked him how he felt while listening to it – she wanted him to remember that surge of adrenaline, and the power of the music, and to use that on court if he was having a rough day and needed to find a way of raising his level. She encouraged him to learn languages, to sing, to read poetry, including the works of Russian romantic poet Alexander Pushkin, and to 'breathe consciously'. If you want to know why Djokovic thinks differently to most athletes, you can't ignore Gencic; she taught him to open his mind.

Djokovic was in the middle of a Grand Slam – Roland Garros in 2013 – when he was told that Gencic had died. Unable to attend her funeral, he wrote a letter, which his mother read out. Djokovic called Gencic an 'angel' and thanked her for her patience, support and 'enormous love'.

*

'Golden child' or tennis 'alien'? At ten years old, Djokovic had a 'cosmic energy' about him on the tennis court. The first time Obradovic saw the young boy play, he immediately picked up on that energy, which almost felt as though the child wasn't quite human, as if he were an extra-terrestrial. 'Novak didn't play the best tennis then. His technique wasn't supreme in that moment. But everyone around him was going, "Whoa" as you could feel and see some energy. Like he's from outer space. Like an alien.'

Djokovic's father had brought his son to Obradovic, to a tennis club in Belgrade's suburbs, to ask the coach what he thought of the boy's prospects. Aside from Djokovic's alien-like energy and obvious talent, there was another reason why Obradovic was left 'in complete shock' from this first encounter: the child's professionalism. It wasn't just that the 'quiet boy' had packed a tennis bag – which he had been doing for years – but that, without being asked, he had started warming up, running around the court. Other ten-year-olds had to be introduced to the idea of preparing your body for practice, and then reminded; Djokovic already knew what was required. Obradovic was astounded by the focus that Djokovic brought to every shot, and how he also already had a cool-down and stretching routine.

At the end of their first practice session, Obradovic asked Djokovic: 'What do you want from tennis? What's your goal?' Djokovic was clear: 'I want to become number one in the world.' Obradovic replied: 'That's easy to say but there are a lot of things that you have to do to get there.' Djokovic wasn't fazed: 'It's OK. I will do everything that's necessary to get there. That's my dream and I believe I will get there.'

Električni Orgazam, or Electro Orgasm, are a rock band from Belgrade who were big in Yugoslavia in the 1980s. Unbeknown to them, they played a significant role in Djokovic's tennis development, helping him to become the greatest returner in history. Obradovic, whose two loves are tennis and music, took his guitar on to the practice court one day and played Djokovic a song by Electro Orgasm called 'Everyone in Yugoslavia is Playing Rock 'n' Roll'. He wanted to show Djokovic that returning an opponent's serve has much in common with playing and listening to music: it was all about rhythm. 'Listen, Novak, you have to follow the rhythm of the song,' Obradovic said. 'And then you'll feel the rhythm in your return, in your movement, in everything. It's like a song. It's all connected.'

As Obradovic said to Djokovic as he played his guitar, 'the music is in between the notes'. The message he wanted to pass on was that everything in tennis and music is about timing, so being a great returner is all about 'having good rhythm and doing something at the right moment'. He was asking Djokovic to notice everything about his opponent's serve. He wanted him to listen to the sound of the ball being struck as he was going to be reacting to that as much to the sight of his opponent's service motion. Obradovic encouraged Djokovic to become attuned to an opponent's service rhythm: his hands, the way he tossed the ball into the air, how he moved his body and the racquet towards the ball, how he hit the ball and everything about the racquet. 'You will have that rhythm of reading and reacting,' said Obradovic, who also introduced Djokovic to the Beatles, playing him 'Yesterday' and many of their other songs.

But, in many ways, his lesson about Electro Orgasm went beyond the tennis court. Before he put his guitar away, Obradovic had one more message about rock 'n' roll: 'The most important part, Novak, is this: if you hear and understand the music, you will become a happier person.'

2

SACRIFICE

Sleepless and on edge, Srdjan Djokovic would sometimes walk the streets at night. In desperation, he had been borrowing money from loan sharks to pay the bills for his teenage son's tennis. On one of his midnight walkabouts, he was arrested after attracting the attention of the police, though after explaining that he was just a tennis dad with money problems, he sat with the officers in the station, laughing and drinking brandy until morning.

That was one light moment at a time of immense financial stress. No wonder Srdjan, the most obsessive and relentless of tennis fathers, had an occasional wobble about how everything was going to work out. There were moments, recalled Djokovic's boyhood coach, Bogdan Obradovic, when Srdjan and his wife Dijana considered abandoning a project – which had sounded fanciful from the start – to help their first born become a tennis immortal. 'Novak's parents would have been so tired from it all and they would have thought about stopping. They would have been thinking: "I just can't do it anymore." If they didn't have to take

Novak to the tennis courts again in the morning, all these problems would go away.'

Obradovic, who was close to the family at the time, said Srdjan was 'crashed emotionally', exhausted from the financial strain of trying to fund his eldest son's tennis career. Srdjan was working 15-hour days but that was never enough. It was impacting his health. 'Srdjan would say that he had done everything he could have done and yet they still didn't have any money,' Obradovic said. 'Their family was getting crushed. It was a huge problem. At that time, there was a big economic crisis in our country. The sanctions were there and everything, including food and gasoline, was very expensive. They were struggling so much. I would listen to these stories from Srdjan about how he couldn't handle all the expenses and he was trying to find sponsors. I could see that Novak was having problems with his racquets, with his strings, with his shoes, with his travelling expenses, with everything. As Novak was suffering, everyone around him – me included – was suffering too. We struggled so much. Lots of bad things were happening with money and everything. That was a very tough period of times when everyone around Novak was completely exhausted by it all.'

These experiences, extreme as they were, galvanized Djokovic, who was left thinking how failure wasn't an option, how he didn't have any choice but to make a success of himself. 'Srdjan did a good thing in trying to keep the money issue from Novak but of course Novak knew some of what was going on and there was pressure on him,' Obradovic recalled. 'But even at that time, even at that young age, Novak was mentally strong and was able to handle that great pressure. That's the kind of person he was then and still is now.'

They had never been a wealthy family and, as Djokovic has disclosed, they lost everything during the war, including the restaurant in the mountains. In the hardscrabble, post-war years, Djokovic's parents were having to find the money for his tennis career at a time when many families were purely focused on survival, on hustling for the coins and notes to feed themselves that day. Those tennis expenses jumped when, just months after the bombing campaign finished in 1999, Srdjan and Dijana sent 12-year-old Novak to train at the Niki Pilic Tennis Academy outside Munich – while Pilic gave them a discount, the fees were still painfully high. For all Djokovic's promise, he didn't have any decent sponsors; the Serbian economy had been shredded by war and sanctions, and it was proving a challenge to find international companies who wished to be associated with a Serbian athlete.

In desperation, having sold the family silver, and having already borrowed from friends, Srdjan turned to loan sharks. 'Criminals,' Djokovic has called them, recalling how Serbia was a dangerous place then. Mostly, the loan sharks charged Srdjan 10 or 12½ per cent interest on his loans – which was already punishingly high – but when they sensed just how urgently he needed the money, they pushed that rate up to 15 per cent. There were periods, Djokovic's mother has recalled, when her husband was borrowing from one lender just to pay back someone else. On a couple of occasions when Srdjan didn't repay a loan shark on time, he had a knife held against his throat.

There was a time when Djokovic travelled with his father to Paris to compete in the junior tournament at Roland Garros and his mother, who had stayed behind in Serbia with his brothers, didn't have enough money to buy any bread. Too often, Djokovic's brothers suffered because all the family money had gone on the young athlete's training and food, and it pained Dijana – and Srdjan too – that they couldn't always provide the basics for all their children. Everything was about Novak, everything they had was invested in him.

'There wasn't a lot of money in Serbia at the time so, even though Novak's parents were paying less than the other families who had children at the academy, I could see that it was a tough time for them,' said Pilic, whose wife affectionately called Djokovic 'Jacket', because when he first visited the academy he didn't seem to have one. 'That lasted for three or four years. Novak's parents were doing everything they could to get that money for Novak as they believed in him. They had three kids, but everything they earned then went on Novak and his tennis.' They also didn't have the same energy for their other children. 'Only Novak mattered,' Srdjan once told *Newsweek* – it made him sad to realize he couldn't give his other two sons even 1 per cent of the fight and power that he had put into furthering Novak's dreams.

With Serbia then regarded as a pariah nation, Djokovic often couldn't fly directly from Belgrade to wherever he was competing as a junior. The only option was to take a bus to Budapest, more than 320km (200 miles) away in Hungary, and take a flight from there. 'We waited on the border for so many hours,' Obradovic recalled. 'We had to get a visa for every single country and waiting for those visas was also horrible – we would wait for hours and hours, not knowing whether we would get those visas or not. It was very tough during Novak's junior career. In fact, it was really terrible. I really don't know how he resisted all those problems and then, as an adult, became the best of all time. This is an incredible story.' Serbia's 'bad reputation in the world' – as Djokovic once put it –

caused all kinds of difficulties. When Djokovic eventually arrived at tournaments, some of the people he met weren't so welcoming, with a few recoiling when he told them he was from Serbia (others, who hadn't heard of his homeland, thought he had said he was from Siberia).

Somehow Djokovic still became the Under-14s European champion, and then the Under-16s champion. Somehow the Djokovic family got through that time. If Djokovic's parents went to bed thinking they couldn't continue, Obradovic said that in the middle of the night or early in the morning, they would have suddenly thought to themselves: 'We're going to keep going, just one more step'. 'That's some strange energy. You don't know what's pushing you that much,' said Obradovic, who suggested it was Djokovic himself who kept the project going. 'With everyone around so exhausted, Novak was somehow finding the energy to renew everything and to wake everybody up and give every one of us our energy back.'

To keep the family's spirits up, Srdjan would sometimes talk about the sports cars that they could buy when Novak achieved superstardom. But mostly there was no escaping their daily reality. Djokovic can still recall the moment – which sounds cinematic but was dreadful to experience – when his father slammed a ten-Deutschmark note down on the table and said: 'This is all we've got.' That money would have to feed all five of them. For most of Djokovic's childhood, his parents tried to keep their financial struggles from him – they didn't want him to appreciate just how poor they were – in the hope he would only have to think about his tennis. But there were times when Srdjan and Dijana could hide it no longer. The drama was intentional: Srdjan was telling a young Novak that he would have to take some responsibility, that they were all in this together.

This, the scrappiest of tennis origin stories, could easily have come to nothing. Djokovic's parents knew there was a risk that their son could have got injured or lost interest in the sport, and then all the money and effort that had been put into the project would have been for nothing. But that never happened. Djokovic's love for tennis never dimmed.

What kept Srdjan going through those times was his belief – which he shared with those around him – that his son would go on to become the greatest of all time, a view that he gladly shared with everyone on the Serbian tennis scene. At first, Djokovic's mother thought her husband was being ridiculous – how could he possibly say that about a child? But Srdjan was persuasive and Dijana started believing that too.

Extraordinary as it might sound, conversations about Djokovic becoming the GOAT – which would have put grand ideas in his head – started as far back as Belgrade in the 1990s. 'Novak's dad wouldn't shy away from saying publicly that Novak, when he was just a boy, was going to be the greatest of all time,' said Dusan Vemic. 'Since Novak was very little, Novak's father didn't change his tune. Lots of players say that their family are their biggest supporters but everybody in Novak's family was very clear on where they were heading and every single day Novak would prove them right and they would then become even more clear. Novak's father has a very strong character so you probably felt he believed what he was saying even more. I don't think many people thought he was wrong for too long. Novak's father did a good job of surrounding him with true professionals, who were also very emotionally involved and who would protect Novak.'

There were moments when Djokovic resented his parents. When he didn't feel as though he was growing up in the best possible environment or when he didn't like how his father was speaking about him and his life. But, as Djokovic has reflected, that was a normal phase of life as a teenager or young man to feel that way. Mostly, as Djokovic told his friend and wellness entrepreneur Chervin Jafarieh, he felt enormously grateful that his parents' sacrifice allowed him to live his dreams. Years later, at the 2010 US Open, some would mock Srdjan for wearing a T-shirt with an image of his son on the front. But the New York fashion police would have been more forgiving if they had known a little more of what Djokovic's parents had been through to help their son play in the Arthur Ashe Stadium.

*

The other students at Niki Pilic's academy used to get 'chicken skin' – or goosebumps – from seeing Novak Djokovic's hyper focus and intensity up close every day. He never eased off. Djokovic was relentless, even as a teenager, and the other kids weren't used to being around that. Sure, it was inspiring but, at the same time, it also made them uncomfortable, appreciating the gap between what they were doing to chase their tennis ambitions and what Djokovic was willing to give for his dreams each day.

Djokovic might not even have been the most talented boy at the academy. According to Djokovic's old roommate, Cosmin Georgescu, the most gifted of them all was Ernests Gulbis, who is said to come from one of the wealthiest families in Latvia (in years to come, when he was competing on the ATP Tour, there would be rumours he would travel to tournaments in his father's private jet, to which he would say, with a smile on his face: 'Yes, and I have a helicopter, a submarine and a spaceship.'). Gulbis was more of a natural talent, Georgescu said. But Djokovic had an edge over Gulbis, and everyone else there, because of his desire for hard work. In Djokovic's teenage universe, there were no off days. Not once did Georgescu hear Djokovic say, as a few kids at the academy sometimes did, 'I'm tired – today I don't care'. 'Novak was always working his ass off,' the Romanian recalled.

Every day, Djokovic was the same. His peers at the academy used to 'gossip' about Djokovic's 'calculated', 'strict' approach to tennis, though never in a bitchy way, more whispering behind his back in awe and astonishment.

Named after the writer Ernest Hemingway, Gulbis was the rich kid with a moneyed, artistic background and 'cool clothes', often going out after hours when he had practice in the morning. When Georgescu shared a room with Gulbis, he sensed that the Latvian 'didn't give a shit'. Gulbis was 'more interesting to hang around with – he was a cool guy'. Djokovic was also fun to be around, but never as fun as Gulbis was, principally because he was there to work, to better himself. Away from the courts, Djokovic would josh and joke around with his friends, he would watch films, and he would talk about girls and life, and very occasionally he went out to the Munich bars until around 10pm. But he was always firm: night-time was for sleeping and not for partying. 'Novak was way more serious than anyone else at the academy. You didn't see that same commitment from anyone else and you don't see that today from anyone either,' Georgescu observed.

On the Munich practice courts, Djokovic was always drawn back to his antithesis, as the pair were the best two players of their age group. From their family backgrounds to their personalities to their approaches to tennis, Djokovic and Gulbis were wildly different. 'I think their backgrounds must have been a factor in how they approached tennis,'

Georgescu said. 'But Novak never spoke about his family's financial situation. As a Serbian guy, it would have been harder but I think that would have been an extra motivation for him. I remember Niki gave us some life advice on what it's like when you have everything on the table and also when you don't have anything on the table. Novak grew up in a much rougher environment than many of us. But he never complained about anything. He was very, very mature for his age. I feel as though Novak was born with a champion's mentality, like it was in his blood.'

There was one place that Gulbis – a future Roland Garros semi-finalist and world number ten – did care deeply and that was when he and Djokovic were on the court, getting competitive. When Djokovic and Gulbis played practice sets, 'there was fire on the court', according to Georgescu, with the rivals swearing at each other and breaking racquets. 'They would play for hours. They never wanted to stop.' It turned out that, more often than not, toiling away on your tennis and fitness (Djokovic) tended to trump pure natural talent coupled with a more casual, rebellious approach to tennis and to life (Gulbis). Djokovic didn't need much extra encouragement back then that he was on the right path towards tennis greatness but every time he won a set off Gulbis must have been a moment of validation.

Pilic, a Croat who appeared in a Roland Garros final in the early 1970s, didn't accept players at the academy under 14. He made an exception for Djokovic, who was just 12 years old, because he could see his potential. 'Jelena Gencic called me a couple of times and said she had this kid and she couldn't teach him anymore. She asked if I could take him,' said Pilic. 'Novak came to the academy. My wife was talking to Novak and said he was a very bright young boy. And then I started practising with him and I was delighted. When we found Novak, it was like discovering a diamond in a mine. Over the months and years, he shone brighter and brighter.'

Djokovic listened to Pilic's every word; he wanted to download all his expertise. He told Pilic that he didn't want to waste his opportunities or waste his career. 'Novak is very intelligent and disciplined and he was trying to make the most of my knowledge and experience so he could improve himself,' Pilic said. 'He was a young man with incredible concentration – he was very coachable. He wanted to learn. I didn't know that Novak was going to be number one in the world for more than four hundred weeks or anything like that but I knew he would be international class. He was winning junior titles and – my experience is long – I could just tell.'

Djokovic regards Pilic as his 'tennis father' and 'mentor'. It can't have been easy for Djokovic, being in a different country to his family, especially as his parents couldn't afford to visit him for several months after he arrived. 'It was a tough time. But my wife and I, we looked after Novak like he was our own son – and he never forgot that,' Pilic said. 'We were warm to him. We wanted him to feel as though he could open up and talk to us about anything and that if there was a problem, we could solve it together. When he was older and he had left the academy, he used to come back to see me and to practise before tournaments in Germany. Some coaches give a lot to players and they get nothing back. I've always got a lot back from Novak. I get respect. We message and we still talk, though not as often as we used to, and see each other once or twice a year. If Novak wins a title, my wife and I will talk to Novak's parents to say congratulations. We talk about everything, about life.'

Pilic would tell the other students how Djokovic was a future elite player and not just because of the way he hit the ball and how he moved, but because of his hunger and his ambition. Djokovic had a vision of where he wanted to be along with a plan about how he was going to get there: by grinding day after day. Georgescu recalled how Djokovic would work on his tennis and fitness until he was almost at the point of physical collapse – he was sometimes about to drop down with exhaustion – and then he would work some more.

*

One of the weirdest episodes in Djokovic's career started, of all places, at a dinner in Scotland. It was April 2006 and with Great Britain hosting Serbia's Davis Cup team that weekend, the Lawn Tennis Association had put on a function at a hotel on the outskirts of Glasgow. It was an evening that promised the usual small talk and tennis chit-chat. But then Djokovic's mother, Dijana, approached Stuart Smith, the then president of the LTA. And she wasn't making small talk: Dijana was telling Smith how the Djokovic family wished to explore the possibility of Novak becoming British. Dijana speaks good English; there was no confusion or ambiguity about what she was floating with Smith and the LTA, though it was unclear whether Novak himself knew anything about this approach at the time.

'Novak is Serbia and Serbia is Novak,' Dijana once said, speaking from Belgrade when emotions were running high during the 2022 deportation dramas before the Australian Open. Spend a few days in the Serbian capital, talking to Djokovic's old neighbours in Banjica and to the members of the Partizan Tennis Club, and you realize there is plenty of truth in what she said. Given how Djokovic is now an unelected figurehead of Serbia, and the strength he has taken from representing his nation, it feels odd to consider how close he came to becoming British. Understandably, it's an episode that some within Serbian tennis don't like to dwell on, that peculiar moment in time when the Djokovic family considered moving to London in a switch that would have seen Novak become Andy Murray's Davis Cup teammate.

Contrary to how this episode has usually been presented, it was – as confirmed by Roger Draper, who was then in his first month as chief executive of the LTA, and someone else close to these conversations – the Djokovic family who approached the LTA and not the other way around. While a teenage Djokovic was already in the top 100 by then, it was far from clear how high he could go in tennis, and no one was predicting that he would win multiple Grand Slams or become one of the greatest players of all time. Djokovic's parents were still under extreme financial stress; they needed more support and they seemingly weren't getting it from the Serbian Tennis Federation, whose president and officials were also at the Glasgow dinner. 'Novak's career was fairly static at the time and his parents obviously felt as though his career needed a boost,' said one insider at the LTA with knowledge of what was discussed.

Perhaps the wealthy LTA, with all the millions of pounds they received every year from Wimbledon, could give the Djokovics the money they needed? 'The message we were getting from the Djokovic family was: "Novak's not getting the support he needs – and he needs some serious support to become number one in the world",' recalled Draper. 'Novak was a rising star at the time, as was Andy. The Djokovic family came and said to Stuart, "Can we have a discussion about it?" Stuart then briefed me and I said: "There's no harm in having a discussion".' But Draper didn't want to meet Djokovic's parents in Glasgow that weekend as he was concerned about being rumbled. He passed on a message to Dijana and Srdjan: 'Let's get the Davis Cup tie out of the way because there are media here in Glasgow and we don't want anyone hearing about it.'

A few weeks later, Djokovic's parents got in touch with the LTA again: 'We're coming to London. Can we meet up?' A hush-hush tour of the LTA's national training centre, which at the time was at Queen's Club in west London, was arranged. That evening, Smith and Draper had an informal dinner with the Djokovics at Smith's home in Kent. Draper and Smith discussed how the LTA could support Djokovic's career, just as they were then offering their full financial backing to Murray, who is a week older than Djokovic. Draper's recollection is that they didn't discuss any hard figures and the LTA weren't dangling jobs, a car and a London home in front of Djokovic's parents, as has sometimes been suggested. But there was no doubt that the LTA were interested in putting together what Draper regarded as the Davis Cup dream team of the future: Djokovic and Murray. Srdjan and Dijana talked about their other tennis-playing sons, and how they also needed support. But, from Draper's perspective, the LTA were only ever interested in Novak.

'Like any parents, they wanted the best for their child and they felt as though they needed the support to get Novak to where he wanted to be,' Draper said of Djokovic's parents. Draper was left feeling as though Djokovic was potentially on the way to London. This wouldn't have been unprecedented. Over that Davis Cup weekend in Glasgow, Djokovic had beaten Greg Rusedski, who in the 1990s had switched his own allegiance from Canada to Britain. Dijana Djokovic could see that Britain in 2006 was actively looking for heroes.

There was just one snag – the security guard on the gatehouse outside Queen's Club was Serbian, and he had recognized Djokovic's parents as they walked in. The tour hadn't been as hush-hush as Srdjan and Dijana had hoped. People in tennis were gossiping, as they tend to. Word was starting to get around, in London and then in Belgrade, that something was potentially up. The LTA was getting calls, including from the media, and fobbing them off that Djokovic's parents were just visiting London and that it was all very innocent. The Djokovics were more than a little spooked, according to Draper: 'There was a feeling that they had lost control of the story.' In a behind-the-scenes email rally between Belgrade and London that stretched through spring and most of the summer, the LTA and the Djokovic family continued to exchange messages. Just after Wimbledon, Draper was very direct with Srdjan and Dijana, asking them something along the lines of: 'Are we going to do this or not?'

From Djokovic's side, becoming British had never felt right. But he had understood that it wasn't just about him and his emotional needs and wanting to stay connected to his country, his language and his friends and wider family. Ultimately, the Djokovics decided to walk away from the discussions they had started. By late summer 2006, when Draper bumped into Djokovic's parents in New York at that year's US Open, it was clear to him that the conversation was over. Perhaps because of that Serbian security guard on the Queen's Club gatehouse, who had alerted people in Serbian tennis. Maybe, Draper has said, the Djokovics had been able to use the meeting with the LTA as leverage to get what they wanted from the Serbian Tennis Federation. Years later, when Draper's son Jack played Djokovic in the first round of Wimbledon in 2021, Draper was reminded of what might have been.

It's fun, Draper suggested, to consider the parallel universe in which the Djokovics said yes and Novak was the one who said boo to Fred Perry's ghost, which had been haunting British tennis pretty much ever since the 1930s. It would end up being Murray who would become Britain's first male Grand Slam singles champion in more than 70 years, since Perry, when he won the 2012 US Open. Murray had that golden moment when he won the 2013 Wimbledon title, as the first home men's champion in 77 years, by beating Djokovic in the final. Had Djokovic also been British, Murray's triumph would have been stripped of most of its emotional power – after all, Djokovic had already won Wimbledon by then, in 2011. But Djokovic becoming British would have meant depriving himself and Serbia of so much more, of the symbolism that went far beyond the tennis court. For Djokovic, and for Murray, it ended up being a smart decision for the boy from Belgrade, the teenager who was said to have grown up off the tennis grid, to have remained a Serb.

There had already been one great Serbian-born player who had won multiple Grand Slam singles titles. But Monica Seles had switched nationality during her career, becoming an American citizen. Djokovic's career was going to be different – anything he achieved in tennis he was going to do as a Serb, not as a Briton or any other nationality. In the end, Djokovic was able to stay true to himself, to play as a Serb, which would bring him some peace and strength. Psychologically, that was big for Djokovic.

'It was important for Novak to show that no one could buy him,' said Jelena Jankovic. 'Even when Serbia was in a difficult situation and couldn't support him financially as Britain was offering to do, he showed that he still had that love for his country. I'm sure that he continues to appreciate the decision he made to turn down Britain and to play under the Serbian flag. Novak was born in Serbia, he's Serbian, he feels Serbian and he should stay Serbian. He should never change his nationality. No money should ever change that.'

It wasn't just Britain; other countries would have been interested in tempting Djokovic to play for their flag. 'This is how it goes sometimes, that athletes from small countries are signing contracts with big countries,' said Bogdan Obradovic. 'The possibility was there for Novak to play for Britain. But I feel as though Novak's family were talking lightly, that it was never a serious thing. From a young age – I think he was 12 – Novak started to have dreams of winning the Davis Cup for Serbia. Representing your nation gives you so much energy, so much belief, as a tennis player and Novak wouldn't have that with Britain.'

Could Britain's money have spoiled and softened Djokovic? He saw the riches of the LTA, and the shiny facilities in Britain, and on reflection he realized that all that support wouldn't have been good for him. Because, he reflected, having the best of everything doesn't make you a winner. Plus, all that money would have come with a price attached, which would have been – as Murray could confirm – being built up and then knocked down.

Over the years, it has become harder to imagine how Djokovic could ever have been anything other than Serbian, and how he could have coped – on and off the court – with pretending to be British. Shortly after winning his first Grand Slam title at the 2008 Australian Open,

Djokovic sent a video message that was played on a giant screen as an estimated 150,000 people demonstrated in Belgrade after Kosovo had declared independence. 'We are prepared to defend what is rightfully ours. Kosovo is Serbia,' Djokovic said. On an emotional night, protestors attacked several foreign embassies, including setting the United States embassy on fire. Djokovic, whose father was born there, once described Kosovo as 'the centre of Serbian history, the cradle of Serbian humanity'.

Holding a white marker pen, Djokovic continued to make his feelings clear at Roland Garros in 2023 – at a tournament where you might have imagined he would have been fully focused on achieving tennis immortality by becoming the first man to win 23 Grand Slam singles titles – when he wrote on a television camera lens that 'Kosovo is the heart of Serbia – stop violence'. While the Kosovan Tennis Federation accused Djokovic of raising tensions between Kosovo and Serbia, and he was also admonished by France's sports minister, he was unmoved. That was what he believed and he stood by his comment.

'The history of our country is cruel,' Djokovic once said. With Serbia's challenging past, and Djokovic's elevated status, it was almost inevitable that there would be some controversy along the way. Such as the outrage when he was photographed sitting at a table with the notorious Milan Jolovic, a former commander of the Drina Wolves paramilitary unit that was involved in the Srebrenica massacre when more than 8,000 Bosnian Muslim men and boys were killed in 1995. Or the video that showed Djokovic singing at a wedding with Milorad Dodik, a Bosnian Serb politician who has described the Srebrenica massacre as a 'fabricated myth' (though that relationship had soured by 2023, when a hot mic caught Dodik insulting the Djokovic family).

As much as he can, Djokovic has tried to represent Serbia in a positive way, to make others, including his own countrymen, rethink their view of the country. 'Serbia used to be known for wars and bad things,' said Jankovic. 'During those difficult times for Serbia, I think athletes, and especially us tennis players, were the greatest ambassadors for our country. We changed how people saw Serbia. We became known as a country with incredible athletes, including legends in sports like Novak who has broken all the records.'

Gangsters and drug-dealers used to be among the role models for Serbian kids, Djokovic's mother once said of the hard, sometimes lawless 1990s and early 2000s. Her eldest son has helped to change that, making a life for himself off the back of hard work and, through that, becoming a symbol of a new, re-energized Serbia. A Serbia moving on from the pain and the darkness. Djokovic's father put it more bluntly: at the worst possible moment in Serbia's history, Novak was sent from god to show that it wasn't, as some might have thought, a nation of murderers and savages.

3

CROSSROADS

Clown prince, they called him. He was the showman, the funny man, the Djoker. And yet, for all the goofing around and the smiles and the silliness, there were fears and doubts bubbling. You might not have guessed it from watching him gleefully impersonate Rafael Nadal's habit of picking wedgies out of his pants, but, in his early twenties, Novak Djokovic sometimes felt uneasy about his place in tennis and where he was heading. There's no physical contact in tennis but you can get roughed up in other ways and being around Nadal and Roger Federer wasn't always good for his psyche.

Something was eating at Djokovic. An extrovert who was more introspective than most, tennis's great thinker felt as though he hadn't found his true purpose. In that moment – already a Grand Slam champion after winning the 2008 Australian Open, and yet still 'a child' compared to the man and athlete he is today, according to his then coach Todd Martin – Djokovic was looking to understand his place in the sport. What was his destiny? What did he want to accomplish? 'At that stage of Novak's career,' recalled Martin, who was part of Djokovic's coaching team in 2009 and 2010, alongside the long-term Marian Vajda, 'he was at a crossroads, considering what his purpose or destiny was. He was asking himself: "What would be an appropriate objective for my career?"'

Djokovic knew he could easily have continued as the third man of tennis for years to come, picking up the occasional Grand Slam when Federer and Nadal were off their games, and there would have been no shame in that. While Djokovic didn't feel sorry for himself, he would have heard the voices around him who sometimes excused some of his results, and it's possible that would have got into his head and affected how he felt about his tennis and himself. There would have been congratulations for his sporadic successes; commiserations for playing in the sport's golden era.

'If Novak had ended up being third in the world for ten years behind Roger and Rafa, I think everyone would have patted him on the back and said he was one of the great players who was accidently born into the wrong generation,' said Martin. 'I don't recall Novak ever saying words to the effect of "Oh woe is me. I'm having to play against Roger and Rafa". But I think those around him – and I don't blame them – excused some of Novak's shortcomings at that time. That would have been in Novak's mind until he was able to take full responsibility for his successes and failures.'

But what if Djokovic wanted more than being the third man of tennis? What if he thought there was a way he could raise himself up and become the sport's central protagonist? 'Novak isn't like us mere mortals. He knew he had greatness inside him,' said Martin. But the Serb had to decide whether he actually wanted to bring that greatness out. Did

Djokovic dare to fully commit to his tennis? While Martin could sense that Djokovic had a curious and intelligent mind, it appeared as though the athlete hadn't reached the point where he had taken full control of his life and of his tennis. 'Novak definitely wasn't there when I was helping him. He just wasn't ready,' Martin said. Djokovic wasn't yet the obsessive athlete who would go on to snaffle so many Grand Slams: 'Novak was immature so he sought distraction. It's painful, right?'

The contradictions inside Djokovic meant that, while he was immature in some ways, he could also be wise and philosophical. Early on in their partnership, Djokovic told Martin, and a group they were sitting with, how 'the champion comes from within'. It was a comment that suggested to Martin that Djokovic had a 'calling to be great'. 'Novak, from war-torn Serbia, and then just 22 years old, sounded like a wise soul. Novak is highly philosophical and thoughtful, which likely comes from being well read. Novak is a good student of life. For him to have said that, at that stage, I imagine that was partly down to his innate wiring, and some product of his childhood and the education he received, as well as the responsibility that was placed on him early in his life.'

When a young Djokovic played Federer or Nadal, it sometimes felt as though he was afraid to win. Afraid because he had too much respect for them, because he was intimidated by them. Once, before going out to play Nadal at Roland Garros, the Majorcan was bouncing around the locker-room, sprinting and kangaroo-jumping, and, in Djokovic's head, that shared space suddenly felt very small. To add to the claustrophobic edge, Djokovic could hear the music that Nadal was listening to as it was leaking out of his headphones. They hadn't even got on court yet and already, in Djokovic's mind, he had sensed that Nadal had something over him and he was 'pissed off'. A naïve Djokovic hadn't appreciated that messing with an opponent's head was part of the game.

Here was another lesson that Djokovic could learn from Federer and Nadal: that the competition starts long before the first point, or even before you emerge from the locker-room. Djokovic would realize he could do the same to others, that his body language and actions before a match would show, as he told *60 Minutes*, that he was 'ready for a battle, for a war'. Djokovic was looking to Federer for guidance on how to organize his tennis and personal lives and yet still be a champion who carried himself with class and dignity on court, while Nadal was showing the Serb how to bring an uncompromisingly competitive spirit to matches.

In the early days of his rivalries with Federer and Nadal, Djokovic felt as though he was getting his 'ass kicked'. They were already multiple Grand Slam champions; he was still finding his way. 'Age is the biggest factor here, as Novak was the youngest of the three,' said Chris Evert. 'Roger and Rafa were already the established stars and Novak was the up-and-coming guy. I'm sure when he was on the way up, it would have been intimidating for him to have played against those two. But, as a young guy, you keep playing and you realize how much you want to win majors. You realize it's not personal. You don't necessarily want to beat someone as much as you want to win. The more you play someone the more it becomes robotic or mechanical and the emotions and the nerves aren't there so much. You also realize that the guys you're looking up to are humans with their own weaknesses as well. Once Novak beat each of them for the first time, they would no longer have been on a pedestal. He would have looked at Roger and Rafa as if they were down at his level.'

One of the challenges for Djokovic was that – when he wasn't playing Federer or Nadal – tennis was sometimes too simple for him. He was able to beat almost every opponent without much of a strategy, and by simply getting the ball back into the court one more time, but that was an approach that would ultimately drain him. It also meant that Djokovic wasn't thinking tactically as much as he otherwise would have done. 'Against 99 per cent of the players out there, Novak was so good and so athletic that he could just refuse to miss,' Martin said.

'In some ways, the game was too simple for Novak against nearly everybody. He could beat these guys by just refusing to lose but that workload ultimately catches up with an athlete. Probably the one guy that Novak had the most open mind against was Rafa. During Novak's early twenties, he had a great record against Rafa because he knew that if he didn't attack and didn't take risks, Rafa would bludgeon him like Rafa bludgeoned everybody else. Novak also had to figure out how to attack the players that he beat just by refusing to lose.' What he hadn't developed yet – this came later in Djokovic's career and will be explored in the final chapter – was a resistance to failure.

While all that was going on, Djokovic was, like all young athletes, learning to cope with all of his failures being picked over in public, which is going to affect how you feel about your place in the sport and whether you're willing to bring your greatness out. 'These athletes have millions and millions of people who witness and critique their failures,' said Martin. 'Athletes such as Novak, if they're going to be great, ultimately must come to terms with that. They say: "I'm going to fail sometimes no matter what. I can choose to embrace that and fail forward." It's relentless on social media. There's no avoiding it now. If you're a really good tennis player, but not great, your successes are there but your failures typically aren't. If you look at the greats, whether they win or lose, it's front and centre. It's on TV, it's in the traditional media, it's in everyone's social media feed, and so on.'

The lowest point for Djokovic didn't come against Federer or Nadal, but against Jurgen Melzer. Having led by two sets to love in his quarter-final against the Austrian at Roland Garros in 2010, Djokovic went on to lose and was so distraught that he cried and sobbed and let it all out; for the first time, he wanted to walk away from tennis. Even stronger than that, he wanted to run away from tennis, to get away from the people and the environment and all the pressures that had been building up around him. Djokovic couldn't see a reason to continue playing. He had already won one Grand Slam and been ranked third in the world but he couldn't envision achieving his dreams of holding the Wimbledon trophy and becoming the world number one. It felt – having worked towards those dreams since he was a child – that his universe was collapsing. If he couldn't even beat Melzer on clay, what chance did he have against Federer and Nadal at any of the slams?

Most coaches, Djokovic would later reflect, would have tried to say something motivational and uplifting, to quickly make the player feel strong again, but Vajda was giving Djokovic the chance to address his vulnerabilities. Vajda encouraged Djokovic to cry, helping him to 'liberate' all the emotions he had been experiencing. Djokovic was, to borrow his phrase, spilling his guts out. And if Vajda hadn't been there, if he hadn't been a shoulder to cry on, Djokovic would have felt even more alone. 'Nole went through this crisis that helped him to touch his demons, to touch his dark side. That was useful for him,' disclosed Igor Cetojevic, his confidant and former adviser on nutrition and life. 'Any kind of crisis is helpful. Sometimes we have to be in that position so we can recalculate, so we can see where we are and what we can do. That's when you have to go back to basics and reset your directions with your GPS. You're like a Ferrari which has gone off-road and now you're putting yourself back on the highway.'

At moments of failure, Djokovic has found it has been helpful to ask himself: 'Why are you playing tennis? What motivated you to play in the beginning? Why are you still playing it?' Stepping away from tennis to reflect on whether he wished to continue, Djokovic went looking for his inner child. He wanted to go back to how he had felt as a young boy in Serbia, and to rediscover that pure love for picking up a racquet and swinging at the ball. If Djokovic was going to end up returning to the circuit, he wouldn't do so just because that's what everyone expected of him. If he was going to keep on playing tennis, it would be because he still had a boyish sense of fun and joy. He hoped that his relationship with tennis could be raw and so simple again, that his motivation for training and travelling and competing could come from the purest source. As much as Djokovic had support from Vajda, and from his future wife Jelena and his parents, this was fundamentally something he had to do for himself. Within a few days, Djokovic was able to connect with his inner child, and there was a voice in his head reminding him what tennis had always been to him, which had brought him to the court in the first place, as well as what the sport could still be: 'Hey, it's a game – go play.'

What Gebhard Gritsch, Djokovic's fitness trainer, called the player's 'reinvention' – into the disciplined, hardened athlete we see today, mixing a child-like love for tennis with a ferocious commitment – began with that defeat to Melzer. 'When I started with Novak in 2009, he wasn't the guy we see now,' Gritsch said. 'He had some days when he wasn't so focused or that disciplined, though of course he was still young. I would say from 2010 onwards he really changed and became very focused, with his main objective to become number one. One of the crucial moments was his loss to Melzer in Paris. That match really hit him. He was very disappointed in himself and in the whole situation. Novak took some days off and he did some soul-searching. After that, he changed his attitude towards many things. He realized he had to focus, do everything right and go into the details.'

For some time, Martin said, Djokovic would have been asking himself: 'I've got greatness inside me, but can I bring it out? Do I dare bring it out? Am I brave enough to bring this out?' Knowing Djokovic as he does, Martin said that there must have come a moment when the athlete would have looked at himself in the bathroom mirror and given himself a pep talk that ultimately propelled him to 'out-of-this-world success'. Martin imagined the motivational speech for himself would have gone something like this: 'It's time. It's time for me to put it on the line enough for me to risk failure. I need to be courageous, test my potential and do everything I can to be great.'

Most players in tennis's toughest era downgraded their ambitions. Fair enough; they were being realists. But some in Djokovic's inner circle said that, blips aside, Djokovic never allowed himself to think like that. Dusan Vemic disclosed that Djokovic never tried to rationalize – as most players would have done – that he was the world number three. 'Novak always believed he was number one even when he was number three. He was never content with the fact he was number three. Novak never tried to rationalize not being number one. He just kept at it,' Vemic said. 'As a world-class athlete, the more experience you gain, you feel better in those moments, and you start to solve the puzzle more than you don't. He always believed he deserved to be a champion because he believed in himself and in his hard work and his lifestyle. He felt it was just a matter of time. He had unwavering belief in himself.'

It took time for Djokovic to start feeling as though his rivalries with Federer and Nadal would get the best out of him. In Federer and Nadal, Djokovic had a way of measuring where his game was and whether he was progressing as an athlete. Instead of being demoralized by Federer and Nadal's greatness, Djokovic came to take inspiration from what they were accomplishing, to see whether he could get there too. As Djokovic once remarked to his friend Chervin Jafarieh, he needed those rivalries. Playing at the same time as Federer and Nadal had forced Djokovic to reach greater heights. Would Djokovic have won more Grand Slams if it wasn't for Federer and Nadal? Possibly, but you can't say for sure as without those two he might not have had the same level of motivation. This can you say with near-certainty: Federer and Nadal made Djokovic a better tennis player; they propelled him to greatness. Chasing Federer and Nadal, Djokovic put himself on a trajectory to winning more majors than anyone else.

'Being the third guy helped Novak rather than hurt him,' said Craig O'Shannessy, Djokovic's former strategy coach. 'Novak thrived in that situation because those other two guys were excelling so much and doing things that hadn't been done before. If you're the third guy, and you're seeing what the two guys in front are doing, then you're going to be thinking: "If they can do it, I can do it too." I think that in a way having Roger and Rafa in front of him kind of deflected a little bit of the attention and at the same time also gave him something to aspire to. Those three guys owe a lot to each other. They all copied each other over the years with the ways they were playing.'

Being friends with your rivals wasn't possible. Tension was inevitable. In his early years on the tour, Djokovic felt as though Federer was unhappy with how the Serb was 'behaving', including how he openly discussed his intention to become the world number one (but he never felt as though he took it too far and disrespected the tennis elders). 'I remember thinking at the time that it was a good thing when Federer was saying things against Novak, when he was complaining about Novak's behaviour or something like this, as that meant that he saw him as a threat,' Ronen Bega, his former fitness trainer, recalled. For extra motivation, Djokovic would look to see if others were being treated better than he was behind the scenes, such as receiving superior shampoo and soap when showering or even being handed a fluffier towel. Djokovic has a better relationship today with the younger generation – with the likes of Carlos Alcaraz, Daniil Medvedev and Jannik Sinner – than he had with Federer and Nadal back then. Some observers hold up Evert's relationship with Martina Navratilova as an example of how tennis rivals can be friends, but they weren't truly close when they were both competing, so she appreciates how Djokovic couldn't be pally with Federer. 'When you're in competition with someone, you don't want to go out for dinner with them and be vulnerable and reveal your true feelings as that's going to give them an edge,' said Evert. 'It's only when you retire, and when you're no longer competing with each other, that you can be friends and human beings and not competitors.'

As was clear after that defeat to Melzer in Paris in 2010, Djokovic's self-belief was enhanced by his 'beautiful relationship' with Vajda, who coached him to 20 of his Grand Slam titles from 2006–17 and then from

2018–2021. 'Relationships are interesting things between people and sometimes great minds might not work well together. But somehow those two individuals – Novak and Marian – really complemented each other in so many ways,' said Vemic, who saw that dynamic up close, from the inside. 'Marian grew as a coach, as a mentor, as an older brother or uncle. He allowed Novak to grow. It was just a beautiful relationship that brought the best out of both of them. Marian helped Novak to believe in himself. A tennis player could be very well coached, he could have learned so much, but that doesn't matter unless he believes in himself. In the critical moments on court, we're alone and we have only a split-second to make decisions. The more we trust ourselves and our abilities, the better the outcome will be. For Novak, his relationship with Marian helped him to back himself in those moments.'

Think of Vajda as the Jedi Master of the courts. 'Marian was like Yoda,' said O'Shannessy. 'Marian was somebody who kind of sat in the background a little bit. But when he spoke, his words mattered. He has an incredible amount of experience. He knows the game inside out. He knows the players. It was an absolute pleasure to work with him, and to see their relationship, because each day I was learning too.'

Some coaches are good at what they do but can be a drag to be around, draining you of energy. Vajda was serious when needed and also light-hearted when required. That, in essence, was why his relationship with Djokovic endured. 'Marian's got a really good attitude about him. He's a fun guy to be around. He's a guy who smiles a lot and cracks some jokes. He laughs as well as being very serious,' said O'Shannessy. 'Marian was a great fit for Novak because Novak needed somebody who knew what they were doing but also at the same time wasn't a pain to be around, and who wasn't so serious the whole time. Their personalities really meshed together. Novak had a tremendous amount of respect for everything that Marian did. That included helping Novak when he was doubting himself and going through some difficult times – being a coach isn't just about the strategy and the strokes and the technique.'

Vajda's aura and energy allowed Djokovic to maintain a positive outlook on life, even when results weren't going his way. 'Marian is an incredible person,' said Gritsch. 'He had a great aura and energy and in the long run that was extremely positive for Novak. And not just for Novak but for the whole team. It's not easy to go out and prepare in the best possible way day after day after day. For this, you need to have a lot of positive energy. That's why Marian's energy was super important for everyone in the team. Obviously as a coach you do a lot of other stuff but the positive energy that he brought to the team was exceptional compared to other coaches. There aren't many great coaches who have such an aura and such a high level of positive energy. Everyone around Marian was profiting from that energy.'

If Djokovic could just move up two spots in the rankings, that would be huge. 'That doesn't sound like a massive leap,' said Martin, 'but when you know how far number three was from number one at the time, it really was massive.' In that era, winning one major was no guarantee of adding any more. Djokovic was aware that he wasn't exactly going to glide through the rest of his tennis life, picking up Grand Slams. But, as Martin said, Djokovic was prepared to work on himself. He sensed that Novak was thinking: 'I wonder what I could do to get better. Let me look into this.'

Bringing the greatness out would mean re-learning how to eat, how to breathe, how to think.

4

THE MAN BEHIND THE DJOKER

No athletes get more television close-ups than tennis players; during the change of ends, when they're seated, cameras keep on zooming until it's borderline intrusive. The director and the viewer are getting a player's face, and their psyche, in HD. It's an individual sport; there's nowhere else, apart from the other side of the net, for the cameras to go. Television is one of the reasons why they say tennis reveals character. Out there on the court, on your chair, you're exposing your psychological make-up to the crowd and the television audience. As much as you might want to, you can't hide who you really are. But what if, a few years into your career, after you have already won a first major title and become a leading figure in the sport, you shed one on-court personality and create another? That sounds like a stretch, almost impossible, but that's what Novak Djokovic did.

Dialling down his Djoker persona – suppressing the showman within and cutting back on the on-court fun – was the revolution that Djokovic needed as an athlete. Djokovic had been the Djoker when he won his first

Grand Slam title at the 2008 Australian Open. By 2011, the season when he achieved his childhood dreams of winning Wimbledon and becoming the world number one, Djoker was no more. Or, at least, Djokovic was no longer the full-on Djoker. He was, at most, Djoker-Light. Something curious had happened with Djokovic early on in his life on the professional tour, during his Djoker phase. Doing impressions of other players was, you might say, when Djokovic was truly himself. That sounds paradoxical but he was showing he had some spirit and a sense of humour. That he had something about him other than otherworldly tennis skills. But Djokovic also came to realize that, for all the laughs and the good times, being the Djoker wasn't good for business.

So he changed. He reinvented himself and became a more subdued and sensible athlete. In the future, the fun side would still surface occasionally when he was on court, such as with his victory dances. There would still be glimpses of the Djoker. But, for the most part, Djokovic had archived that side of his personality. But you have to wonder: at what cost, when having fun was such an important element of his character? Who was Djokovic without some of his inner joy, especially as he understood that the crowd wanted to see players' personalities as well as their forehands?

'Novak became more and more subtle on the court,' said Dusan Vemic. 'That's just been his journey of finding who he is. Stopping the impressions was part of his growth. One moment, Novak would have felt as though that was the right thing to do and then, in the next moment, he would have felt that it was OK not to be the guy who makes those reels.'

If Djokovic wasn't a tennis player, he once said, he would have liked to have gone into the entertainment industry. Among the big hitters in men's tennis, Djokovic is by far the biggest extrovert, the one who was happiest showing his human side – and a bit more besides. That was obvious from watching his turn in the karaoke booth at Roland Garros one year, which a French broadcaster had arranged for some of the players. Djokovic got carried away with Gloria Gaynor's 'I Will Survive', singing or perhaps shouting out the lyrics with gusto, and finishing the song shirtless like Iggy Pop. Even more daring was his appearance at a fashion show at a tournament in Montreal one summer – after discarding his robe, he stood there in just his underwear, which wasn't something that you could have imagined Roger Federer doing. Which, in a way, was the point; Djokovic was seen as the rebel, as the young man who wanted to tear down the tennis establishment, and doing things differently just fed into that. On his very first appearance in the main draw of the Grand Slams, at the 2005 Australian Open, Djokovic had been keen to add to the theatre of it all – he asked the hairdresser to dye the front of his hair for his opening round match against Marat Safin (which his mother wasn't too happy about).

Away from tennis, Djokovic didn't take himself too seriously. When Belgrade hosted the 2008 Eurovision Song Contest, Djokovic made an appearance, hurling a giant tennis ball into the audience, an act that signified that the voting was open. While he was up there, with millions watching across Europe, he accepted the hosts' invitation to break into song. In that situation, confidence wasn't an issue. 'It's not that Novak has ever tried to be an entertainer for the sake of tennis, that's just his personality,' Chris Evert said. 'Roger and Rafa are a lot more inside themselves. They're a lot more introverted than Novak. They're shy by comparison. Novak has always been a strong guy.'

For some time before his talent for mimicry became public knowledge, Djokovic had been entertaining his team and his friends in private. To send up Maria Sharapova, which he used to enjoy doing more than any of the other impressions, he would go through her pre-service routine, including pretending to sweep long hair behind both ears, as well as fidgeting with strings and staring at the backstop. Djokovic would stuff a towel down his T-shirt and pretend to be Serena Williams (when Williams's friend Caroline Wozniacki did something similar, padding her top and skirt with towels to imitate Williams's curves, some found it offensive but the American said she didn't consider it racist). Djokovic's repertoire of impressions also included Federer and Andy Roddick, plus some of the past greats, such as John McEnroe, his idol Pete Sampras and his future coaches Boris Becker and Goran Ivanisevic.

Closely observing and copying how other players moved on a tennis court was something Djokovic had been doing since he was a child, as his first coach Jelena Gencic had encouraged him to watch videos of leading athletes and to emulate how they were hitting their strokes. Years later, when Djokovic was establishing himself on the tour, the first thing that many tennis fans would have learned about him was that he was an impressionist.

At the 2007 US Open, an on-court interviewer invited Djokovic to perform some of his impersonations and the 20-year-old was very happy to do so. The crowd loved that. He was living it up in New York City that summer, reaching his first Grand Slam final, which he lost to Federer. In addition to Sharapova, Djokovic had actor Robert de Niro sitting in his guests' box in the Arthur Ashe Stadium. Djokovic looked like the extrovert that tennis had always said it wanted, even though he wasn't mimicking other players because he thought it would endear him to the crowd; he was doing it because it made him smile. Writing in his book *Hitting Back*, which was published in 2008, Andy Murray noted that 'many people like [Djokovic's] personality, including his famous impressions of other players. He does great take-offs of players' serves. The best ones are Roddick and Sharapova, and Nadal tugging at his shorts'.

Djokovic was sufficiently self-aware to appreciate that from time to time he pushed it too far. He was realizing that being humorous on the court possibly wasn't helping his cause. He wanted to be seen as a tennis player, as 'a big champion' and not a comic who happened to be good at tennis, and he wasn't getting that balance right. During that 2007 US Open, Djokovic felt as though he was getting more compliments for his impersonations than he was for the quality of his tennis, even though he had gone deeper into a Grand Slam than ever before. It left him wondering: 'Guys, am I here for the impersonations, entertaining, or to play tennis?' If there was a moment when Djokovic felt as though he was going to have to tone down being the Djoker, it was when he was serving in a big match and he heard a spectator shout out: 'Hey Novak, do the impersonation of Sharapova, we like that, make us laugh.' How about the actual tennis? As the spectator told Djokovic very plainly, that was boring him. What was Djokovic exactly, a tennis clown or an athlete?

Maybe, for a time, he was both, and a successful combination of the two. Even as the Djoker, Djokovic had always been serious about his tennis – you don't win a first Grand Slam by playing for laughs during the points. As a tennis player, as an individual athlete, you play for yourself first and if that makes anyone else happy – such as your compatriots watching back home or inside the stadium – that's a nice bonus. But that theory was stress-tested the day that Djokovic won the 2008 Australian Open. Landing a first Grand Slam is hugely significant for any tennis player. But it felt even more momentous for Djokovic when he lifted the Norman Brookes Challenge Cup. It wasn't as if he was, say, an American joining the long list of champions from the United States; he was the first player from Serbia – which, as we have established, in tennis was like coming from nowhere – to score a major. Djokovic couldn't claim his victory just for himself; it felt as though it was also Serbia's. He had got there just before his childhood friend Ana Ivanovic, who would snaffle the women's singles title that season at Roland Garros.

The performance that stays in the memory from that fortnight was Djokovic's tennis in the semi-final when he defeated Federer – who had reached the final of the previous ten Grand Slams – in straight sets. While Federer wasn't at his best that night, and it would later emerge that the Swiss had been weakened by glandular fever, Djokovic was poised and classy in the Rod Laver Arena. Djokovic didn't have everything his own way in the final against Jo-Wilfried Tsonga – he dropped the opening set, perhaps disturbed by picking up on how his family, dressed in T-shirts spelling out 'NOLE', didn't appreciate being seated next to a large group of vocal French fans. Djokovic found a way of dealing with the power of the unseeded Frenchman and the occasion, stopping the cries of 'Allez Tsonga'. No doubt it helped that he had played in a major final once before. Djokovic was 20 years old. He wasn't quite one of tennis's teenage prodigies – like Nadal, who held the Roland Garros trophy just days after turning 19 – but he also got there quicker than Federer, who had been 21 when he had his breakthrough at Wimbledon.

Djokovic partied until 4am in the locker-room, after a local band was invited inside to play for him and his team and other guests. 'Novak was acting like a kid with all the excitement of winning his first Grand Slam,' recalled Craig Tiley, the CEO of Tennis Australia, who was then the tournament director of the Australian Open. 'The band played all night and it was great to see Novak having so much fun.' While he was still the Djoker at the 2008 Australian Open, he was far less enthusiastic than before, and he had to be persuaded by an on-court interviewer to do his Sharapova impression for the Melbourne crowd. Increasingly, Djokovic felt as though he was coming under pressure to perform – he was being forced – which was bound to take the fun out of it.

Some players clearly didn't mind Djokovic doing impressions of them. Djokovic joked Sharapova would 'kill' him after doing his spoof of her for the umpteenth time. If Sharapova really had been bothered, she wouldn't have sat in his player's box at the 2007 US Open. But Djokovic could see that other players weren't laughing. Nadal wasn't thrilled in the beginning. Federer, the most influential voice in the locker-room, observed: 'I know some guys weren't happy. Some guys might think it's funny – he's walking a tightrope, for sure.' While it's an individual sport, tennis is much more collegiate than some might appreciate – you're travelling the world together, and before and after matches, you're in the same space as your peers. Djokovic enjoyed making the crowd laugh and smile, but if that was going to irritate others, and bring bad energy into the locker-room, it was time to stop being the tennis jester. Being the Djoker hadn't just started to 'hurt' his tennis; he once acknowledged it risked 'hurting everything'.

One of Djokovic's closest friends, Janko Tipsarevic, said it would have been boring if Djokovic had carried on doing impressions throughout his long career. How many times do you want to see Djokovic picking out wedgies like Nadal? 'When Novak was a young kid on the tour, I think it was fun for him to do impressions but if he had carried on doing that for the next 15 years or so, that would have been kind of dull. Novak changed and evolved, and that's how it should be. You're not the same person in your thirties that you were as a teenager or in your early twenties.' Some might say that Djokovic suppressing his Djoker has meant that he hasn't been able to fully express himself on court but Tipsarevic would disagree. 'Even though he's no longer doing impressions, Novak is still expressing himself. And, in my opinion, he's still very entertaining and funny.'

'Novak still wears his emotion on his sleeves,' Vemic said. 'He doesn't shy away from being in front of the crowd and expressing himself as an athlete and as an entertainer and a role model and a mentor. That's his spirit, that's who he is. If you put Novak on the spot today, he would probably still be able to mimic some of the current players and their serves and forehands and backhands and whatnot. He's an extraordinary athlete so can copy anyone and everyone, even the little intricacies of their technique and behaviour.'

Djokovic wasn't going to do anything that hurt his primary goal: to win. But he had to ease himself off the impressions. Sometimes Djokovic just couldn't resist, such as the occasion he did an impression of Nadal right in front of the Spaniard at the trophy presentation ceremony after the 2009 Rome final. Or the time at the 2009 US Open when he mimicked McEnroe on court after a match, even teasingly shouting out,

'You cannot be serious', but that was different. That wasn't going to risk possibly enraging his peers in the locker-room. And, anyway, McEnroe seemed to appreciate the teasing, leaving his commentary booth to play some points with Djokovic.

But there can be no doubt that, for a long while now, Djokovic hasn't been the Djoker, that he hasn't been the showman of old. Every tennis player wears a mask, according to psychologist Daria Abramowicz. Athletes aren't revealing their true selves to the public because they're creating psychological safe havens where they're able to feel healthy and calm. That's become more prevalent since social media created a culture around athletes that stirred up, in Abramowicz's words, 'a lot of hate and judgement'. Djokovic's Djoker phase came before the age of Twitter and Instagram and haters casually telling athletes that they wished their families all died of cancer (for female tennis players, getting called a bitch online can be a regular occurrence). Djokovic probably wouldn't have used the word safe haven at the time. But he was retreating ever so slightly from the public stage. One of the sport's great extroverts was choosing not to reveal his authentic self. Keeping that mask on can be hard, Abramowicz said, as it costs you more energy than being your authentic self. But what choice did Djokovic have?

And, in other ways, Djokovic is extremely open. As we will examine later, when it comes to articulating his ambitions, along with discussing the fears and doubts in his head, he could hardly be more transparent.

The Djoker hasn't been killed off completely. Djokovic's millions of followers on social media, on Instagram and X, will know that his handle is a combination of his two nicknames, 'Djoker' and 'Nole'. Djokovic didn't mute all the fun. He has been game with his sponsors. For one commercial for his racquet supplier HEAD, Djokovic went wing-walking and played some tennis on top of a flying plane, while in another advert, he put on a blonde wig and pretended to be Sharapova.

To celebrate Halloween one year, he walked on court at an indoor tournament in Paris wearing a Darth Vader mask, and one summer before Wimbledon he was playing an exhibition match outside London when – and this was written up as a striptease – he took his shirt off while the crowd clapped and then twirled it around his head. From time to time, he has impersonated players, though it doesn't happen too often now. One such occasion was when he did an impression of Andy Murray at the players' party at the Monte Carlo tournament in 2023 (Djokovic also dressed up as the rapper Snoop Dogg at the same event). To make himself smile on the practice court at the 2023 US Open, he revived his Djoker show by performing some of his old favourites, such as his Sharapova piss-take. A few days before the 2024 Australian Open, Djokovic hosted his 'Novak and Friends' charity event and it was an illustration of how you can achieve tennis greatness, often enduring some heavy stuff to get there, while still having a lighter, humorous side. Totally at ease in the Rod Laver Arena, he was joshing with other tennis players and with a selection of Australian athletes.

As Jelena Jankovic said: 'Novak likes to joke around. He's a funny guy.'

*

Maria Sharapova used to say that if she was going to do an impression of Djoker-era Djokovic, she would have stood at the baseline, as if preparing to serve but never actually hitting the ball, instead endlessly bouncing a tennis ball: 'I'm just going to stand here and bounce the ball for a really long time before I serve. We're going to be here all day long.' Djoker's no more but you could do the exact same impression now – while Djokovic has tried to stop bouncing the ball to excess, because he's fully aware that it aggravates others and it also annoys himself, he's been unable to quit. People call it a habit but it's more than that: bouncing that ball meets some psychological need within Djokovic.

For all Djokovic's mental strength and resilience, playing professional tennis is up there as one of the most trying sports; a game invented for English garden parties, for the Victorian leisure class, can put great rips and tears in a modern athlete's psyche. On top of everything else that makes tennis so demanding – the burden of the travel plus the changing circumstances every tournament, with a new surface, often new balls, new conditions, new surroundings and new people, and the almost inevitable defeat as only one player ever goes undefeated – the long pauses and breaks between points aren't helpful. There's too much time to feel, too much time to think. Much more time than most other sports. 'Most of the time as a tennis player, you're not in your prime – you feel like shit,' said Abramowicz. Djokovic will have those days. And even when everything goes well, there will still be moments of low-level anxiety or times when he feels as though he needs to compose himself.

For all his mental greatness, Djokovic can't always be mentally robust. He's imperfect and bouncing that ball is a way of controlling his anxiety. By focusing on the ball, he's able to clear his mind and get composed. Bouncing the ball also provides Djokovic with an opportunity to regulate his breathing: he'll often be breathing through his nose to release some of the tension and manage his stress levels. When Djokovic is facing a break point, or it's a pivotal part of the match, he will often bounce the ball for longer as he tries to cope with the tension he is feeling. 'It seems as though Djokovic is managing the anxiety inside him,' Abramowicz said from observing him on the tour. While Chris Evert, a tennis great and an insightful observer of the modern game, suggested that Djokovic was 'quelling the nerves and trying to calm himself down'. 'It's also possible that, as he bounces the ball, he's being thoughtful and he's thinking about where he's going to serve. He's visualizing the point ahead.'

If you sometimes feel yourself counting the bounces before Djokovic serves, you're not alone. Djokovic used to count the bounces to ensure he was doing an even number when serving from the deuce court and an odd number from the ad court. He's stopped doing that – there's no number he's trying to hit – but when he approaches the baseline, ball in hand, he doesn't know how many times he will need to bounce the ball before starting his service action. Djokovic will keep on going until he feels as though the tempo is right and it's the moment to toss the ball up.

Earlier in his career, Djokovic sometimes felt as though he had no control over his hand – he had no ability whatsoever to stop the bouncing – and he would often end up with cramp along with a sore back from all the time he spent holding that position at the baseline, wondering whether he would ever get to serve. As Djokovic couldn't explain why he was bouncing the ball so much, how could he possibly deal with it? The worst was a Davis Cup tie against Australia in 2007 when he almost got to 40 bounces before one serve.

While in recent years it appears as though it has become less of a problem, the bouncing continues. It's natural that some spectators and opponents get enormously frustrated with Djokovic's bouncing of the ball – and feel as though they are stuck in a loop which will never end – but it's possible to look at this differently. It's not a psychological trick designed to aggravate and destabilize opponents. It's a moment when you get to see more of the real Djokovic and you're reminded of his vulnerabilities and imperfections as a man and as athlete. That's not a criticism – he has said himself that he's a flawed human being and not an almighty demigod. Djokovic's achievements are all the more interesting and admirable because he's imperfect.

5

FOOD FOR THOUGHT

Novak Djokovic's decision in 2010 to ditch the gluten in his diet, long before it was fashionable – as well as making other adjustments, such as reducing how much meat he was eating – is often presented as the career move that transformed everything for him. In the end, it was. But in the early days going gluten-free, and all the other changes to his nutrition, was becoming dangerous for Djokovic: he appeared to be getting close to the red zone. His fitness trainer Gebhard Gritsch was the one who was alarmed; some days, he had noticed, the Serb didn't have the energy to get through all his training sessions. Djokovic couldn't do what was required to continue as an elite athlete. Gritsch had picked up on how Djokovic's muscles were slowly and quietly disappearing; he was becoming 'weaker and weaker'.

Listening to Gritsch speaking openly about one of the most critical periods of Djokovic's life, you appreciate that switching to a gluten-free diet wasn't without its complications. As Gritsch noted, 'for a top athlete, everything is fragile', and this new-look Djokovic appeared to have taken his fresh approach too far; he had gone beyond what Gritsch saw as 'the limit' and simply wasn't consuming enough calories. From Gritsch's perspective, the tennis player's nutrition had become a genuine concern; Gritsch had several conversations – which must have felt urgent at the time – to explain to Djokovic why his body was low on energy and why he was losing muscle tissue.

'There was a process and, at the beginning, the changes to his nutrition helped him a lot. But there were also stages when it was almost getting dangerous to his health and to his energy supply as an athlete,' Gritsch said. 'Nutrition-wise, it wasn't just going gluten-free; he changed a little bit more. He also reduced his meat intake. It was the same as it would be for anybody who goes that way – you lose weight and basically you feel better, but there's always a limit. You come to a stage where you have to ask, "Are you getting the necessary nutrition to be a top athlete and to get through the workload every day?" At certain times, he didn't have energy for the training, and that was concerning for me. It was a very difficult thing. Nutrition-wise, it wasn't easy to get him to the right level.'

Gritsch needed to be direct and honest in his conversations with Djokovic. 'The amount of food he was eating just wasn't enough to maintain the workload. What happens then is that muscles disappear slowly and then your motor is getting weaker and weaker. He was always trying to optimize but it can go both ways. It's difficult to find the right balance. I spoke to him several times. I tried to explain what was happening to him physiologically.'

In time, with Gritsch's help from 2009 to 2017, from 2018 to 2019, and then for a third collaboration from 2024, Djokovic would go on to become impossibly stretchy and flexible, celebrated for his bendy, almost rubbery legs and for looking as though he could jump into the splits at any moment. Gritsch doesn't think there has ever been a more flexible tennis player. In years to come, Djokovic's explosive movement was also unparalleled – every other player worked on that, too, knowing how important that first step was when reacting and moving towards the ball, but they didn't have his discipline and good genes. Genetically, Gritsch said, Djokovic was always the perfect package as a tennis player and, later in his career, he would become the greatest athlete to have ever swung a racquet. But that was in the future. In 2010, it didn't look so certain that Djokovic would achieve the physical conditioning to make the most of his athletic genes. In Gritsch's view, this was getting 'dangerous' for Djokovic.

Gritsch was clear with Novak: 'You're not putting enough calories into your body. You need to find a balance.'

Getting that balance right would be critical. How Djokovic reached that state would also be an indication of how the Serb's mind worked, and how he processed information, including warnings from those close to him.

*

'How many Grand Slams are there in a year?'

The man asking that question was the doctor who – with the help of a slice of white bread – would change the course of tennis history. It was directed at Novak Djokovic and his team, who, just before screaming with laughter, replied as one: 'What? How can you not know that?' But Doctor Igor Cetojevic hadn't entered Djokovic's world in the summer of 2010 because of his tennis knowledge or even because of any enthusiasm for the sport – he cared so little for tennis that he didn't even know the proper terms. He would, for instance, call a match a 'game'. That's a mistake that often infuriates anyone who plays or watches tennis but Cetojevic got away with it, as well as his genuine enquiry about the number of majors in a season, because of his easy, smiley nature. Talking to him now, you can appreciate how he brought some lightness and laughter to the Djokovic camp. Cetojevic's WhatsApp profile picture is graffiti of a smiling cow saying, 'go vegan', and he often punctuates his messages with the sunglasses and flexed bicep emojis.

What this Bosnian-born Serb did know about was 'energetic medicine', which is based on quantum physics and is focused on the energies and vibrations in the body. While rooted in traditional Chinese teachings, it became more prominent in the 1980s because of the technologies that had been developed that had allowed practitioners to measure those vibrations. Even so, it's still considered alternative; Cetojevic said he takes an 'unusual' approach to medicine. When people hear how he uses pendulums to find the 'holes' in a body's atmosphere, they think it sounds like magic. Cetojevic explained he didn't just examine a patient's physical body; he was also interested in their mental body and their emotional body, along with their spiritual body. And, just as you might expect from a specialist in energetic medicine, he brought good energy to his life and to his work.

Djokovic's association with Cetojevic would be transformative. It would change Djokovic's body and his tennis life. Without Cetojevic, Djokovic wouldn't put together such an astonishingly good season in 2011 and play such punchy tennis beyond that. But that wasn't all. Linking up with Cetojevic would shape Djokovic's thinking, giving him a new playbook for tennis and life. Djokovic would learn how taking an alternative approach – opening your mind, stepping away from the mainstream and daring to do things differently – could work for him. He would realize he didn't have to eat as everyone else ate. Or think as everyone else did. Djokovic would learn, Cetojevic said, that he didn't have to be 'trapped in the mass media' as 'he could think for himself and take his own path in life'.

'You could say I've had an impact on how Nole thinks as well as how he eats. He's an intelligent guy. When you're a young man and you try something and you get some results, you're going to be receptive and you're going to start doing research for yourself. You're going to be even more curious and you're going to be thinking, "OK, what else can I do?"'

Djokovic's future approach on health and wellness – including some of the more New Age stuff and deciding against having a vaccine during a global pandemic – can be traced back to Cetojevic. Djokovic's association with Cetojevic wouldn't have worked out if the athlete hadn't already been through the shift in his mindset, committing to getting the greatness out of himself. Other tennis players might have been reluctant to engage with an alternative doctor in the first place. They might not have even taken the meeting. But Cetojevic has said Djokovic has a 'beautiful open mind'.

It was open before Cetojevic popped up in his life. Seeking out knowledge had always been a thrill for Djokovic. He looked for it in books. And he didn't read much that was lightweight or fluffy. Djokovic was surprised, perhaps also a little amused, when he was handed a copy of Andy Murray's 2008 autobiography, *Hitting Back*. Murray had written a book? Djokovic had been under the impression that the Scot, a rival since their junior days, didn't even read books. Djokovic, meanwhile, had always been a big reader. At that time, he was reading a biography of

Nikola Tesla, as he was intrigued to find out more about the Serbian inventor's death in a Manhattan hotel room and who – conspiracy theory alert – might have wanted him dead. Djokovic would also read books such as one about a neuroscientist who had a near-death experience and a spiritual awakening. There was a time when Djokovic would spend some evenings with Jelena arranging – and then rearranging – their extensive library of books and would recommend books on consciousness and other topics.

Djokovic has been known to quote the Greek philosopher Socrates: 'All I know is that I know nothing'. When Cetojevic had got in touch, Djokovic had been receptive to new ideas, and finding some way to elevate himself above his status – as Jelena was calling it – as the third man of tennis. In 2010, Djokovic and Cetojevic were sitting in a restaurant in Split in Croatia. Cetojevic handed Djokovic a slice of bread. Djokovic was curious: 'What do you want me to do with this bread? Eat it?' Cetojevic laughed. He had something else in mind.

Sometimes, Djokovic thinks, the universe conspires to help you on your path. Ordinarily, Cetojevic wouldn't have given a moment's thought to Djokovic's efforts at the Grand Slams. But, in January that year, Cetojevic had met a friend for coffee who was a tennis enthusiast and who had urged him to take some interest in this young Serb who was playing the Australian Open. That was how Cetojevic, lying on the sofa in front of his television at home in Cyprus, found himself watching Djokovic's quarter-final against Jo-Wilfried Tsonga in 2010. It wasn't just that Cetojevic wasn't much of a tennis fan; he also wasn't 'a TV guy'. If you believe in karma, as Cetojevic does, that was how he switched on and tuned in for that match. It wasn't the first time that Djokovic had suffered a breakdown on court. But this was infinitely worse than anything he had experienced before. Cetojevic didn't have to be an expert on tennis to see that Djokovic had been 'playing nicely' and then suddenly he couldn't do a thing, as if someone had switched him off and drained him of all energy. Clogged up with sticky gluten, negativity and deep, dark, existential despair, Djokovic was fading fast.

He was weak and empty, unable to catch his breath between points, unable to compete. Djokovic's vision blurred and the court, which had looked so wide at the start of the match, now appeared narrow. There was an overwhelming, terrifying sense of being powerless and helpless. Djokovic, who had led by two sets to one, was physically and mentally 'broken' towards the end of his five-set defeat, with his racquet so heavy in his hand that it felt as though he was swinging Thor's hammer. He was a tennis player hollowed out from the inside. Off-camera, Djokovic requested a bathroom break and he returned to the locker-room where he felt as though he vomited away all his remaining strength. Tsonga, meanwhile, was bouncing and bustling around the hard court, full of energy and life and ambition. 'The end came quickly and mercifully, like an execution,' Djokovic would later write in his book, *Serve to Win*. Djokovic lost the final set 6–1, which is sometimes called a 'breadstick', just as a 6–0 set is a 'bagel'. Breadstuffs were more of a problem than Djokovic could have realized.

It was the lowest, most desperate moment of Djokovic's career and for his supporters this was excruciating to watch; Cetojevic, a newcomer to tennis, was intrigued. He didn't understand all the technicalities of Djokovic's tennis. He didn't even have a grasp of the basics. But – backed by his studies in Chinese medicine at a college in Belgrade along with a degree from the Indian Institute of Magnotherapy in New Delhi – he took issue with the commentator saying, not just once but a few times, that Djokovic's struggles could be explained by asthma. Cetojevic, who felt as though he could read people, even those thousands of miles away whom he was only seeing through his television screen, didn't think that sounded right.

Maybe asthma could have affected Djokovic's breathing and performance if he had been competing in the morning, but this was an evening match. And, anyway, Djokovic had been physically fine when building a lead at the start of the match before his body went into meltdown. If this had been asthma, that would have affected Djokovic from the opening set. Cetojevic was talking back at the television so loudly that his wife, who had been in the kitchen, came to see what was going on: 'Who's playing?' When Cetojevic responded that it was 'this Serbian guy', his wife instantly encouraged him to offer his assistance. 'She was pushing me, saying, "If he's a good guy, go, go help him". If it wasn't for her, I never would have made contact.'

The way it usually works at the highest levels of tennis is that you go through your big existential struggle – confronting and then fixing the physical, technical or psychological flaws in your make-up – and then all being well you have your breakthrough and win your first Grand Slam title. But that wasn't the Djokovic narrative. If he had imagined that, after winning his first major at the 2008 Australian Open, he would quickly pick up a few more, it didn't work that way. Far from surging and soaring, he was regressing. He didn't win another that season, the year after or even the season after that. He didn't even appear in another major final in 2008 or 2009. Djokovic had won that first Grand Slam title before undergoing a personality adjustment, before dialling down his extrovert

Djoker persona and becoming a less excitable presence. Djokovic had also become a major champion before sorting out what was happening in his body, or before he ever knew there was anything to sort out. Djokovic's story was unusual in tennis: first, the maiden Grand Slam victory and only then afterwards did he experience the big struggle, which saw him flirt with the idea of quitting.

It's often said that tennis is a mental game and that's undoubtedly true. But if you can't keep moving around the court over five long sets, or even three, having the best mind on the tour isn't going to count for much. Watching Djokovic play in his mid-to-late thirties – when he has been showing remarkable athleticism and stretchy, rubber-limbed flexibility – it can feel odd recalling how in his early twenties, he was often physically vulnerable.

Since he was a boy, Djokovic had often experienced breathing difficulties, forever feeling 'stuffy' and blocked up, and not getting the oxygen his muscles wanted. It was worse at night, when there was the occasional sense of being 'suffocated'. From talking to Djokovic, Cetojevic believed the player was struggling with insomnia, and that he had become resigned to bad, broken sleep, among all the other health issues that were crowding in on him and his enjoyment of tennis and life. 'It was normal for Novak not to sleep well,' Cetojevic said of Djokovic's insomnia. 'If you're eating something wrong, your body is smart and trying to get rid of it. It's not allowed to calm down at night. You know what's important for a sportsman? To have good rest. To rejuvenate in the night. Novak wasn't always able to do that.'

Djokovic tried to address his health issues; he had an operation to fix a 'deviation' on his nose and had been to see a Belgrade opera singer to learn breathing exercises. But still he had issues. There were clues on his face that something wasn't quite right. A few years later, Jelena was going through old photos of Djokovic at the time and she noticed that he often had a swollen upper lip and that his nose was puffy. As Djokovic got older, his physical issues intensified, particularly when he was on court, which was far from ideal. Combine that weakness with the psychological pressures and emotions of playing elite-level tennis and you have a volatile, unsettling mix.

There were days when Djokovic felt as though he had concrete in his legs and as though he couldn't get air into his lungs. He wasn't good in the heat. It was also taking him a long time to recover.

When he was new on the scene, a teenage Djokovic had developed the last thing any athlete wants in a sport as demanding as tennis: a reputation for fragility. The first year he played Roland Garros, in 2005, he took the opening set in his second round against Argentine Guillermo Coria – which was a promising start against such a decent clay-court player – only to feel as though he couldn't breathe out there on the clay and he retired during the third set. Even more alarming for Djokovic, and for those watching, was how he repeatedly needed medical attention for breathing problems during his opening match at that season's US Open. As first appearances in New York go, it wasn't a happy one. While Djokovic ended up winning the match – beating Frenchman Gael Monfils in five sets – the crowd were dubious about what was real and what wasn't. As Djokovic left the court, he heard the boos.

If some of Djokovic's peers in the locker-room suspected that Djokovic was sometimes too feeble to keep up, Federer was one player who suggested that the Serb occasionally made the most of his injuries to throw opponents off their rhythm. 'I don't trust his injuries. I'm serious. I think he's a joke, you know, when it comes down to his injuries,' Federer said at a Davis Cup tie between Switzerland and Serbia in 2006 after suggesting that Djokovic had been calling for the trainer too often while playing Stan Wawrinka. When Djokovic stopped his semi-final against Federer in Monte Carlo in 2008 – citing a sore throat, dizziness and breathing difficulties – he heard what some people were saying about him. He was hurt by suggestions that he abandoned matches whenever he was losing.

Retiring from any match won't sit easily with any tennis player; that's an even more desperate situation when you're deep into a Grand Slam. But it was happening all too often with Djokovic. A year after stopping against Coria in Paris, Djokovic reached his first Grand Slam quarter-final at Roland Garros in 2006 where he was to play Rafael Nadal, but after losing the first two sets he retired because of a back injury. Djokovic's aim of winning Wimbledon appeared closer than ever when he advanced into the semi-finals in 2007, but after splitting the first two sets with Nadal he felt as though he could play no more. His body felt exhausted, he had a sore back and he had barely been able to walk on the morning of the match because of an infected blister on his little toe.

A pattern was emerging. As his old friend Maria Sharapova has observed, there was a long while when Djokovic's body wasn't at the level of his tennis. She used to watch him and wonder: 'Are you ever going to get your shit together?' The most dispiriting of all Djokovic's Grand Slam abandonments was at the 2009 Australian Open. For the first time, he was back at a major as the defending champion, giving him special status, and yet he faded in the heat of Melbourne, retiring from his quarter-final with Andy Roddick. Djokovic was cramping. He also felt an all-over soreness and couldn't move as he wanted. Djokovic felt as though he could no longer fight against his own body. Federer, who never liked to retire from matches, took a swipe at the Serb, 'He's not a guy who's never given up before . . . it's disappointing', adding: 'I'm almost in favour of saying, you know what, if you're not fit enough, just get out of here.'

The previous summer at the US Open, Roddick had made a joke about Djokovic's physical readiness for competition, suggesting that the Serb was suffering from a comically long list of injures and ailments: 'cramp, bird flu, anthrax, SARS and the common cold and cough'. What Federer and Roddick couldn't have known at the time was that Djokovic wasn't faking or exaggerating his injuries; the feeling of helplessness and powerlessness was all too real. Djokovic was training hard, stretching diligently and he thought he was eating well, and yet in matches he would often feel as though he didn't have the strength or the power to compete.

A weakened body meant a weakened mind – he was going into matches wondering when the physical collapse, possibly even the emotional collapse, would happen. 'If your body isn't functioning well, that's obviously going to affect your mind. You're not going to feel good,' said Gritsch. 'As a player, you're looking for two things. You want to maintain a good energy level. It's also just as important to maintain a good focus throughout the match. If you're not in top shape physically, then both are very difficult.'

People talk about one-slam wonders. Was that the direction Djokovic was heading in? If his career was going anywhere, it was regressing rather than kicking on. Two years after beating Tsonga in the 2008 Australian Open final, he was facing the Frenchman again in Melbourne, this time in the quarter-finals, and the match played out very differently. Cetojevic – who signs off his emails with a quote from Hippocrates: 'let food be thy medicine and medicine be thy food' – believed something was up with Djokovic's digestive system, which could have resulted in a build-up of toxins.

The next day, Cetojevic had a coffee with the same friend who had suggested that the doctor tune in to watch Djokovic. He told his friend he was sure Djokovic didn't have 'asthma' and indicated he was open to helping the player. His friend said he would get in touch with someone who knew the Djokovic family. Djokovic's father called soon afterwards. But before Djokovic and Cetojevic could meet, the athlete had another Grand Slam meltdown, against Jurgen Melzer at Roland Garros, which made him consider quitting. Djokovic returned to the tennis circuit. He reached the semi-finals of that summer's Wimbledon, where he lost to Czech Tomas Berdych, and from there he travelled on to Serbia's Davis Cup tie against Croatia, which was where he had a first meeting with Cetojevic.

You can be as sceptical as you wish but there's no doubt that you can divide Djokovic's career into two parts. The time when he was eating a lot of gluten and then the mostly glorious rest of his career, which started the moment that Cetojevic placed a slice of white bread on his stomach in the summer of 2010. At the restaurant in Split, Cetojevic firstly pressed down on Djokovic's right arm, with the player pushing back. Next came the great tennis experiment when Cetojevic put the bread against Djokovic's stomach and again pressed down on his right arm; Djokovic sensed he was weaker. Djokovic wanted to be sure that he was definitely weaker when exposed to the bread so Cetojevic did the test again. Once more, Djokovic could feel how gluten was weakening him.

Reading that, perhaps you're unconvinced by this 'kinesiological arm test'. But Djokovic used to talk about a party trick that illustrates how your body can be weakened when you place something against it. First, Djokovic has said, test a friend's arm strength. And then put their phone against their belly and test them again. Djokovic suspected that your volunteer won't be able to push back with so much strength when they have a phone on their stomach as 'the radiation from the cell phone causes the body to react negatively and weakens the arm's resistance, just as a food you're intolerant to will'. Djokovic has said that once you've seen how a phone can affect someone's body you might question whether you want to carry it around all day in your trouser pockets.

Djokovic is aware that some of what he has said and written about Cetojevic might strike people as 'truly unbelievable, but, then again, so were the results'. Some have doubted the bread test. Cetojevic didn't sound at all bothered by the sceptics questioning the science. He doesn't need to feed his ego, and he knows who he is and why he does what he does. There are some people who have 'small knowledge' and 'limited perception'. 'I don't find it [frustrating] when others are sceptical. Not at all. That's just a question of knowledge. People are coming from different realities and levels of knowledge. I'm an open guy and I accept opinions from everybody. What works for me doesn't work for everyone. Results are key.'

While Djokovic didn't have coeliac disease – an auto-immune disease that can cause the sufferer to have an adverse reaction to gluten, which is a protein in wheat – a blood test showed he had a high intolerance. It also showed what he wasn't. He wasn't, as he wrote in *Serve to Win*, 'a hypochondriac, or an asthmatic, or an athlete who just folded when the matches got tough'. He was an athlete who, for too long, had been eating all wrong.

If a gluten intolerance wasn't alarming enough for the son of pizzeria owners, the tests also revealed a dairy intolerance and how he was mildly sensitive to tomatoes; his body didn't get on with the three core ingredients in a margherita. Gluten had been everywhere in Djokovic's childhood. With Italy nearby, Serbs ate a lot of Italian food – pizza and pasta – and it often seemed to him as though there was a bakery on every corner, and if you had wanted to, you could have had a different basket of bread every day. Often when Djokovic had been eating a pizza, he had had some bread on the side. If bread had always been a key food in Serbia, that was particularly true during the war. When money was tight, it was making cheap bread which, Djokovic said, 'sustained' his family and so many others. Bread wasn't just something that Djokovic ate; it represented so much more than that.

No one adored eating wheat products more than Djokovic did and he has sometimes wondered whether the amount of gluten that he put into his body as a child had created the intolerance which caused him so many problems as a man. Cetojevic said that was possible, though he couldn't be certain as everyone has different reactions to different 'triggers'. 'I'm not against people eating pizza. In moderation, it's not a problem but it's not a good idea to eat it a lot as then you'll have it in saturation. You're getting close to the edge and your body can't handle it anymore.' Djokovic had thought he had been fuelling his body for competition, but the problem, as Cetojevic saw it, was that the athlete had been putting 'diesel into a Ferrari'.

A few years earlier, in what sounded a bit like an intervention, his then fitness trainer Ronen Bega had introduced Djokovic to a nutritionist who went to the player's apartment and removed everything in his fridge. 'The nutritionist opened Novak's fridge and she said to him, pointing at the food inside: "Listen, this isn't good, this isn't good, this isn't good." She removed everything from his fridge and threw it away and took him to a supermarket and they went grocery shopping together,' Bega said. 'It wasn't for nothing that I brought the nutritionist to his apartment. I brought her because I had seen what he was eating. Fatty things like sausages. And as an athlete you can't eat like this. After that, Novak changed how he ate, so the process started in my time, though nothing like as extreme as what happened later when I was no longer working with him when he went gluten-free.'

The way that Djokovic had felt on court for so long had been terrifying, but so was learning how to eat again with Cetojevic, abandoning all the foods he had adored since childhood. But there was a determination to Djokovic. When Cetojevic asked him to go gluten-free for two weeks, he initially had some cravings for bread, pizza dough and sweet rolls, but they soon passed. Very quickly, he could feel the difference. No longer was he feeling drowsy and slow in the mornings; he had an energy that he hadn't felt in years. When the 14-day trial was over, just to confirm how cutting out the gluten had given the athlete a full reboot, Cetojevic asked Djokovic to do something surprising; to go back one time and eat a bagel. In the morning, Djokovic felt rough and heavy, as if he had been drinking whisky all night. Think of that as a gluten hangover, an experience he would never put himself through again.

Throughout the whole process of changing what he ate, and how he thought about food, Djokovic was forever asking: 'Why are we doing this?' If he was going to rip up his diet and start again, he needed to be clear in his mind how it would benefit him. Cetojevic would joke with Djokovic that he had 'a German mentality'. 'When we use that expression in Serbia,' Cetojevic explained, 'it's to describe somebody with a good preparation and a strong determination to achieve their goals.'

*

If what you eat matters, Cetojevic told Djokovic, *how* you eat is also key. That was why he advised him against eating in front of the television as that would mean 'splitting' the physical, mental and emotional bodies and also splitting emotions. 'If you're watching TV while eating, that can be the beginning of allergies as every allergy has an emotional background. Food is coming unprepared into the body and it's reacting differently.' In an era of fast food, and unthinking consumption, Djokovic was going against the mainstream, eating as slowly and consciously as he could. As well as no TV while eating, he also wouldn't be checking his emails, messaging or talking on the phone as otherwise he would be risking losing some of the food's taste and the energy. Djokovic addressed the mouthful he had chewed, giving it clear instructions about what he wanted it to do for him. When eating protein in the evening, for instance, he would say: 'I need you to repair the mess I made.'

The greatest change in Djokovic was how he felt, which was stronger, faster and fresher, even more flexible. Now that he was eating right, he could breathe and he had more energy, focus and mental clarity than he'd had in years. In short, he was reinvigorated. For the first time in years, he was sleeping well. Groggy, glutenous Djokovic was no more: he was getting out of bed in the mornings and feeling as though he was ready to 'tear into the day'. These days, Djokovic considers himself a deep sleeper – he doesn't wake during the night and he gets the eight and a half hours of sleep he desires, which he regards as the most important of all his recovery routines.

Being in shape, in Djokovic's head, has always been about more than the physical side. 'Novak spoke about the mental side and emotional side a lot. It doesn't matter, for instance, if you practise your backhand a lot but your mental and emotional side aren't stable. Under pressure, your weakness will appear,' Cetojevic said. 'You're doing physical training to be in good shape. But you're also doing emotional training to be in good shape. You're doing mental training to be in good shape. And spiritual shape. They need to be all aligned together. He was very responsible and very aware. He has goals. And you need to work towards them every day.'

When Gritsch had started working with Djokovic in 2009, the fitness trainer had looked around at the competition and had seen that a good number of the other players had packed on the muscle. 'That was a time when you went into the locker-room and saw the other athletes and you just had the feeling, "Wow, there's a lot of muscle mass here, there are some really heavy, strong guys around". And I was convinced that that wasn't the way. Those players had too much weight and there was too much pressure on the joints. There was too much mass to move around when you're playing for hours. I felt as though that was impossible to maintain. Novak wasn't so light when I started with him. Later he reduced weight. For a top player, even a couple of kilos is a big difference.'

Djokovic hadn't linked up with Cetojevic with a view to getting slimmer. But the effect of the new regime was troubling for Gritsch. Some of Djokovic's family and friends were also concerned he had lost too much weight. It took a while, and almost reaching a 'dangerous' stage, before Djokovic was able to find the balance he needed. 'That was something that Novak had to manage, getting the balance right,' Gritsch recalled.

Cetojevic became such a central figure in Djokovic's world that the doctor accompanied the athlete to tournaments where he noticed other players weren't eating the right foods to prime their bodies for training and competition. After a while, Cetojevic tired of life on the tennis circuit and stepped away as a member of Djokovic's team. But his influence remained. Every title that Djokovic has won since going gluten-free owes something to Cetojevic's intervention in his life.

Gluten wasn't the only thing that Djokovic cut from his diet. He also stripped out dairy and refined sugar. For a while, he had been feeling as though digesting red meat was taking too much energy from him, which would have been better spent on his next training session or match, so he moved towards being plant-based, with no animal products. With Cetojevic's encouragement, Djokovic began the process of changing almost everything about his nutrition and hydration; he would soon be starting the day with warm water and lemon to detoxify his body before sipping on celery juice and later having a green smoothie with various algae, fruits and super-foods. Foods that would give him mental clarity and make him feel good and perhaps even boost his longevity as an athlete. Djokovic learned to keep it light with his nutrition, especially in the mornings before training – he didn't want to eat anything that would take too much energy to digest. That meant lots of fruit as well as quinoa, millet, wild rice and sweet potatoes and sometimes regular potatoes too, though never fried but boiled or steamed.

About half of what Djokovic eats is raw, he has disclosed. Others have said how Djokovic counts salad leaves and carrots at the lunch table and can be extraordinarily specific with his drink orders in a café; when asking for a mint tea, he will request that they squeeze the leaves. Djokovic likes cherries and wild apple cider vinegar for their anti-inflammatory properties, though he doesn't just drink the vinegar; he also applies it to any blisters on his racquet hand to help the skin heal.

You might expect someone of Djokovic's monastic self-discipline to be teetotal, but he has the occasional glass of wine. It's not an alcoholic drink, in Djokovic's mind, but a holy drink. He prefers Italian wines, finding French wines too strong.

Encouraged by the doctor, Djokovic would become such a convert to this way of eating that, in addition to writing a book about it – *Serve to Win* – he would open a vegan restaurant in Monte Carlo and he would be executive producer for *Game Changers*, a Netflix documentary about the power of eating plants. For someone who used to love cookies and sweet rolls, and who would eat sugary energy bars before practice and matches, he was remarkably disciplined. He got into the routine of checking the colour of his urine at the same time every morning to ensure he was hydrated but not too hydrated (he liked to have 'a little bit of colour').

Bogdan Obradovic was sitting at a table with Djokovic once, eating some lunch after a practice session, when an alarm went off on the player's phone. It was to alert Djokovic that a year had passed, to the minute, since he had last eaten chocolate. 'Now it's exactly one year since I last had a piece of chocolate in my mouth,' Djokovic said to his then Davis Cup captain. This is the player who, after winning a Grand Slam, asked someone to break off a square of chocolate – just a single square and dark rather than milk chocolate – so he could remind himself what it tasted like. Obradovic laughed at the memory of Djokovic setting alarms about abstaining from eating chocolate: 'I said to Novak, "You're crazy, man." But he likes to practise tough things and to show himself he can do it and that he can get through it without any problems. Maybe he has other alarms on his phone, too, for other challenges. Novak's a very interesting person. He has created his own world and he's playing in it.'

6

FUTURE PERFECT

Novak Djokovic was already thinking about the long game; he was looking almost 20 years into the future. When they're new on the scene, tennis players tend to be focused on what's right in front of them. The next tournament, the next match, the hit that morning. Djokovic was – is – different. It wasn't by luck he would still be winning Grand Slams when he was closer to 40 than 30 years old; that was an aspiration he had been working towards since he was barely out of his teens. The first thing a 21-year-old Djokovic had said to Gebhard Gritsch – when they met in Belgrade in the spring of 2009 at the start of a first collaboration that lasted for almost a decade – was that he wished to be healthy when he was 40.

'Novak told me he didn't want to train in a way that his body suffers too much as he wanted to be in top shape when he was 40,' Gritsch recalled. 'That was very important to him as he knew a lot of athletes are done when they are in their early to mid-thirties. Good on Novak for having that as an objective when he was still only 21 as I know so many athletes who can't even walk properly when they are 40. They have been destroyed by their coaches with the intensity of their training. I studied sports science in Austria and the base of our knowledge came from Eastern Germany and from Russia, but I was convinced I couldn't use their training concepts and methods with Novak. They had destroyed so many athletes. I was convinced that was the wrong way to go with Novak.'

Avoiding 'classic, tough, high-intensity' workouts would also help to prevent injury, with Gritsch saying that 'risk management' has always been key to how he has worked with Djokovic. They would spend as much time on trying to avoid injury as they would on any other aspect of his fitness. 'I was very aware of what could have happened and what the consequences could have been. The worst thing for an athlete is to be injured – you're sitting at home and you can't do anything. For an athlete of that dimension, how much would he miss out on if he was injured and couldn't do anything for six months? And, with the recovery process, who knows whether he could ever go back to the same level again? That's why keeping Novak injury-free was always the main objective.'

At the start of their collaboration, it was plain to Gritsch – and to others in the team – that Djokovic had a problem with his endurance. Or what Gritsch referred to as 'tennis-specific speed endurance'. At the Grand Slams, where men's matches are the best of five sets, players can be out on court for up to four or five hours and sometimes even longer; they're not constantly running but need to sprint and have short, explosive bursts of energy. 'Everyone in the team was very much aware that he had issues with that,' Gritsch said. Another task for Gritsch was making Djokovic more efficient, as he initially 'didn't have a good relationship between input and output, and you need to be efficient if you're on court for hours'.

There was lots to fix. When Gritsch met Djokovic, he felt as though the athlete was spending too much time lifting weights in gyms and wasn't having 'enough fun'. Far better for him to go outside, spend time in nature and play a mix of sports for greater variety and mental stimulation. Over the years, with his foresight and dedication, and the advice of Gritsch and others, Djokovic would turn himself into tennis's most dynamic mover.

You sometimes fear for Djokovic's ankles when he slides around a tennis court – on clay, hard or grass – but he knows what he's doing: he's more skilled at that move than anyone else in tennis. Walking around barefoot as a child, something his parents suggested, has given him extremely flexible ankles. Skiing also helped. If Djokovic is the Spider-Man of the tennis universe – capable of hitting winners while sliding, doing the splits and what looks like extreme yoga – that has come from years of spending just about every spare moment stretching. No one becomes that flexible without making stretching a central part of their life. There have been times when Jelena has been talking to Djokovic when – without warning and while keeping the conversation going – her husband has gone into some next-level stretch.

It was Niki Pilic, at his academy outside Munich, who told Djokovic that becoming more flexible would supercharge his game. That comment resonated with Djokovic. For years, Gritsch would encourage Djokovic to stretch. Not that he needed much persuasion. 'Novak's the kind of guy who if he's really convinced that's something important, he will do it on a daily basis,' Gritsch said. 'I said to him that stretching will help his flexibility, which is important and he said, "Don't worry, I'll do it every day". He was disciplined then and he spent so much time on it. That flexibility has obviously been very important for his game.' While preparing for the 2024 season, Djokovic posted 'a challenge for the brave' on social media, inviting his followers to try to replicate one of his stretching routines, which required great balance as well as high levels of flexibility.

*

No one can ever say for sure but if it hadn't been for that slice of white bread that Cetojevic held against his stomach, Djokovic possibly wouldn't have won another Grand Slam. He had been regressing. But after Cetojevic became involved, good things started to happen for Djokovic again. At the 2010 US Open, he reached his first major final in more than two and a half years, which he lost in four sets to Rafael Nadal.

At the end of the season, he did something even more extraordinary, leading Serbia to a first Davis Cup title with victory over France in Belgrade. For a small country which didn't previously have much of a tennis history, it was a startling achievement, which Djokovic celebrated – along with his teammates – by shaving his head. By the time the 2011 season began, Djokovic's hair had grown back, but the effects of that Davis Cup win stayed with him. Winning the Davis Cup had galvanized him, showing what was possible and how he could find more energy within himself. 'That was a crucial moment for Novak. That was the moment when he went over the line. And he did that with his team, with his country, which brought him so much energy and power,' recalled Serbia's Davis Cup captain Bogdan Obradovic. 'Novak learned how to trigger that energy again in the future so he could do even more than he believed was possible. That was something so valuable.'

Janko Tipsarevic, who was also part of the winning team, agreed that victory in the Davis Cup helped propel Djokovic to do great things in his solo career: 'I'm quite sure that winning the Davis Cup with friends gave him the momentum in 2011.'

That was clearly a positive development but Djokovic had only been able to perform at that level – including winning both of his singles matches in straights sets in the final – because he had gone gluten-free. Cetojevic, the man who didn't care about tennis at all, had set Djokovic on a path that would see him put together one of the greatest seasons in tennis history. 'Nole was like a diamond in the dirt before. He needed to be clean and polished a little bit.'

Of all the voices in Djokovic's team, Cetojevic was the one who was boldest about what this new, gluten-free player could accomplish in tennis. When Cetojevic was told there were four Grand Slams in a season, he responded by informing Djokovic and his team that the Serb would win a minimum of three majors in 2011, if not all of them. 'You don't know what you're talking about,' Djokovic and his team said. Cetojevic had said it in a jokey way, but he was serious and said to the group: 'I believe in myself, you're good at what you do and we have an exceptionally talented player.' Everyone laughed, but Cetojevic also sensed that the others were 'scared about the possibilities' of what Djokovic was capable of.

Re-energized, Djokovic had also taken the time to reimagine his game. He was hitting the ball with greater force than before and he had also been working on his service action with his coach, Marian Vajda. Djokovic was an altogether better player than he had been a year before. Going gluten-free changed his mindset too – knowing that he didn't have any physical issues, he could push on in matches without the concern that, any minute now, his body was about to fail him and he would soon be running on empty.

Suddenly, Djokovic was a different player. Suddenly, he had a physical authority on the court. For so long, he had been behind Federer and Nadal in the world order, but now the third man was behaving like the alpha male. 'A monster year,' Nadal said of Djokovic's 2011 season, which was an accurate assessment of the ferocity of the tennis he played that year. Twelve months earlier, Djokovic had been physically and mentally depleted in his quarter-final against Tsonga; in 2011, he was an altogether different player, not even dropping a set in his semi-final against Roger Federer or against Andy Murray in the final. Three long years after winning his first major, and around seven months after he had considered quitting when emotions were running high at Roland Garros in 2010, he had his second Grand Slam.

From the start of the year until a semi-final against Federer at Roland Garros in early June, Djokovic was unstoppable and often unplayable, winning 41 consecutive matches (add in the two singles rubbers from the Davis Cup final the year before and his streak was 43 wins). No one in Djokovic's era, not even Federer or Nadal in their prime, had dominated like that – it was the best start to a season by any male player since John McEnroe in 1984 when the New Yorker won his first 42 matches. Djokovic's defeat to Federer would be his only loss all year at the Grand Slams. Looking back, you wonder whether Djokovic receiving a walkover in his previous round messed with his rhythm and momentum. Djokovic knew that his streak was going to break at some point, as you can't go on winning forever, but it was just unfortunate that it came in that moment when he was so close to a first title in Paris.

Cetojevic had been inspired to hear Djokovic's story of making his own Wimbledon trophy as a boy and dreaming of one day lifting that golden cup for real. 'It was beautiful for Nole to have had that imagination, and to still have that inside him, and it was also inspiring for my brain to hear that,' the doctor said. When Djokovic's dream became a glorious reality on Centre Court, after overcoming Nadal in the final, it was time for Cetojevic to step away from tennis: 'Nole had a real Wimbledon trophy – the process was over.' After 12 months on the tennis circuit, inside a world that had previously been so alien to him, the doctor felt as though his work was done. He had some good times, but he had had enough of some aspects of life on the road, including the waiting around for matches to start, and he felt as though he should get back to his other patients in Cyprus.

For the first time, but not the last, the champion on a plant-based diet reached down and nibbled on some blades of Centre Court grass; it somehow tasted of his own sweat and also wonderfully, surprisingly sweet, like nothing he had eaten before. Everything was happening fast for Djokovic, as reaching the final had propelled him to the world number one ranking – it was the first time in more than seven years that someone other than Federer or Nadal had had that status. He was 24 years old. The boy who at night had hidden from the bombs in a basement bunker, emerging during the day to practise amid the destruction, was officially the best player in the world with the ranking computer catching up with what everyone in tennis had thought for a long time.

This was Djokovic's triumph, but it also felt like Serbia's and when he returned to Belgrade, more than 100,000 people gathered in the city's central square to celebrate with him.

There was even more to come at the US Open where Djokovic came from two sets down against Federer in the semi-finals – remarkably, that was the second year in a row when he had saved two match points against the Swiss at that stage of the tournament. Victory over Nadal in the final carried him to a first US Open title.

With three Grand Slams, as well as seven other titles, and seventy wins from his seventy-six matches, Djokovic had dominated men's tennis. Two of those defeats had been in the round-robin stages of the final tournament of the season, the ATP Finals in London, by which stage Djokovic would have been exhausted from the long tennis year. Of all the numbers that season, arguably the most significant was that Djokovic had won ten of his eleven encounters against Federer and Nadal, the supposed overlords of men's tennis. Two of Djokovic's victories over Nadal had been on the Spaniard's beloved clay, in the finals of tournaments in Madrid and Rome. McEnroe, who won 82 of his 85 matches in 1984, suggested that Djokovic had put together 'the greatest year in the history of our sport'. But why restrict the comparisons to tennis? Djokovic's idol, Pete Sampras, considered it 'one of the greatest achievements in the history of sports'.

It wouldn't be the last time that Djokovic would win three of the four Grand Slams in a season – there was much more glory to come from his racquet – and in many ways he is a better player deep into his thirties than he was in his mid-twenties. But, given what had come before it, with Djokovic's existential struggles in 2010, and how until then he had been toiling in Federer and Nadal's long shadows, his 2011 season arguably remains his finest season. Never again would Djokovic be thought of a tennis weakling. If you could pick out one match or moment when the locker-room's view of Djokovic shifted, you might go for his victory over Nadal in the Miami final. While Nadal cramped after the match from fatigue and dehydration, Djokovic was afterwards in much stronger physical shape.

The gluten-munching Djokovic wouldn't have coped with the extraordinary physical contest that was the 2012 Australian Open final against Nadal. But the new Djokovic came through, taking almost six hours to win what was the longest Grand Slam final in history. A year later, Djokovic was victorious in Melbourne again, beating Andy Murray to become the first man in the Open era to win the Australian Open three years in a row.

Cetojevic, the man who was instrumental in that success in Australia and around the world, is still in touch with Djokovic. The doctor has told Novak how he doesn't tend to watch his matches at the Grand Slams – as he finds them too long and doesn't want to potentially spend up to six hours in front of his television – but he does continue to take notice of the results. Talking to Cetojevic, you sense he feels enormously satisfied with helping Djokovic. He continues to receive grateful emails from Djokovic's fans around the world, which typically go along the lines of: 'Dear doctor, I don't know you, but thank you so much for what you did with Nole. I'm also gluten-free myself now.'

7

A TENNIS ORIGINAL

Why drink from the tap or slug an Evian, as other tennis players do, when you could be sipping 'pyramid water'?

Novak Djokovic goes deep underground – beneath ancient Bosnian pyramids or what some regard as a giant, pointy hoax – to drink this healing pyramid water. This water is said to have been exposed to the mystical energy of these supposedly ancient pyramids, and to vibrate at a different frequency to other waters. Pyramid water is apparently about so much more than the physical benefits. Djokovic finds this water in the tunnels below the pyramids, guided by his friend Sam Osmanagic, a fedora-wearing archaeologist, businessman and author who has been called the 'Bosnian Indiana Jones'. Osmanagic, who announced to the world in 2005 that he had discovered the Pyramids of the Sun, the Moon, the Dragon and Love, suggested this pyramid water enhances Djokovic intellectually and emotionally. Ordinary water that you might get from a tap or a bottle merely quenches a thirst; pyramid water is going to restore Djokovic in just about every way.

Djokovic likes this water so much, according to Osmanagic, that every time he visits the pyramids, he fills up several bottles to take home with him. And whenever Osmanagic drives from Bosnia to Belgrade to see Djokovic and his family, he loads up his car with this special water to present to them. The water comes with quite the backstory. 'If there is a paradise on Earth, then it is here,' Djokovic has said of Bosnia's 'Valley of the Pyramids' near the hill town of Visoko. Djokovic has spoken of the 'miraculous energy' at the pyramids, which Osmanagic and other believers have said were constructed by an ancient civilization during the late Ice Age. There isn't a mummy in sight at Visoko, said Osmanagic. Don't think of pyramids as tombs, he suggested, but as giant energy amplifiers. According to Osmanagic, scientists have concluded that the pyramids emit 'energy beams' that can transmit information faster than the speed of light and it's possible, he said, that could allow humans to communicate with other galaxies (so making the pyramid something like an intergalactic hotline to any aliens out there).

There are, it must be noted, a few sceptics about these pyramids and the supposed energy they are giving off to water, visiting humans and the seeds of fruits and vegetables (Osmanagic claimed that the pyramid energy could change the DNA of the seeds, making them grow faster, richer and healthier). Many geologists would say these 'pyramids' are natural formations, nothing more remarkable than a cluster of pointy hills. The European Association of Archaeologists have called it a 'cruel hoax' while a group of Bosnian academics have appealed to their government to stop Osmanagic, saying he is embarrassing the country. Osmanagic has ridden this out, suggesting that his critics are 'jealous' of his discovery, including the Pyramid of the Sun, which at

220m (720ft) tall is even bigger than the Great Pyramid in Egypt, making it the largest pyramid in the world. While Djokovic appreciates that there are 'doubts' about the authenticity of the place, he has suggested that you have to visit it to fully understand and appreciate what is happening there.

Taking a different view sits just fine with Osmanagic, who, in his book *Alternative History*, suggested that Adolf Hitler didn't shoot himself in Berlin in 1945 but escaped to live in an underground base in Antarctica. If the pyramids are controversial, that means the pyramid water is too (you might say that there's also a lot of bad energy around this mystical drink). Osmanagic isn't, he said, in the 'healing business' and he understands he must be careful about any health claims he makes about the pyramid water. However, he did say that some people have said that drinking pyramid water reduced their blood pressure or regulated glucose in the blood. This is apparently the cleanest water you could imagine, free from viruses, bacteria or fungi. If you were to freeze the pyramid water and look at its molecular structure under an electron-microscope, you would see it's hexagonal, said Osmanagic, and that's apparently the most powerful geometrical shape for energy. Meanwhile water that has been treated with chlorine or fluoride is 'deformed'. If you live in a city and run the tap, the water that comes out might have metal and plastic residues. Everything about the pyramid water is very agreeable, said Osmanagic, even its mildly alkali pH level of 7.45, which is the same as our blood.

'Novak really appreciates the water from the pyramids. He can see it brings him benefits,' said Osmanagic. 'When Novak comes here, he always gets supplies of the water.'

Djokovic had been following the story of the Bosnian pyramids for a while before he connected with Osmanagic and then spoke over the phone in an amiable, four-way conversation with their wives. Djokovic visited for the first time in 2020, curious to know more about how the pyramids, including how, according to Osmanagic, they amplify energy. One of the things that Djokovic and Osmanagic have in common is a fascination with Nikola Tesla, a Serbian inventor and engineer, who, among his other work, once said he had created a death-ray that could melt the engines of enemy aircraft. Djokovic has read a lot on Tesla and even named his dog after him. 'Tesla said that if you are to find the secret of the universe you need to view it through the energy frequency and vibrations,' Osmanagic said. 'That's exactly what we do. Novak really appreciates that.'

As Osmanagic told Djokovic, the concentration of negative ions, or electrified molecules, inside the pyramid tunnels is higher than anywhere else in the world, which would mean that the air is around 50 times richer and healthier than what you'll find at the top of a mountain. Such a high concentration of negative ions could boost your immunity, Osmanagic has said.

In Djokovic's view, the pyramids are among 'the most energetically powerful places on the planet'. Being there fills him with energy and gives him 'the strength' he needs for 'future challenges in tennis and in life'. Going to the pyramids can have an immediate impact on Djokovic's mood. Tennis is played 11 months out of 12, which is the longest season of any major sport, and has made it challenging, even between tournaments, for Djokovic to properly relax. Osmanagic hopes that Visoko has become a sanctuary for Djokovic, away from the pressures of being a star athlete. The day after losing in the Roland Garros final one year, he travelled to the pyramids and, according to Osmanagic, he looked happy, which made it seem as though he had quickly processed the disappointment. When Djokovic visits, he likes to meditate, drink the water, walk the 'energy tunnels' – which he would recommend to every athlete looking to recharge and recuperate – and play some basketball. Osmanagic has built some basketball and tennis courts at the park he has created from what was previously 'swampy, neglected' land. One summer, Djokovic came almost straight from winning Wimbledon to open the tennis courts.

To give Djokovic some 'archaeological excitement', Osmanagic took the tennis star on a private tour down tunnels that are off-limits to the public and 'a human foot hadn't been in for thousands of years'. 'It was a little risky, I must say,' Osmanagic disclosed of their expedition 25m (82ft) underground, which involved wading through clear, chest-high water that was a chilly 11°C (52°F) without any safety rails or support (though they did wear protective and waterproof equipment). When they reached a dry section of a tunnel, they sat down. Immediately, both felt 'this beautiful energy' going through their bodies. There was also – even though getting there hadn't been without risk – a sense of calm and safety, which Osmanagic likened to being inside his mother's womb. 'It was just a special feeling that you can't fully put into words. The excitement and the beauty and the calmness of the place,' said Osmanagic. 'That was a special moment in our lives.'

Osmanagic spoke about his 'sincere' friendship with Djokovic, and how they are showing others in the Balkans how one man born in Belgrade and another from Bosnia can get along famously, vibing on energy tunnels, basketball and pyramid water. Among all the other reasons he admires Djokovic – including for his empathy – he values his friend's intellect: 'Novak is very intelligent. What does that mean? He has the ability, in a new situation, to find the right response.' Osmanagic also appreciates Djokovic's open mind: 'We are what we drink. We are what we eat. We are what we think.' Osmanagic said Djokovic is open to receiving ideas before deciding what is best for him. 'He's open to different philosophies and beliefs. People are different. If everyone followed the same rules and the same routines, and everyone thought the same, why should we live?'

Why, Osmanagic asked, would anyone possibly have a problem with Djokovic having an open mind? While Osmanagic knows about pyramids – he said he has visited every single one in the world – he's obviously unaware that, in tennis, if you try to do anything outside the norm, you can be viewed with dark suspicion.

*

In simpler, gentler times – before Novak Djokovic – tennis used to think that Andre Agassi was dangerously avant-garde. All because the Las Vegan, who would coach Djokovic many years later, wore acid-washed denim shorts over hot-pink cycling shorts and bleached his hair. Today, tennis can still feel like the most traditional and emotionally buttoned-up of sports. Spiritually, Centre Court at Wimbledon is the home of tennis, a place where they are still playing on the same surface that was used at Victorian garden parties (beautifully striped rectangles of lawn) and where the dress code is still very 19th century (all white). 'In this environment, it's not always easy to be accepted,' said Gebhard Gritsch.

Enter Djokovic, who cares little for convention, and who is always eager to explore new and alternative ways of doing things. It turns out that the bio hacks – drinking celery juice before dawn, going

gluten-free, going years without eating a single square of chocolate –
were entry-level stuff. There's also the New Age spirituality, the belief
in the paranormal and the edgy science; anything legal he believes will
supercharge his life on and off the court. He's no Agassi ('image is
everything'). Superficially, there's nothing remotely provocative or
rebellious about Djokovic, with his sensible haircut and his preppy
Lacoste T-shirts and his lack of piercings or tattoos or ostentation. You
must go inside his mind to discover why he's so unconventional; to
appreciate why he makes some people in tennis uncomfortable, and why
others snigger, though of course there are many who counter that, as
well as being the most successful male tennis player of all time, he's the
sport's most original thinker.

The first thing Djokovic does every morning, he once said, is pray,
including giving thanks for 'the opportunity to continue my evolution
as a multi-dimensional being in this realm' (he's also grateful for his
body, his family, his senses, his big bed and beautiful sunrises). From his
perspective, Djokovic's greatest achievement isn't the dozens of Grand
Slams he has won or the hundreds of weeks he has spent at number one,
but his open mind.

Djokovic had a closed mind once; he felt emotions such as resentment,
revenge and hatred. But then he came to understand, he has said, the
power of opening up his mind to different dimensions and horizons of
self-care and self-development. Djokovic became a more joyful,
emotionally balanced, calm, peaceful and fulfilled human. Djokovic
gained a greater appreciation of who he was. And how if he doesn't like
the reality he is in, he can change what's happening on the inside – and
the vibrational frequency he's resonating on – and that will alter the

reality. And yet there have been times when Djokovic being open-minded and thinking, and speaking, so differently to others in tennis – you don't hear any other players talking about expanding their consciousness and being truth-seekers – has made him feel isolated and lonely. It's not just that people in tennis don't understand Djokovic; he has also felt as though they don't accept him. Even worse, Djokovic has felt as though he has been labelled as 'the black sheep of the herd'. The greatest, but also the outcast.

You can be surrounded by others on the tennis circuit – by members of your team, and by your fellow players and other friends – but still feel a kind of loneliness. 'In a team sport, you obviously train together and spend time together. In an individual sport, there's a possibility of feeling lonely and to spend a lot of time thinking about yourself, especially if things aren't going well,' Gritsch reflected.

People inside tennis shouldn't be so judgemental, said Chris Evert. 'This is a guy who studies a lot, who investigates and gathers a lot of information, who asks a lot of questions, and he's looking at every alternative medicine, everything new that comes up on the scene to make his body stronger and healthier. More than any player, he's up on that. He has every right to talk about it and you should respect it. I don't always agree with everything he says but you can't be judgemental. I admire that he's not afraid to broach any kind of subject, whether controversial or not. I've always liked Novak and have always respected his professionalism.'

Seeking out pyramid water is just the start of it. Djokovic has spiritual life coaches. He also has beliefs that can make others in tennis uncomfortable.

As Maria Sharapova said to Djokovic once, he took a risk by choosing a different path and pushing against the norm. Even the way he has made his entrance on court has set him apart from others. There have been times when Djokovic has looked up at the sky while walking out, giving thanks for being there, and touching the playing surface to build a connection between his heart and the court he would be playing on. Djokovic was imagining, as he once told his friend and wellness entrepreneur Chervin Jafarieh, that there was 'a huge energetic ray of space that connects the heavens and the court'. He was at one with the court. Deeply spiritual and self-aware, Djokovic has recognized he had made himself look and sound mystical or even like 'a complete lunatic'. As Djokovic has explained it, his post-match victory celebrations have seen him drawing 'the energy from the heavens' and sharing that love with everyone gathered around the stadium.

Djokovic knew others would think he was being unnatural, artificial or fake, as that's the reaction you get when talking openly about energy and souls. You're going against the pattern of thinking and behaving that almost everyone else has absorbed from society. At first, these practices didn't always sit right with Djokovic. Was this all fake? Was he making a fool of himself in front of other people? While he gave up the routine for a bit, he then went back to doing it and after repeating it enough times – as he likes to say, human beings are mechanical beings – it became part of him. Not just a habit, but a powerful habit. He had started to really believe in what he was doing.

You can understand how it was possible for a rumour to have spread that the tennis player had bought up the world's entire supply of donkey cheese, which he supposedly wanted to supply restaurants in Serbia. Fake news, Djokovic has said, but many had believed the story, which tells you something about how others perceive him.

The most fascinating aspect, though, is: why? Why keep your distance from the tennis mainstream? Why has Djokovic bought into all this? And also: how? As in: How does any of this help him to win Grand Slams? It helps a lot, according to Gritsch, who said it has been fundamental to Djokovic's greatness. Over the years, when spending 40 weeks a season with Djokovic while priming the Serb's body for competition, Gritsch has also peered inside Djokovic's head and seen how he thinks. Gritsch recognized that taking an unconventional route was the only option that was available to Djokovic; he couldn't have got where he has by sticking to the mainstream. 'If you want to understand Novak, you should know that he's a smart guy – he's very intelligent – and that he doesn't have an average approach to life. And I mean in all situations in life and not just tennis. When it comes to his thinking pattern, it's not like the average . . . His logic is not comparable to my logic and to other people's logic but it's logic and it works. He has his own way and it works for him,' Gritsch said.

'Novak came into life in certain conditions, growing up in Serbia, and he wanted to be the best player in the world and to achieve that, he had to go his own way. He's not coming from a developed country and he didn't have rich parents. Basically, he needed to develop his way, his personality and his mental toughness. It's not easy in this environment to be accepted and to be a leader. I would say that he did what was necessary to become the number one and to become as successful as he is. In my eyes, you have to accept that. It's unbelievable what he did. If he had been the same as everyone else, he would never have reached that stage.'

When raising a tennis champion, Srdjan Djokovic found a way by doing things differently. In that respect, his eldest son is the same.

Others might think that some of what Djokovic does is alternative or even strange, but, as he has won so much, it has clearly been working for him, so why change his approach? Djokovic absorbs information from a lot of sources and then uses what he can if he believes it will enhance his tennis, according to Gritsch. 'Obviously, tennis is his life and I don't think anyone knows more about tennis than Novak does. He knows the game and he doesn't forget important things. He can accumulate things and use them to his advantage.'

As a boy, Djokovic wasn't alone in being transfixed by Wimbledon and all its traditions. Plenty of other kids get hooked on the lawns. Perhaps he took that further than most by idolizing Pete Sampras, the most vanilla of all grass-court champions. So far, so ordinary. Everyone grows up, but it's quite a jump from that conventional kid to the New Age Nole. Wimbledon was never the biggest influence on a young Novak, though; war was. As Djokovic has recalled, growing up under communism, you weren't taught to be open-minded as leaders preferred it if you could be 'easily manipulated'. Djokovic's willingness to go against the consensus, to do things differently, can partly be seen as a reaction to that, to ensure he didn't become another unthinking face in the crowd who never stops to question what we have been taught to believe. From a young age, from some of his first conversations with Jelena Gencic, Djokovic wanted to keep his mind open. At a time of war, having an open mind felt even more necessary. Djokovic was also pushing against something which had started long before war: the idea, advanced by communist doctrines, that there was only one way to think, live and eat.

Conformity is for others. Seeking out the radical and the unconventional makes Djokovic feel free, as if he has escaped the government's – and society's – mind control. The more unusual it is, and the more it clashes with mainstream thinking, the more reassured he is doing the right thing. Others will dispute Djokovic's views. That doesn't always stop him; might it even embolden him? Call him weird or bonkers if you wish. To his ears, weird might just sound like encouragement. Scepticism can be important, Djokovic has said, but scepticism can also stop you from being open to new ideas. In this age of logical, rational thought, Djokovic has noted, people are forever asking for proof, when sometimes it might be worth giving something new a try and seeing whether it works for you or not. That, he has suggested, should be the proof you need. Djokovic doesn't think that most people are willing to analyse themselves or to be open-minded.

Be your own person. Be curious. Be inquisitive. Avoid reading newspapers (online or print editions) or watching the television news (though, as he's on social media, others show him what is being written and said about him). That's the Djokovic approach to tennis and life. Some would suggest there is a darker side to Djokovic's wariness of the mainstream and what's supposedly 'proven' – when you start questioning everything, you're going to be reluctant to get vaccinated in a global pandemic. For now, let's keep the focus on how, with his views on wellness and health, Djokovic might just be tennis's answer to Gwyneth Paltrow. Well, almost. The big difference between Paltrow and Djokovic is that – unlike the actress and Goop entrepreneur – he isn't trying to sell you anything. And while Djokovic might use his 'platform' to gently encourage others to 'liberate themselves' and to explore what's out there, he also doesn't want to come across as being preachy, as he knows that no one likes being preached at. Djokovic believes what he believes because he thinks it will enhance his physical and mental health, as well as his spirituality.

He is used to the sniggering and the tittering, to being called weird, wacky and a bit woo-woo; he does it anyway. Life would be easier for Djokovic if he played it safe, and generally did what everyone else in the locker-room does – Andy Murray was once considered 'out there' for doing Bikram yoga and eating large helpings of sushi – but then the Serb would feel as though he wasn't being true to himself. To be conventional, Djokovic would suggest, is to put a limit on yourself. 'Novak's a student of life,' said Dusan Vemic. 'Even when he has retired, he will still be like this. If he gets to his fifties and he decides that he wants to play jazz, for instance, you can be sure he will try to learn to play the saxophone at a top level. Novak will continue growing and trying to make himself a better human.'

A member of the Serbian Orthodox Church (that's just about the only time that you'll see his name and orthodox in the same sentence), Djokovic prayed almost all day on a visit to Hilandar, a monastery on Greece's Mount Athos that was founded in the 12th century by the first Serbian Orthodox bishop. He thought it was the holiest place he had ever visited. But Djokovic doesn't want to limit himself to Christian places of worship. There's a Buddhist temple in Wimbledon, a place of serenity within half a mile of the grass courts, where the orange-robed monks have been accustomed to seeing him meditate under a tree or by the lake. Walking around the 2-hectare (5-acre) site, Djokovic would have seen the Buddhist sayings on the wooden boards, including the one which read, 'though one may conquer a thousand men in battle, the one who conquers himself is the greater warrior'. As a serial champion – who has conquered a few opponents in his time – that could have resonated with him.

Djokovic is celebrated for his flexibility, for his impossibly rubbery legs. When, actually, the most elastic thing about him might be his mind. Djokovic leans into all sorts, opening his mind to a great mix of ideas and practices, some of which are beyond the imagination of others.

Sharapova teases her friend for being a tree-hugger. But Djokovic doesn't go wrapping his arms around just any trunk; he feels a connection with one particular fig tree in Melbourne's Botanical Gardens that he considers an old friend. For more than 15 years, Djokovic has been going back to that tree (and he's not saying which one as he wants to keep that for himself). He likes the look of the roots, branches and trunk and whenever he has a chance he climbs that tree, strengthening their bond and possibly tapping into its energy and wisdom. There are countless demands and pressures on an athlete making tennis history. Being alone with that tree, the most dependable of friends, makes Djokovic feel grounded. When Nick Kyrgios asked about the tree at the 2024 Australian Open, Djokovic said the secret was to take off your shoes, climb to the highest point and hang upside down for precisely 33 minutes and 3 seconds. It was a joke, of course, but was there also some truth, people were left wondering, in what Djokovic had said?

8

LONE WOLF

In the beginning, Novak Djokovic was sceptical, even uncomfortable, about Pepe Imaz's teachings of 'amor y paz' or 'love and peace', with the Spaniard also big on the transformational power of very long hugs, and a believer in telepathy and telekinesis (the ability to move objects using the power of your mind). Djokovic had an open mind, of course, but even for him all this love and peace was too much. His younger brother Marko had moved to Marbella on Spain's Costa del Sol, where Imaz has a tennis academy, and Djokovic couldn't see how Imaz's philosophy could further Marko's ambitions at the time to play professional tennis: 'If you're all love and peace on the court, the other guy will beat you.' Djokovic didn't get it. He wasn't supportive of his brother's life choices.

But Marko impressed on Djokovic how Imaz was helping him to address something inside him. When Marko was standing in front of Imaz, he felt free, he said, because the Spaniard looked at him with love rather than judgement, and that allowed him to overcome his depression. For the first time in years, Marko was able to tell Novak, along with their other brother Djordje, as well as their parents and his friends, that he loved them. From Imaz's side, his conversations with Marko had been nothing less than 'divine'.

In time, Djokovic felt himself drawn to Imaz's energy. He liked how Imaz was always smiling, even when they were having a tricky conversation. Imaz went deeper about 'love and peace'. Imaz would pray for Djokovic and talk to him about the importance of doing 'inner work' and of 'universal love'. It was in the months after a disturbing, third-round defeat at the 2016 Wimbledon Championships – when Djokovic was going through a rough patch both professionally and personally, and when he would have been in greatest need of some love, peace and hugs – that he was first publicly linked with Imaz. Some were saying that Imaz was somehow responsible for Djokovic's downturn in form. Presumably they were unaware that Imaz had been in Djokovic's ear before that, and 2015 had been one of the best seasons of his career.

Djokovic was comfortable enough with Imaz's teachings to appear on stage with him in a conference room in Marbella in 2016 – where the audience had been encouraged to close their eyes – where he spoke of looking inwards and establishing a connection with the 'divine light'. By then, Imaz had become one of Djokovic's spiritual life coaches. Imaz would be part of Djokovic's inner circle and coaching team for two years and was possibly an influence for even longer.

Hugging is so beneficial, Imaz has written, that it 'should be prescribed by doctors'. 'It is a powerful cure that we still don't know enough about. Hugging heals hate. Hugging cures resentments. Hugging cures tiredness and alleviates sadness. When we hug, we drop our armour. We instantly forget the things that made us lose our calm.

Hugging gives our soul peace. When we hug, we stop being on the defensive, we allow others to approach our hearts. When we open our arms, we open our hearts too.'

The world should be hugging out its problems, Imaz seems to be saying. Much of Imaz's thinking can be traced back to traumatic younger years when he despised himself and felt empty inside. He tried to fill that emptiness with food, and that only made him feel worse. When his self-loathing and bulimia were at their most extreme, Imaz was vomiting up to eleven times a day, and he came close to death, spending two weeks in a coma. Not long after, he was in a lift when he met a woman, aged about 50 and wearing sunglasses, who said to him: 'You don't know me but I've been waiting for you and I can see your pain and suffering.' This spiritualist told him that Imaz had appeared in her meditations and dreams and she invited him to come to her home the next day where she began teaching him 'The Big Truth'. That included suggesting that he should look up David Icke, an English conspiracy theorist and the self-proclaimed 'Son of God', who has claimed that the world is controlled by alien lizards.

While lizards aren't part of Imaz's own teachings, some of his other views will seem 'out there' to some observers. As part of a 23-day programme of discovery, Imaz has encouraged students to send 'pleasant thoughts' to a container of boiled rice with a 'love' sticker on the side and to transmit negative ones to another container labelled 'fear'. Do that for 23 days and then open the containers, and you will apparently see that the rice inside the 'fear' container has 'deteriorated' more than the 'love' rice. In between hugging humans at his tennis academy, you can always cuddle the giant teddy bears labelled 'love' and 'peace'. Imaz has often worn T-shirts with a heart shape on the front along with a heart-shaped necklace.

How does Imaz's philosophy square with the combative Djokovic we have all seen on court, the one who has broken a few racquets, said some salty words and ripped a few shirts? John McEnroe, who knows something about expressing emotions on a tennis court, said that 'bringing in somebody who wants to give people a lot of hugs does not necessarily translate to having that killer instinct'. As McEnroe said while Djokovic was working with Imaz, 'you don't want to get into a situation where it is all peace and love and then have to go out and try to stomp on somebody's head in competition'. Imaz wasn't suggesting that Djokovic should become a pacifist on court. As a former player who was once ranked inside the world's top 150, Imaz understood that tennis is an explosive sport. Through love and peace, he has said, you can move beyond fear, tension and a blocked emotional state on court and achieve a harmony that allows you to play with power and intensity.

A new, loving Djokovic would write 'Amor y Paz' on the lens of a television camera after matches, and Imaz would thank Djokovic, privately and publicly, for promoting love whenever he had a chance. In Imaz's eyes, Djokovic was an innovator in elite tennis, someone who valued how he was developing as a human more than his success as an athlete. Djokovic was changing how he found happiness – it was no longer based on whether he was winning tennis matches or not.

Almost inevitably, Djokovic was teased, even ridiculed, for getting all deep and dippy with Imaz. 'Guru' wasn't a word that Djokovic ever liked to use about Imaz. Maybe Djokovic felt as though 'guru' conjured up visions of a mythical figure. That it would invite ridicule for people in tennis to be saying he was travelling the world with a guru. Djokovic would have liked it even less if he heard that one media organization had nicknamed Imaz the 'Cuddle Guru', which didn't seem to be taking him seriously as a member of Team Novak. Imaz would have expected this hostility towards love as he had been 'taunted' for years by some people inside tennis. As he wrote in a blog post, you have to be brave to speak out about love as that will only invite others' 'sharp judgement'.

Off the court, you could detect Imaz's influence on Djokovic. In 2018, Novak was promoting a documentary series he was in, *Transcendence — Live Life Beyond the Ordinary*, when he spoke openly about his beliefs in the paranormal. In an interview with *ShortList* magazine, Djokovic expressed his view that telepathy and telekinesis were 'gifts from the higher order, the source, the god, whatever'. Djokovic was aware, he said, that some people would suggest he knew nothing about these topics, but he was attracted to them and wanted to share what he had learned so people could 'explore their superpowers'.

Was it possible that all that peace and love could have created conflict within Djokovic's team? Imaz has said that he had always got on well with others who worked for Djokovic. But Imaz's presence, and all the chatter about it, felt odd for some of the other members of the Serb's team. 'It was a little bit strange for the team [having Imaz around] and the situation,' said Gebhard Gritsch, who was part of Djokovic's inner circle at the time. 'Obviously for the media it was something for them to jump on because it was something extraordinary that was happening in Novak's team. But I think there was too much noise about it. Pepe faced a lot of criticism from the press. All I can say is what I think of Pepe personally and how I found him – I think he's an amazing guy, with an academy that is helping troubled children. He's definitely some kind of guru. But Pepe didn't come into the team and put pressure on anything. Because Novak's brother works at Pepe's academy, Pepe was always in Novak's outer circle of friends and acquaintances. At a certain stage, Novak thought he could benefit from talking and being with Pepe for some time.'

There have been suggestions that Imaz's approach wasn't always compatible with the thinking of Novak's more traditional tennis coaches. When Djokovic asked Marian Vajda in the spring of 2018 to coach him again – they had stopped working together the year before – the Slovakian expressed his reservations about working with Imaz, and soon the age of peace and love was over. Djokovic and Imaz don't appear to be as close as they once were. But the connection isn't completely broken. Imaz still speaks fondly of Djokovic while, at the time of writing, Imaz's website suggests that Marko continues to work for the Spaniard. Djokovic also lives in Marbella.

In his efforts to become a better human being as well as a better tennis player, Djokovic has had another spiritual life coach in Zarko Ilic, a Reiki healer but also, in the athlete's view, so much more than that. Ilic has described Reiki, which is believed to have originated in Tibet and was then reimagined in Japan, as 'a natural healing technique using high-frequency energy'. In addition to 'curing the body, calming the mind and cleansing yourself of negative emotions', Reiki 'more importantly, teaches you how to adopt a more spiritual, healthy attitude towards life'.

Djokovic and his wife turned to Ilic to help them to grow spiritually. 'He's helped my wife and I to open our minds even more and to understand how we can have internal conversations with ourselves.

I didn't know how to do that. I didn't know [how] to verbalize my emotions,' Djokovic told his friend Jay Shetty. 'My wife was ahead of me and that's where we struggled in our relationship because she was trying to dig things out of me and make me share more but I wasn't able because I didn't know how. She was like, "Speak to me, what do you feel?" and I was like, "I don't know, I feel something." Zarko was very helpful with that.'

Ilic has been trying, he has said, to be a guide to the modern man. While 'searching for the light and walking towards it', Ilic had found peace, serenity, joy and balance in his life, and he wished to share that knowledge with Djokovic, Jelena and his other clients. Ilic was once such a central figure in Djokovic's life that he was among the close group who celebrated in the locker-room after the Serb won his first Roland Garros title in 2016. Away from tennis, Djokovic and Ilic went on a trip together in 2018 to the Grand Canyon in Arizona.

Humans aren't Djokovic's only advisers – he also has wolves as his 'spiritual nature guides'. As a young and impressionable boy, Djokovic was hiking through the forests in the Serbian mountains near where he grew up when he encountered some wolves. While it was a frightening experience, it also left him feeling connected to the wolf. When the adult Djokovic said one summer at Wimbledon that he had brought a 'wolf energy' to the lawns, it just sounded like a good line, a crowd-pleaser that got some laughs. But he wasn't joking; he had meant what he said about channelling the wolf – one of the national animals of Serbia – when he was on court. Sometimes, Djokovic has said, the wolf energy has caused him to howl or scream out, but mostly it has been useful. When Djokovic is able to balance that wolf energy with an inner calmness, it helps him to understand when to attack on court and when to ease off. Wolf energy also means having the freedom and space to roam.

Maybe the grazing GOAT – the one who celebrates winning Wimbledon by nibbling on the Wimbledon grass, which 'tastes of sweat' – is actually a wolf. Djokovic has recognized it hasn't always been easy for his wife Jelena to live with the wolf of the tennis world. 'It can be very stressful to run with the wolf. I know that she doesn't enjoy it at times,' he has said. 'It's kind of living on the edge with the wolf.'

Djokovic's friendship with Wim Hof, an excitable Dutchman known as 'The Iceman', has been built on a shared belief in the power of the mind, and how mastering what's going inside your head can help you to conquer the external world. Using breathing techniques and mind control, Djokovic's 'dear friend' has climbed Kilimanjaro in just his shorts and also got most of the way up Mount Everest in a similar state of undress before turning back as he felt frostbite in his foot. Hof also swam more than 50m (165ft) under the ice, which was a record, and once sat in an ice bath for the best part of two hours. Inspired by Hof, Djokovic has had ice-cold showers for years and one winter in the Italian mountains – after doing some breathing exercises on the bank to 'soothe the pain' – he sat down in an icy stream, in just his underwear and a pair of Crocs, for almost two minutes.

Djokovic hasn't always liked to categorize himself as an athlete as that seems so limiting; he feels as though he's so much more than that. And why limit yourself when you could be expanding your consciousness? It's Djokovic's view that everyone is more than what they think and what they feel with their five senses. When Djokovic realized that – as he once told his friend Jay Shetty – it opened up a different universe and dimension to him, and his inner evolution and growth quadrupled. That left Djokovic feeling calm but also exhilarated and excited about 'everything that life has to offer'.

Every day, Djokovic likes to do some self-care work. When he doesn't have much time, that might just mean a short prayer or two minutes of meditation or breath work, but at least it's something, and he has stayed disciplined. Working on his habits is important for Djokovic. It's very possible, he has noted, for you not to be able to recall a single moment in your day and that's because you have been constantly distracted, possibly by your phone. Djokovic, while highly disciplined in so many ways, has noted how a phone can be addictive and he adores Instagram. That's why he is trying to stay in the present, so he is able to be more aware and to be able to remember some of the moments. Djokovic has tried to bring the same focus to his life off court as he has to his tennis life. Sport has taught him how he can accomplish anything he desires, and he has tried to bring that same approach to all aspects of his life.

Keeping a journal has brought Djokovic some inner peace. While Djokovic's 'second mother' Jelena Gencic had initially encouraged him to write down his thoughts every day, he stopped doing that for a few years until he met his future wife Jelena – an enthusiastic reader and writer – and he got back into it. He has found that writing down his thoughts has enabled him to release tensions in his mind. Djokovic has discovered he has learned more about himself in the harder moments – when he has been feeling down and discouraged – as then he has been able to go deeper with his writing. Should he wish, he can go back and see how he was feeling during previous bad times, and how he got through them. An old-school approach – taking pen to paper rather than tapping something out on his phone or laptop – has allowed Djokovic to organize his thoughts around two fundamental questions. Who are we? Why are we here? It's in moments like those that Djokovic has truly felt like a truth-seeker, digging into questions that he believes are at the centre of what it is to be a human.

It's unlikely that any other Grand Slam champion has spent so much time exploring whether Earth is a planet, a realm or a matrix.

*

If Rafael Nadal is obsessed with the arrangement and positioning of water bottles – moving them on court near his chair so the labels are facing the end he is playing from – Djokovic thinks deeply about what goes inside, about what you can do with water if you just open your mind. There was amusement and a little outrage when, in an Instagram Live with Chervin Jafarieh, Djokovic claimed you can detoxify polluted water, changing what's in your glass at a molecular level, through the power of prayer and gratitude because water listens to what you're saying to it. According to Djokovic, prayer and gratitude can transform dirty water into healing water: 'Scientists have proven that, that molecules in the water react to our emotions, to what is being said.' In Djokovic's view, prayer and gratitude can also transform toxic food into something edible.

Djokovic aired his claims in a conversation with Jafarieh during the pandemic, as part of a series of chats called 'The Self Mastery Project'. Jafarieh, the founder of wellness brand Cymbiotika, was strongly in agreement: 'They say if you had specific thoughts, specific emotions onto the water, if they were happy thoughts, if they were good thoughts, they created a molecular structure that had a geo-prism based on sacred geometry, meaning there was symmetry and balance,' he said. 'On the opposite end, when you give water pain, fear, frustration, anger, that water will break apart.'

You can see why Djokovic was drawn to Jafarieh, whom he describes as 'my dear friend, my Persian brother from another mother and a wonderful soul'. From his side, Jafarieh has said Djokovic has one of the most beautiful souls he knows, and that they are connected in spirit and bloodlines. When Jafarieh claimed 'a global shift will occur when each individual finds the courage to awaken from the mass amnesia', it no doubt resonated with Djokovic's belief that we should be keeping our minds open and resisting the mainstream view that there's only one way of living life. Jafarieh, who has a podcast called Wake the Fake Up, is big on trampolining and 'longevity mushrooms'.

Maybe you're a non-believer; you're not convinced that water can be altered at a molecular level through positive emotion. But Djokovic knows it to be true because he has seen that with his own eyes (there are parallels here with Pepe Imaz's boiled rice experiment). A few years before his lockdown chats with Jafarieh, Djokovic recalled observing an experiment in which a researcher filled two glasses with the same amount of water, which was from the same source. In this 'test of Eastern medicine', the researcher 'nurtured' one glass with 'positive energy – love, joy, happiness, all the goodness of life'. The other one received 'negative emotion – anger, fear and hostility'. The researcher even swore at the negative glass of water. Several days later, the researcher returned to the two glasses of water. 'The difference in the waters after a few days was immense,' Djokovic wrote in Serve to Win. 'The water that had negative thoughts and influences directed at it was tinted slightly green, as though algae was growing inside. The other glass was still bright and crystal clear.'

Dippy or dangerous? Or both. Or neither, if you can just open your mind. Who can say for sure? Djokovic's views on purifying water weren't welcome in all quarters, with influential tennis broadcaster Mary Carillo 'very disturbed' by what she heard, calling his views 'dangerous stuff' and asking him to back down (which he didn't). Tennys Sandgren, an American player, was more mocking of Djokovic's thoughts on water purification, writing on social media, 'If Novak doesn't get Covid I'm gonna start blessing my water with positive vibes' and then, 'I told my water it was very handsome anyway'.

*

Djokovic's views have sometimes collided with science. Believing that our bodies are 'self-healing mechanisms', and 'trying to be as natural as possible', he resisted having an operation on an elbow issue that bothered him for two years. Djokovic hoped his elbow would heal naturally and holistically. Andre Agassi, his coach at the time, wasn't a fan of that decision. After seeing the MRI scans, Agassi urged Djokovic to have an operation as soon as possible to deal with the issue. In the end, Djokovic relented and in early 2018 he had the first major operation of his career. On waking up, he cried for three days. The guilty feeling lasted longer. He felt as though he had failed himself. But the operation seemed to fix the issue and Djokovic would go on to win a bunch of Grand Slams.

Every year on tour, it feels as though Djokovic brings fresh, challenging thinking to tennis. He hasn't ever settled; he's forever finding new ways to rough up convention. At the 2023 French Open, the tournament where he would win his 23rd Grand Slam title, Djokovic had a small patch taped to his chest, a small and much-discussed piece of nanotechnology that he suggested was inspired by Iron Man's superhero suit. 'When I was a kid I liked Iron Man a lot – so I try to impersonate Iron Man,' Djokovic observed, and it was hard to say whether he was joking or not. The manufacturers, Tao Technologies, think of their TaoPatch as 'a human upgrade device' that converts body heat into 'microscopic beams of light' that supposedly stimulate the central nervous system. Inevitably, there have been sceptics, as there always seem to be when Djokovic has introduced something to the tennis world, with one doctor telling *Forbes* that it was 'pure pseudoscientific gibberish'.

Of all the tech that Djokovic has brought to the sport, a giant, pressurized 'space egg' was what really got tennis's chattering classes going. In keeping with the size of the thing, there was a big fuss when Djokovic's use of the spaceship-like chamber was first mentioned in the summer of 2011 – during the US Open, he was said to have been staying with a friend in New Jersey who owned such a machine and was said to have been alerted to the benefits. By simulating high altitude and compressing the muscles, this hyperbaric chamber was said to have been legally boosting his blood cells while also removing lactic acids and stimulating stem-cell production.

Keeping in shape has involved the ancient – such as capoeira, a Brazilian martial art that is a combination of dancing and fighting – and the very modern.

Mostly, Djokovic is open about his beliefs and the ways he tries to reach a higher state of enlightenment and performance. Occasionally he chooses to be more mysterious, such as when he was inhaling from a drinks bottle at Wimbledon in 2022, saying only that it contained a 'magic potion', which some observers thought could have been an isotonic powder. Later that season, there was a curious episode at an indoor tournament in Paris in the autumn when Djokovic's team prepared a drink for him in the middle of a match while arranging themselves in their seats to prevent a spectator from filming what was going into the bottle. If Djokovic's entourage had wanted to avoid people becoming interested in what he was drinking, it had the opposite effect. For a few days, the mystery of Djokovic's bottle and his secretive team was the main subject of conversation in tennis, prompting some absurd theories about what had been going on courtside, including the suggestions that rules had been broken. As Djokovic's wife Jelena wrote on social media, there wasn't anything 'dodgy' going on; it was simply that Djokovic's team had wanted some things to remain private.

The norm at Grand Slams is that players practise on their days off between matches. That helps them to stay in a groove. But Djokovic was prepared to do things differently in Paris in 2023 – the day before the final, he was walking in a forest outside the city with his family, enjoying being in nature. He felt as though he wasn't about to forget how to hit the ball. He was right.

Tennis players are notorious copycats. There aren't too many secrets in the locker-room. If you see another player doing something new and they're suddenly surging on tour, you're going to try it for yourself. See previous trends for hiring big-name super-coaches and going gluten-free. Ditching the breadbasket was one trend that Djokovic did help to push. Others saw how going without gluten had transformed his game and wanted some of that success for themselves. But that might be one of the few Djokovic innovations that has caught on in tennis. You have to wonder whether other players don't believe that any of this has been helping Djokovic to conquer tennis. How do long hugs and being a water-whisperer help you when you're deep in the fifth set of a Grand Slam final? Maybe they believe that Djokovic has been successful despite all the unconventional stuff, and not because of it.

Waking early, often before sunrise, Djokovic starts his day with prayer, gratitude, and a couple of long, deep breaths before hugging his wife and running off to see his children. Contrast with Murray, who when discussing his morning routine with Djokovic, plainly stated what he does first: 'I go for a pee.' Murray is part of the tennis orthodoxy, in many ways a conformist (as well as a fine champion). The orthodoxy doesn't interest Djokovic. He's partial to 'aerial yoga', hanging upside down and getting a different perspective on the world to any other tennis player.

Inside the basement shelter – beneath a Brutalist apartment block in Belgrade's Banjica neighbourhood – where Djokovic spent many nights during the 1999 NATO bombings.

One of the thick steel doors to the bunker, which was originally built as an atomic shelter in case of nuclear war.

As a boy, Djokovic often played at the Partizan Tennis Club – today it has a friendly, understated, unassuming vibe and doesn't make too much of its Djokovic connection.

Djokovic's old neighbours in Banjica are very fond of him – for his generosity as much as for what he has accomplished on a tennis court.

An old military building in Belgrade that was bombed in 1999 and never rebuilt; this is a city where you don't have to look too hard to see the scars of war.

Novak's first racquet was neon pink. He carried it around all day, not ever wanting to put it down.

Djokovic dyed the front of his hair for his Grand Slam debut, against Marat Safin at the 2005 Australian Open.

The week of Serbia's Davis Cup tie against Britain in Glasgow in 2006, Djokovic's family approached the LTA about Novak possibly becoming British.

With his success at the 2008 Australian Open, Djokovic became the first Serbian to win a Grand Slam singles title.

Winning the 2010 Davis Cup brought Djokovic 'so much energy and power', according to the Serbian captain, Bogdan Obradovic.

One of Djokovic's most memorable Grand Slam wins was saving two match points in the 2019 Wimbledon final against Roger Federer.

Djokovic's parents, Dijana and Srdjan, spoke out against what was happening to their eldest son, who spent several days in an immigration centre in Melbourne in 2022.

Djokovic's 'chemistry' with his former coach Goran Ivanisevic 'had its ups and downs, but our friendship was always rock solid'.

Djokovic and his wife Jelena have two children, Stefan and Tara.

Igor Cetojevic (centre) didn't just change how Djokovic eats –
he also transformed how the Serb thinks.

Jelena Gencic, Djokovic's first
coach, told his parents he was
'a golden child' with a big future
in professional tennis.

Sam Osmanagic, who has been
called 'the Bosnian Indiana
Jones', introduced Djokovic
to the Bosnian pyramids.

Pepe Imaz, who was part of Djokovic's team, promotes 'love and peace' and believes in the transformational power of long hugs.

Djokovic won his 24th Grand Slam title at the 2023 US Open, enhancing his status as the greatest tennis player of all time.

9

'I'M DONE'

Novak Djokovic, his mind humming with doubts about his future, was suddenly sure of one thing: he no longer wanted to play tennis. It was the spring of 2018 and he gathered his team, including his then agent Edoardo Artaldi and his wife Jelena, and told them he was stopping: 'You know, guys, I'm done.' The break with tennis would be absolute. It wasn't just that he no longer wanted to play tennis; he also no longer wanted to watch tennis or even be around tennis. Djokovic was 30 years old and he had won 12 Grand Slams; it had been a fine career, and he had had moments when he had been untouchable, but no one was describing him as the greatest of all time, not even close.

'Novak thought it was the end of his career,' recalled Craig O'Shannessy, the Australian who was part of Djokovic's team at the time in his role as strategy coach. 'Novak was going through a period of doubt. We all doubt ourselves at times. It's just that Novak does it on a stage where everybody is watching.' You only had to look at Djokovic then to suspect that something was up: he was so skinny, as he tried to get back to the top of the game after missing the second half of the 2017 season with an elbow injury, that when he took his shirt off you could see his ribs. O'Shannessy was receiving messages from people in tennis who were worried about Djokovic's physical conditioning and the muscle mass he had lost in his time away from the game: 'Craig, please feed him.'

In O'Shannessy's estimation, Djokovic was 10kg (22lb) lighter in that moment than he is today – and all the weight he had lost was in his muscles. That was affecting his game, which was, and is, so reliant on his movement and strength. But mostly, O'Shannessy said, the problem was in Djokovic's head. 'I think it's absolutely normal that Novak went through this period of self-doubt. I think it would have been strange if he hadn't had that at least once in his career.'

It was an existential crisis backdropped by palm trees and blue Florida skies, with Djokovic tipped into retirement by his defeat to Frenchman Benoit Paire in his opening match of the hard-court tournament in Miami. That was his third defeat in a row, a grisly run that had started when he went out in the fourth round of January's Australian Open. After Melbourne, Djokovic had had an elbow operation, the one his coach Andre Agassi had been urging him to have for some time. On his return to the circuit in March, Djokovic lost his opening match in Indian Wells in the Californian desert, which likes to style itself as 'tennis paradise'. For Djokovic, there was only a tennis hellscape, first in Indian Wells and then in Miami.

These were dark times in some of the tour's most Instagrammable stops, with every defeat eroding Djokovic's self-worth and sense of what he was hoping to do. A few on the tour were wondering whether impatience had got the better of Djokovic, and that he had returned to tennis too soon and that it would have been wiser to have waited a little longer before competing again. In the long months in the second half of 2017 when he hadn't been able to play, Djokovic had had this overwhelming sense of claustrophobia, as if the walls were closing on him. But then he had come back and he looked lost.

Without a Grand Slam in almost two years – since his 2016 Roland Garros title – Djokovic was in a negative spiral. Gebhard Gritsch, who had been Djokovic's fitness trainer for eight years from 2009 to 2017, returned to the team in the spring of 2018 and he was disturbed by the Serb's movement. Djokovic's game had been based on precision tennis (as he would disclose in 2023 in an interview with *60 Minutes*, he has often aimed at a target the size of a small coin). Djokovic was the most precise mover in tennis and that was why he had been so good. But, from Gritsch's perspective, it seemed as though Djokovic had become imprecise. He wasn't balanced or stable on court. The rhythm of old wasn't there. He wasn't playing his natural game. Djokovic is someone who likes to be in control. But suddenly he wasn't even in control of the fundamentals – his technique and how to play the sport – and that was enormously frustrating for him. It had previously looked as though there was a machine-like quality to Djokovic's tennis, but that had disappeared, with Gritsch observing: 'Novak was somehow lost. He was out of order.'

This crisis – technical, psychological and then existential – seemed as though it could be traced back to Djokovic's 'shock therapy', which is how he described his decision in 2017 to ditch Marian Vajda, his coach of 11 years, along with Gritsch and his physiotherapist Miljan Amanovic. Think of this as the aftershock: in early 2018, his then coaches, Andre Agassi and Radek Stepanek, hadn't been part of the team for long enough to know how to restore the precision movement. For much of Djokovic's collaboration with Agassi, which had begun in the spring of 2017, the Las Vegan – who wasn't getting paid, and was instead doing it for the pleasure of helping out – found the two of them didn't always see tennis the same way. From Agassi's perspective, he and Djokovic kept on having to agree to disagree. While Agassi had offered up some ideas on conditioning and nutrition, he felt as though Djokovic needed 'ownership over his own process'.

One of the difficulties, Gritsch noted – and he didn't think this was Agassi's fault – was that the American didn't have detailed knowledge of how Djokovic moved. Or how Djokovic should have been moving. 'Novak was the most precise mover on the tennis circuit but then he lost that precision. To maintain this precision movement, you must stay focused every single day in practice because it's very easy to let some different movements come into your game and destroy your precision. It's a very difficult thing to maintain this perfection that he achieved,' Gritsch said. 'But then that precision went and it wasn't possible to get that back with his new team because they didn't have the history with him. I admire Agassi and Stepanek – they're great people – but they didn't know where to start. There was a good reason to hire those guys – for competitive mental performance as they had been there and they understood the pressure – but I don't think they could deal with issues like biomechanics. Novak was in big trouble with his career and he knew that.'

There was something else going on, too. While Djokovic had been away from tennis, he had experienced what life was like away from the circuit, and he had liked it, O'Shannessy suspected. Djokovic had seen what life could offer when you're not forever on planes and practice courts. 'When you step away from the game, you do different things. You have a different life. You have a different view of life rather than going from tournament to tournament, always on airplanes,' O'Shannessy said. 'He probably got a taste of that different life and his tennis wasn't going well so it's only a natural progression to think that maybe this is the end of my career.'

While Djokovic hadn't reached an emotional state where he 'hated' tennis with 'a dark and secret passion', as Agassi said he had done during his own career, he couldn't see the point in continuing. Djokovic instructed his agent to tell his sponsors that he was zipping up his racquet bag. Then he went on holiday to the Dominican Republic with Jelena and their three-year-old son Stefan and their baby daughter Tara. The sport didn't know it – as he didn't announce the news on social media or put out a statement – but he was an ex-player now. Eight years earlier, when the defeat to Jurgen Melzer at Roland Garros in 2010 brought on an existential crisis, Djokovic had thought about running away from tennis; this time, with feelings even stronger, he had gone ahead and retired.

If Djokovic wasn't going to play some tennis on the family holiday, Jelena was. She still loved tennis. Jelena found an old ball machine and enjoyed the simple pleasure of hitting tennis balls. Stefan was also having a go, playing some shots and running around the court picking up the balls. Djokovic was nowhere to be seen. He didn't even want to watch his wife and child playing. It was on the third or fourth day of that trip that something changed. That day, Djokovic – barefoot and wearing beach shorts – showed up at the courts, just to observe. It had been a while since tennis had felt fun to him; the sport had been serious for him for longer than he could remember. But Djokovic could see this was fun. Jelena was having fun and so was Stefan. He asked for a racquet. Teasing him, Jelena said no, but Stefan invited Djokovic to join in: 'Daddy, it's your turn now.'

Still barefoot and shirtless, Djokovic took some balls to the baseline, hit some serves, and then said, maybe to Jelena and Stefan, maybe to himself: 'This isn't bad. This is feeling OK.' The next day, Djokovic accompanied his family to the court. By the end of the holiday, he even came to the courts properly dressed for tennis, wearing shoes and a shirt. Being in nature also helped Djokovic to recharge: he was having a snooze on the beach on that holiday when he felt a wave coming in – not the sea, a big wave of energy. Ten days after quitting, Djokovic was un-retiring: he told Jelena that he would be calling Vajda to ask him to come back and coach him again. 'Between Marian and his wife Jelena, Novak got through that time,' O'Shannessy said.

Not long afterwards, Gritsch was also back in the team again. 'Novak realized he was a fighter and he wasn't going to give up that fast. We had times before when he said it didn't make sense for him to play this shit, so bad. He had had bad times before and he didn't quit that fast,' Gritsch said. 'Novak was born to be a tennis champion and he knows it.'

The way Jelena has described it, Djokovic's tennis sounds like a game of Jenga; sometimes all the wooden blocks must come crashing down on the floor so he can start afresh. 'Novak needs to drop completely down and lose everything and then he can start building another tower,' Jelena said in conversation with American video journalist Graham Bensinger. 'And it's [going to be] an amazing tower.'

Within a couple of days of Vajda and Gritsch returning, Djokovic regained much of his precision movement. 'At the beginning, at the first tournament when I came back, Novak didn't really know what and when and where or how. It was good for him to take a step back to an environment that he was used to. Novak found his way back. He had missed a lot of really good training but, in two days, the basic technique came back, and after one week he was almost back to where he was before,' said Gritsch. 'Novak learned one very important thing during those hard times in 2017 and 2018 – that he has to be able to rely completely on himself when it comes to the technical issues in his game. When we were working with him before, because we knew him so well, if something wasn't running perfectly, we gave him a hint and it was easy for him to solve it and find his form again. Because the new people didn't know him, he didn't have control over his own technique anymore. When we came back, I saw him many times writing down in a notebook some hints at what he needed to do. Novak was doing that because he knew the importance of being self-sufficient.'

No one in elite tennis should expect a smooth ride. But Djokovic's career has sometimes been a jagged line, with some enormous highs – higher than anyone in modern men's tennis has ever been – interspersed with some devastating lows. Djokovic's brief retirement in 2018 wasn't the only moment when it appeared as though he was in crisis, and that his head wasn't fully in the game. Take late spring and early summer of 2016, when Djokovic went almost immediately from the high of Paris, winning Roland Garros for the first time, to the low of London, with an early and abrupt departure from the Wimbledon fortnight. Sure, tennis moves on quickly, but has another player ever gone from one extreme to another as quickly and as abruptly as Djokovic did that season?

*

It was Paris in the spring and Djokovic was drawing a giant heart in the orange-red clay of Roland Garros and then lying down inside it; this looked like the closing scene from a Disney tennis movie when the only emotion was pure, uncomplicated happiness. Hoisting la Coupe des Mousquetaires – the Musketeers' Cup – after winning a first Roland Garros title in 2016 was supposed to have been one of the most joyful and fulfilling moments of Djokovic's life. It wasn't. Instead, from nowhere, he soon felt a kind of emptiness. Then a darkness.

Professionally and personally, winning in Paris was the start of a deeply unsettling time for Djokovic. Here was a victory that Djokovic had obsessed over for years as it would complete his set of the sport's four biggest prizes, putting him in a highly exclusive club of men to have done the career Grand Slam (this was such a significant moment in tennis history that his racquet would sell at auction in 2023 for more than $100,000). Ever since winning Wimbledon and the US Open for the first time in 2011, adding to his Australian Open title in 2008, Djokovic had been consumed by the vision of also being champion of the Parisian clay. Djokovic needed to win that title if he was to be considered as one of the true greats of the game; victory would also fulfil the wish of Jelena Gencic, who died during the 2013 edition. But this was about more than that; Djokovic had suffered so much in Paris, including losing three finals, that it was about proving to himself that he could overcome those failures and hellish memories.

The intensity of Djokovic's preparations for Roland Garros each spring had been heightened by Rafael Nadal. The Majorcan was constantly on the minds of Team Novak, according to Gritsch; what could Djokovic do to give himself an edge against Nadal's heavy-metal clay-court game? Two of his defeats in Paris finals, in 2012 and 2014, had been against Nadal, with the other loss coming against Stan Wawrinka in 2015 in a match that had looked very winnable. 'To win in Paris, with Rafa, was very difficult. How do you beat that guy? This wasn't an easy task. We spent so much energy, put so much intelligence, into winning in Paris, which was the ultimate objective. I had never planned things in so much detail before,' Gritsch said. 'It was so important for him to win. Novak is the kind of person who if he makes up his mind on a goal, and creates this whole thing around a goal, he will do everything to make that happen. We were researching a couple of areas where we thought we could get an advantage on a clay court. It definitely wasn't a normal approach to a tournament. It was a special approach as we thought that would give us a better chance. This was also a long project with many frustrating years.'

Only later would Djokovic realize he had wanted it too much – way too much – to the extent that his happiness was entirely dependent on how he performed on the clay. If Djokovic never won the title in Paris, how could he possibly be content again? 'I got the sense that Novak needed to win that title to be happy,' Gritsch said. But then in 2016 Djokovic achieved that dream, and not by beating Nadal – who had withdrawn before his third-round match with a wrist injury – but by coming from a set down to defeat Andy Murray. Adding to his 2015 Wimbledon and US Open titles, as well as his 2016 Australian Open success, Djokovic completed what was unofficially known as the 'Nole Slam'. It wasn't over a calendar year, but that was a minor quibble: Djokovic was the first man since the 1960s to hold all majors at the same time. And while he was happy, it was only a passing happiness.

Not long afterwards, Djokovic fell into a 'motivational hole', according to Gritsch.

If Djokovic's body and mind weren't completely burned out, they were close. 'Finally, it happened in Paris, but after that match Novak went into some kind of motivational hole. All of us in the team were in that same hole,' recalled Gritsch. 'For months after that – this continued into 2017 – we were mentally and physically exhausted. Once you achieve something important like that, you feel relieved but you don't have the same motivation and the same push inside you to go for it every day because you have something in front of you that you must achieve. Novak was very happy that he won but that feeling didn't last for long. The adrenaline was gone and he didn't feel great. He was very tired and emptied out of an energy, just mentally and physically drained. Novak's tank was almost empty after winning in Paris.'

Chasing that first Roland Garros title, Djokovic had been operating at an extreme level for years. But it was unsustainable. For some time, Djokovic had thought as though he could just go on winning and dominating. As if this sport was straightforward, that he could just keep on banging out Grand Slams. He would discover how wrong he was. 'Novak wants and wants and wants – he wanted to keep on winning – but he's also human. We all have our limits,' said Gritsch. 'By 2016, Novak had already spent a lot of years training and preparing mentally and physically as best as he could, and then performing, but then came the stage when he could no longer maintain that. He couldn't accept that. He wanted to keep on winning. But there's no way you can maintain such a high effort and high-energy environment. It was almost inevitable that he would have a low soon afterwards. That low would be at that summer's Wimbledon, which came very quickly after Roland Garros.'

Djokovic's 'tennis father', Niki Pilic, also sensed that the Serb was going through a low. 'Winning that first Roland Garros title was an incredible achievement but you can't stay at that level for so long,' Pilic said. 'Of course, you go a little bit down. That's normal. Novak is highly motivated – you can see that from how hard he works – but of course there will be some waves in motivation, and it was lower after Paris for a while.'

Falling into a motivational hole was just the start of it; without a first Roland Garros title to fixate on, Djokovic was left confronting some unresolved psychological issues. Looking inwards, Djokovic felt as though there was a small, distraught child in some dark corner of his mind. That child was sobbing and wailing and demanding attention. That's when Djokovic realized – with the clarity that was only possible after he had achieved his goal of winning in Paris – that while he had been nurturing his tennis, and improving every aspect of his game, he had not developed his emotional side. The cost of his devotion to tennis was that he had ignored that inner child. 'If you concentrate all your effort on one thing, then the normal life doesn't really exist anymore,' said Gritsch. 'You don't have a normal life with the weekend off or whatever. You're trying to do everything you can to make things happen and to do that I think you almost have to ignore the other things in your life.'

Djokovic was as dominant as he, or anyone else in modern times, had ever been. He had accumulated 16,950 ATP ranking points, a record, and more than the second-ranked Murray (8,915) and third-ranked Federer (6,655) combined. In holding all four Grand Slam titles simultaneously, he had accomplished something that was beyond Roger

Federer and Rafael Nadal. And yet, in that moment, he felt as though there was something lacking. To soothe the wailing child, Djokovic would have to understand himself on a deeper level than ever before and it wasn't always easy, including the realization that the relationships he had with 'some of the closest people' in his life were shallow and superficial. He recognized that he would have to reset those relationships. There was the realization, as Djokovic told his friend and former monk Jay Shetty, that he had been living a successful life but not a fulfilling life. Up to that point, his only concern had been whether what he was doing would make him a better tennis player. But that was wrong, he thought. From then on, the 'inner work' that Djokovic did would be to help him to evolve as a human being, and not just to further his sporting career. Shetty would take to calling Djokovic, who became a more spiritual person after 2016, an 'inner athlete'.

Just weeks after winning in Paris, Djokovic was in London, on the Wimbledon grass, and he was dealing with issues in his personal life. In the middle of Wimbledon, Jelena informed her husband she would be leaving London for 'a spiritual trip' to Ecuador. Jelena, who felt as though she had given all of herself supporting Djokovic in Paris, and was emotionally spent, said she wanted to do something for herself: 'I'm sorry, I'm just going to go.' Djokovic was supportive of her going to South America, even though the timing, mid-Grand Slam, wasn't ideal: 'You know what, I get it. I'm happy that you want to go and do something for yourself. You deserve it.' It would be a 'beautiful' and meaningful trip for Jelena.

In 2015, an imperious Djokovic had won 27 matches out of a maximum 28 at the majors, with his only defeat in the Roland Garros final. Going into the 2016 Wimbledon Championships, Djokovic had

visions of accomplishing the calendar-year Grand Slam. But, in a twist
that no one had seen coming, he would lose in the third round to
American Sam Querrey, which was his earliest defeat at the majors for
seven years. At the time, that was a shocking result: once you understand
what was happening in Djokovic's head at the time, it's much less so.

Following Wimbledon, it was an emotional Djokovic who lost to Juan
Martin del Potro in the opening round of the Olympics in Rio de Janeiro
for what was one of the most jarring defeats of his career; the pressure
and expectations had built in his head until they had become unbearable,
and he cried as he walked off court (a sore wrist didn't help either). Later
that summer in New York City, Djokovic disclosed he had been dealing
with some 'private issues' during Wimbledon. Resolving those issues,
Djokovic said, had allowed him to 'evolve as a human being' and life
would go on, but he didn't look quite like his usual self in the US Open
final, with a defeat to Stan Wawrinka which hurt him psychologically.

Some of the strongest bonds in Djokovic's life were breaking or being
tested. Boris Becker's player-coach relationship with Djokovic was, the
German said, 'very sensitive, almost intimate', to the extent it felt as
though he was married to the player. If he was to get the best out of
Djokovic, Becker believed he needed to know everything about the Serb,
including how he slept, how he ate and the state of his (actual) marriage
to Jelena: 'Everything matters because he carries that on a tennis court.'
While other young star athletes didn't want to hear the truth from their
coaches, Becker noted, he was impressed by how Djokovic invited him to
speak freely and honestly.

Djokovic had been working with Becker since 2013, in which time his
coach had, among other things, introduced him to chess to improve his

mental clarity and focus, and reassured him he could continue winning Grand Slams. In those intense moments, Djokovic often wanted eye contact with Becker between points; having Becker in his corner gave him additional mental and emotional strength. 'As a player, Boris had been very successful and very competitive himself in the biggest matches,' said Gebhard Gritsch. 'The most important thing he did for Novak was with his mindset and giving Novak the assurance that he was the one who would win the match, that he had prepared well and that he was the best. That helped Novak a lot. With Boris as his coach, Novak knew that he had someone sitting there who understood him and understood how to win an important final, and who could offer a tip or some words that would help him to find the form he needed.'

Djokovic liked the Niki Pilic connection, how Becker also had been coached by the Croat. Under Becker's guidance, Djokovic had won six Grand Slams, including a couple of titles in Becker's happy place, Wimbledon, in 2014 and 2015. But, with Djokovic in a motivational hole after winning Roland Garros in 2016, Becker felt as though the champion hadn't worked hard enough in the second half of that season. He simply wasn't spending enough time on the practice court. On reflection, Becker has since thought that Djokovic's results in the second half of the season were almost a blessing as he had been winning so much that he had forgotten what it was like to lose. Only by losing do you feel the hurt and the pain that push you to refocus and reset.

In December that year, Djokovic and Becker's working relationship would come to an end. Though that wasn't the end of their friendship – they grew closer after Becker was convicted of hiding assets when bankrupt. Becker was so appreciative of Djokovic's support when he was in a British prison that he considered him a member of his family. When Djokovic won Wimbledon in 2022, Becker was so overcome by emotion when watching the television coverage, he cried in his cell.

*

First dates can be awkward and Djokovic and Jelena Ristic's had certainly had its moments. He had felt as though he had had chosen somewhere refined and exclusive; she wasn't impressed by going to a sports bar. Jelena also hadn't been expecting Djokovic to order on her behalf. There was also the excruciating part when Djokovic called a waiter over and said the meat was undercooked and the waiter explained to him that steak tartare was served raw. Djokovic pretended he knew that. Whenever they see steak tartare on a menu now, it reminds them of that first dinner. Djokovic and Jelena once made a video for one of his commercial partners that recreated that moment, a project which indicated how he is happy to poke fun at himself and his failings.

Very early on, Jelena influenced Djokovic. Feeling stressed from her studies, Jelena had got into yoga, and she introduced her boyfriend to downward dog and sun salutations. Jelena studied in Milan, which was close to Djokovic's base at the time, in Monaco. Once she had completed her business course, she tempered her career ambitions so she and Djokovic could spend more time together, a sacrifice which, in Djokovic's eyes, saved their relationship, and he was grateful for that (she also did a master's degree in luxury management at a university in Monaco). Djokovic proposed on an early-morning hot-air balloon ride – he had arranged for another hot-air balloon to come close to theirs and for the pilot to unfurl a giant banner asking: 'Will you marry me?' While it didn't go so smoothly – part of the other balloon caught fire and lost altitude, which panicked Jelena, and then when she saw the banner, she initially thought it was an advertising stunt – she did say yes. Jelena had said to Djokovic that she knew him so well that he couldn't surprise her; that was a balloon ride which proved otherwise.

Before the birth of their first child, Stefan, in 2014, Jelena had mostly been focused on Djokovic and his needs; she would do whatever she could to support his tennis ambitions. She didn't stop to consider what her needs might be. Inevitably, there were some frustrations from Jelena's side, and she sometimes directed those at her husband, even though she knew it wasn't his fault; it had been her choice to support him in that way. Becoming a mother 'shook' Jelena's core, she has disclosed: she recognized she needed to focus on her own wellbeing, and to do something for herself, as only then would she be able to take care of their son. A source of anxiety for Jelena was how to mother a child whose father was, in her estimation, 'a historical figure'. Thinking about that saying that children should stand on the shoulder of their parents, Jelena wanted to raise a son who would, as she put it, 'exceed' his father: the only trouble was that Djokovic kept on pushing himself and his tennis to ever greater heights.

Jelena was telling herself: 'I have this kid and I have to do something special.' That was making her fret. 'I feel like I destroyed me and the vision of who I am,' Jelena said in an interview with American journalist Graham Bensinger. Djokovic has recognized that while his children won't experience the hardship and dangers that he did when growing up, they will have to find a way of dealing with the greater emotional difficulties of being known as 'the son of' and 'the daughter of'. Their journey of self-growth, Djokovic has said, isn't going to be easy. Jelena, meanwhile, was realizing that she wasn't the superwoman she thought she was. Something had to change.

For some time, Jelena had been in competition with her husband. He was being praised for what he was doing on the world stage, but what about what she was doing backstage? Didn't she deserve more recognition? Djokovic has an ego; so did she and it was, she said, 'battling'. Jelena wasn't conforming to the stereotype of what an athlete's wife was supposed to look like and how she was supposed to behave. She was meant to be enthralled by fashion and to be obsessed with her appearance. But, while Jelena liked clothes, that didn't excite or energize her. Vanity wasn't her thing. While she knew she was being judged by some for going her own way, and that could be trying, she wasn't interested in being that glossy athlete's wife. She didn't want to fit in and be what everybody expected her to be. Jelena didn't want – even though she felt as though women weren't supposed to speak up – to be the quiet, meek wife who just sits and smiles gently. Jelena wanted to prove – and this was the root of her competitiveness towards Djokovic – that she could be something other than his wife.

When the university-educated Jelena was introduced as Djokovic's wife – which was every time she appeared at a tennis tournament – she would think to herself: 'OK, here we go, the wife, let me sit and smile.' It would take a big shift in Jelena's mind – and this came after she found some peace – before she could once more 'proudly wear that title' of Djokovic's wife.

Reading books by the psychologist Jim Loehr has helped Djokovic and Jelena to have clarity on their relationship and where it is heading. Though, as Jelena has said, they are a 'passionate couple' who 'collided a lot'. There have been times when her motherly instincts have slowed him down; he hasn't been able to 'fly' as he has wanted. When Djokovic has wanted to do things, and Jelena has said to him: 'Do you know what? We have two kids that we have decided to have together and we have to readjust our choices.'

John McEnroe's remarks about Djokovic and Jelena's marriage in the summer of 2017 – when he made some comparisons between the tennis player and golfer Tiger Woods – weren't welcomed by some around Djokovic. Andre Agassi, Djokovic's coach at the time, spoke to McEnroe about not making hurtful comments. That wasn't the first or the last time that others have commented about Djokovic's marriage – as he has recognized, it's more interesting for others to read that he and Jelena are getting divorced, even when they're not, than how they're in love.

Becoming a father has awakened the inner child that Djokovic had abandoned for years. For the first time in a while, he was joyful and playful again. The other lessons and transformations of parenthood have included learning how much love he was capable of feeling and giving. Djokovic has often felt as though he doesn't have much spare time, but being a father – their second child, Tara, was born in 2017 – has taught him about patience. Both Djokovic and Jelena believe that – contrary to what society says – children are their parents' teachers and masters and can help their mothers and fathers to understand life on a deeper level. When Tara was a toddler, he described her as a healer, who had brought energy to the world and had accelerated their consciousness and awareness for the moment. Of course, Djokovic has also said he and Jelena are teaching their children, that the process flows both ways.

In the past, Jelena had sometimes considered her husband had been selfish about putting so much focus on taking care of his needs. But, as she learned more about what she needed, she came to understand that Djokovic wasn't being self-centred, and that everybody should be doing the same if that allowed them to be energized, loving and giving. What Jelena realized was that peace would come from not being 'a victim of life'; she would be doing things because she wanted to do them and not because she felt obliged or pressured. She had choices. Jelena was going to live her life with purpose and she was going to live it 'full on'.

For his part, Djokovic has spoken of the importance of he and Jelena having the same life goals. 'We have to go on this journey together. It's inevitable that she has to endure the same journey as I do at the same time, otherwise we can't stay together. I'm really grateful and happy that she embarked on the same journey. Her own journey but parallel [to mine],' he told Graham Bensinger.

A strong connection with his wife and his family was key to Djokovic's happiness. 'Novak's a family man,' said Gritsch. 'In order to have a good life, you need to have a good social life and that's not possible for a tennis professional, particularly when you're successful. First and foremost, you have no time. You have so many issues and so many things to do. Everybody wants something from you. You have so many appointments. It's a very, very tough life and there's not much free time. On the competitive tennis circuit, obviously you have a couple of friends – the Serbian guys are pretty close – but that's not the same as a family. A family gives you a completely different satisfaction.'

Dealing with his psychological and emotional issues hurt Djokovic's tennis career, though of course the elbow injury also didn't help. From the high of Roland Garros in 2016, Djokovic wouldn't win another Grand Slam for more than two years, until the 2018 Wimbledon title. Going through that process wouldn't have been easy but it allowed Djokovic to mature, for his emotional intelligence to catch up with his tennis. Once he was through it, Djokovic felt as though he was better at handling his emotions. Better at dealing with life when it wasn't going his way. He was 'super glad'.

10

THE NUMBERS GUY

As much as Novak Djokovic is an emotional character – someone who gets agitated on court and who retires and then un-retires – he's also an analytical man. A numbers guy who understands that the data tells a story that's worth listening to. Hiring Craig O'Shannessy made Djokovic a tennis pioneer; he was the first elite player to employ someone purely for strategy. Marian Vajda was Djokovic's coach, but O'Shannessy would provide the data and the strategies for Novak's matches. With the Australian's assistance, Djokovic would always know how his opponent would play, including the areas where his adversary would make errors. 'The big thing was that Novak would never be surprised,' O'Shannessy said. Djokovic liked to see video analysis. If O'Shannessy was at a tournament, he would deliver the presentation, which tended to include video clips, in person, and often he would go over the strategy for the final time an hour before the match. If he was working remotely, he would email a PDF.

With the hard data and his soft skills, O'Shannessy was helping Djokovic to understand his own game, and also his opponents' tennis.

While Djokovic wanted strategy for every match and every opponent, there were naturally two players he was more interested in. 'There are these two guys that I keep running into on Sundays,' Djokovic said to O'Shannessy when they met in the players' restaurant at Melbourne Park before the 2017 Australian Open, sitting with Vajda as they discussed how the three of them could work together. Djokovic was looking for an edge when he played Roger Federer and Rafael Nadal and he hoped that O'Shannessy was going to give it to him. Djokovic was clear with O'Shannessy: 'We need to know more about them than they know about us.' If Federer or Nadal made any adjustments to their game, however small, O'Shannessy would pick up on it through looking at the numbers, and then make a video for Djokovic's consumption. Of course, there were other players to keep track of, such as Andy Murray (for a short while, people used to talk of the Big Four or the Big Three and a Half). Djokovic had fallen to number two behind Murray, and there was a hunger to get back to the top. 'It was kind of like a new chapter for Novak to be guided by the analytics of the sport. He was all in with that.'

In the three years that he was part of Djokovic's team, there were times when O'Shannessy felt like he was 'working with a 14-year-old boy'. Not because Djokovic was immature – he was quite the opposite – but because of his boyish enthusiasm for tennis. 'Just like a young kid, he was in love with the sport, eager to play and always hungry to get better. He had already been very successful and he knew that he could get better and he could see improvement right around the corner. Novak knew that he could tidy up his game. The number one player wins around 55 per cent of all points he plays – that goes right back through the ages. That means you're still losing around 45 per cent. Novak understood that and that the more he could reduce that percentage the better. There were things he knew he could do better, such as shot selection.' The two of them would be guided by the data. The question was always: 'What are the numbers saying?'

While other players might have been working purely on hunches and intuition, Djokovic was making informed, data-driven decisions about where to hit the ball.

Even on the biggest occasions, such as his 2018 Wimbledon semi-final against Nadal, Djokovic was willing to embrace the data. When the match was suspended overnight because of the tournament's 11pm curfew, O'Shannessy studied the numbers and saw how Nadal was yet to miss a backhand return from the ad court. 'Rafa was obviously hitting it well but Novak had been too predictable. We made the adjustment over the last two sets to serve more to Rafa's forehand. It's kind of counterintuitive on the ad court to serve out wide to the lefty's forehand. But, without that piece of information, Novak doesn't win that match. Novak would have kept going to Rafa's backhand and Rafa would have kept putting every ball back in play. There were no free points there. All of a sudden, Novak had the surprise of a serve out wide. That changed the match and Novak ended up winning in five sets.'

Stretching before an important match serves a dual purpose for Djokovic. He is preparing his body for competition, while also helping to control any nervous tension he might be feeling. Not that Djokovic is a player who gets overcome with nerves. He isn't nearly as relaxed as Federer used to be, but also nothing like as hyper and bouncy as Nadal. 'When I went through the strategy one final time with Novak – this would be about an hour before the match – he was always very calm and relaxed. Now Roger was super-laidback, joking around, and you would look at him and think: "I can't believe he's got a final in 20 minutes." Novak isn't quite like that and he also isn't whipping himself into a frenzy before a match like Nadal. Novak is quite normal. Nothing outrageous.'

Given the circumstances, winning that summer's Wimbledon title, which Djokovic completed with a straight-sets victory over South African Kevin Anderson in the final, was possibly the most extraordinary of all his Grand Slam titles. But that went unappreciated. The Centre Court crowd didn't have any of the context, and how Djokovic had retired less than four months earlier.

But Djokovic didn't learn so much from his victories. When you lose, he once said, you connect on a much higher level than when you win. Defeat is a learning opportunity. Reviewing a loss, and looking at the numbers, was part of the process with O'Shannessy. If they didn't do that debrief immediately after a defeat, when it still felt raw, it happened as soon as possible: Djokovic could still feel the emotions, but they weren't dominating his thoughts and his mood.

Extracting all the information he could from a defeat has long been a key component to Djokovic's greatness. There is a Michael Jordan quote, from an iconic Nike commercial, that resonated with Djokovic, and which he has often quoted to others: 'I've failed over and over and over again in my life. And that is why I succeed.' Throughout his career, Djokovic has tried to extract what he can from his own failures. As a young player, he told *The Times*, he was more emotional after defeats and it would sometimes take him days to get over a big defeat, but in time – and he considered this an important development – he was able to analyse what had happened in a more balanced and a more 'serene and peaceful way'. Djokovic would tell himself: 'In an ideal scenario you want to win. But you are going to learn a lesson. You are going to move on from this experience as a stronger player.'

First Djokovic takes away your legs; then he takes your soul. That was Andy Roddick's analysis anyway. But how does Djokovic do that? It's sometimes said of the Serb that his brand of tennis isn't as strong as Federer's or Nadal's. By which people mean that his tennis doesn't have the same emotional impact as Federer gliding around a court and turning hitting a forehand into an art form or Nadal's whippy forehand, loaded with energy, competitive spirit and heavy, heavy topspin. Djokovic, meanwhile, does everything brilliantly. As the only man to have won each Grand Slam tournament at least three times, he's the most complete male tennis player in history. He's also the best returner to have ever played the game, with his backhand return marginally stronger than his forehand. But you still wouldn't think of Djokovic's return as the defining part of his game, simply because every aspect is at such a phenomenally high level. When Djokovic is on court, you're asked to marvel at nothing, and also everything, all at once.

While everyone has been able to see the greatness with him, as his former coach Todd Martin has observed, they haven't always been able to explain that greatness. 'Roger was remarkably graceful and elegant and won a ton. Rafa is feisty and has a bit of a blue-collar sensibility to him and wins a lot. Novak is in between those two,' said Martin.

As Djokovic's friend Janko Tipsarevic put it, Federer and Nadal 'had a certain amount of flash in their games'. 'Roger and Rafa, who were obviously great, were producing a huge serve or a crazy forehand or a huge passing shot. Novak does everything well,' said Tipsarevic.

'Every single aspect of his game is great. Novak has a great serve, a great forehand and a great backhand, and obviously the best return ever – he does everything so well that he has this ability to pace himself which means that he doesn't necessarily have to do anything special. One reason why Novak's game sometimes doesn't look as appealing as the other two is because the biomechanics of his movement on court are so perfect that it looks like he covers the court with so little effort and that the other player needs to do way more to win the point and therefore makes an unforced error. And, trust me, I've been a victim of this. I played him seven times. When you look at the match from the outside, you think that the other guy is playing like shit. But when you're actually on the court you have to win every point three times in order to actually win it.'

Every time anyone takes to the court against Djokovic, they're willing themselves to play the match of their lives, as this is their opportunity to make a name for themselves. And quite often they do play close to their highest level, and that's still not enough. More often than not, Nick Kyrgios has noted, Djokovic's opponents are left asking themselves: 'What am I even doing out here?' Facing Djokovic, the Australian has said, you start to 'hate' the depth of his shot, which neutralizes pretty much anything you try against him. One of Djokovic's other superpowers is an ability to redirect and change the direction of the point – for most, that could be a risky play, but for him it's not and, as he doesn't adjust his technique, there are no visual clues about what he's about to do, so his opponent has no warning about what's coming next. In years past, perhaps one small weakness in Djokovic's game was that he didn't put enough variety into his second serve, but he is now more than willing to mix it up, making him far less predictable. And after a first or second serve, Djokovic is immediately on you, looking for a chance to take control of the point; there's never a moment to settle or breathe.

If Djokovic doesn't have the same 'flash' – as Tipsarevic notes – as Federer or Nadal, that doesn't matter. 'On Novak's best day, he is a better tennis player than the other two greats were at their peaks,' said Dusan Vemic, one of his former coaches. 'Novak has enough weapons and no holes in his game when his mind is in the right place.'

There's an intelligence to Djokovic's tennis. 'Novak has a strong tennis intellect,' said Jelena Jankovic, who has herself reached world number one. 'He's a complete player and has all the tools and because he's very intelligent, he's able to adapt and use the right tools against different players and find a way to beat them. Some other players might have stronger forehands or bigger serves but Novak can do everything. He has very strong defence – he's very flexible and agile and quick. He gets lots of balls back. He's also able to play strong offence. Novak can adapt and play well on all surfaces, which isn't easy to do. Some other players aren't so good on all the surfaces.'

In Martin's view, Djokovic's return of serve is as good as it gets. 'From a technical standpoint, the biggest thing about his game is his return. I've never seen anybody return serve better. Novak covers more space. He understands that, against a first serve, his primary responsibility is to defend and yet he often neutralizes, if not better. And Novak has the ability to attack the second serve. With Novak, the ball is constantly in play. Free points are remarkably valuable in tennis and he gives so few of those away.'

One of the most extraordinary parts of Djokovic's game – and it's something that many observers don't fully appreciate – is how he's almost always perfectly positioned to hit the ball. Other players sometimes don't get it right. They're falling away as their racquet connects, or they're jammed up because they're too close or they're reaching for the ball because they're too far away. They're having to make compromises with their technique. Djokovic doesn't have to do that. 'Novak takes a lot of little steps and he's exactly where he needs to be,' O'Shannessy said. 'His positioning is amazing . . . and that means that his stroke is amazing and clean. No one does that better.'

It's been said that Djokovic's only weakness is his overhead: the so-called 'Djoko-Smash'. 'Overall, Novak's smash is a weakness. He can miss it pretty badly. Compared to the rest of his game, which is so clean and technically correct, the overhead does stand out as a shot that he misses,' said O'Shannessy.

In O'Shannessy's view, Djokovic struggled more with his smash when he came to the net 'randomly'; if he was clear about the strategy, and what he was trying to achieve from that spot on the court, he generally hit the overhead with much more authority and success. Before the 2018 season, O'Shannessy was in Los Angeles with Djokovic, preparing for the year ahead, and talking about a strategy that would see him finish points with a smash. Djokovic said to him: 'Should I go to the net more?' To which the Australian replied: 'Absolutely. In general, you're winning close to 70 per cent of points at the net and between 50 and 55 per cent at the baseline. That's a great number at the baseline but the net offers a vastly superior percentage.'

Djokovic wanted more: 'How do I get to the net? What's the best way?' O'Shannessy reminded Novak of the options: 'There are four ways. The forehand approach to an opponent's backhand is the best. The backhand approach to the backhand, not as good. Forehand approach to forehand is strength versus strength, not as good. And the backhand approach to the forehand, that's the worst. The forehand approach to an opponent's backhand is going to be your number one way to come in.' Once Djokovic had absorbed that information, he had another question: 'Where do I hit my first volley?' O'Shannessy recommended that Djokovic hit that shot – which would typically be played from around the service line – back behind the opponent: 'Almost always go back behind as that's going to wrongfoot them as if you go for the open court that's going to give them a running forehand. And if you go back behind almost every time they're going to hit a lob on the next shot, which is going to give you an overhead.'

With O'Shannessy's encouragement, Djokovic, while capable of winning points anywhere on the court, was committed to going to the net. Djokovic understood the numbers. If he won 50 per cent of his points at the baseline, that was a good day, but at the net he was going to win two out of every three points. 'Novak went to the net a lot. He still does.'

Djokovic was eager to hit overheads during the 2018 US Open; he went looking for opportunities to deploy the Djoko-Smash. 'In that tournament, Novak's overhead was spectacular. It was really, really good. The reason was that it was part of an overall gameplan, it was part of a strategy, and so it was clear in his head what he had to do,' O'Shannessy said. 'Novak was hitting the forehand approach to his opponent's backhand, then the first volley was back behind his opponent and then he was expecting an overhead, he was wanting an overhead. His overhead was exceptional at that tournament. Championship point against [Juan

Martin] del Potro, he hit an overhead.' Just months after quitting tennis, Djokovic was a Grand Slam champion again.

Victory at the 2019 Australian Open, where he vaporized Rafael Nadal in a one-sided final, would make it three majors in a row. It also set up a chance at Roland Garros that season of another non-calendar-year 'Nole Slam', though he would lose in the semi-finals to Dominic Thiem. Quickly going from 12 to 15 Grand Slams was a big move. What if the un-retired Djokovic, who for a short while in 2018 couldn't even bear to play tennis, was on his way to becoming the greatest player in history?

II
_____

'HATERS ARE A GOOD
PROBLEM TO HAVE'

Other tennis players have critics or detractors; Novak Djokovic has
haters. Their loathing for him can be as grotesque as it is absurd. They
sometimes call him 'Djoko-bitch' and worse. But maybe, Djokovic
sometimes tells himself, that's not such a terrible thing. There's a quote
from his late friend and mentor Kobe Bryant, the former Los Angeles
Lakers basketball player, that Djokovic likes: 'Haters are a good problem
to have. Nobody hates the good ones. They hate the great ones.'

As two ferociously competitive athletes, Djokovic and Bryant were
close. Bryant was celebrated for his relentless pursuit of success, which
he called his 'Mamba mentality'. If you ever saw him in a fight with a bear,
Bryant would say, pray for the bear. He liked to dare others to be their
best selves. Djokovic, who was distraught when Bryant was killed in a
helicopter crash in California in 2020, had turned to his friend for
advice on maintaining a winner's mindset. 'Novak talks about Kobe
Bryant quite a bit. That's not the stereotypical mentor-mentee
relationship that somebody just stumbles upon,' said Todd Martin.

'That's something you seek out. From Novak's side, that required a level of ambition but also a level of humility.'

Whenever Djokovic felt down, and as though his spirits needed uplifting, he would call Bryant, who once wrote a fantasy novel about tennis. And he could be sure that the American would be there for him. While Bryant wouldn't have known all the intricacies of tennis, he understood the emotional challenges of being an elite athlete, and that was what Djokovic wanted from his friend: to talk on an emotional level. Sometimes, when speaking on the phone, Bryant would instantly have words of advice and encouragement for Djokovic. There were also occasions when Bryant wished to mull over Djokovic's issue and then come back to him with a considered opinion. Bryant's counsel was most useful for Djokovic when he was trying to regain his alpha status when he lost his way, because of an elbow injury and other issues, for two years after winning the 2016 Roland Garros title. But you have to imagine that, in the course of those conversations, Djokovic and Bryant would have touched on the tennis player's haters and how he should have been handling the vitriol spewed his way.

At the very least, Bryant's quote resonated with Djokovic and gave him some comfort, as this had been an issue throughout his career, with his fitness trainer Gebhard Gritsch observing: 'Very early on, Novak was made aware he wasn't the darling of the world.'

The haters lurk online where they sneer and snipe. But they're also out there in the real world; from Melbourne to Paris to London to New York, Djokovic has been trying to win Grand Slams while battling the casual unkindness and focused venom of what must sometimes seem like the tennis mob. Ignoring the online hate is easier; you just delete the social media apps on your phone. But you can't mute or turn off the spectators at the Grand Slams. Even at the best of times, centre stage at the majors can be a lonely place, where you are left exposed and everyone gets to peer into your soul. Now try doing that – as Djokovic has so often during his career – when it can also feel as though, in addition to your opponent, you're taking on thousands in the crowd. Sometimes it has just been a few individuals who have gone too far. But there have been matches when the stadium has felt very hostile. All too often during his career, Djokovic has had the crowd against him.

You might well ask: how many Grand Slam titles does Djokovic have to win before more of the public learn to love him, before the haters go quiet? But that might be the wrong way of looking at this – most likely it's his sustained success, winning an unprecedented number of majors, that has been aggravating sections of the public. Bryant was right – if Djokovic had never won a single Slam, if he had never been a tennis great with dozens of majors, no one would have bothered to work themselves into a rage about him. It feels as though Djokovic didn't attract so much venom during his Djoker era. He was a looser, more carefree presence on the tour then, but also less successful so not a genuine threat to the world order of Roger Federer and Rafael Nadal. Even when he was the world number three for so many years, he might as well have been twenty-three for all the attention he was getting in comparison to Federer and Nadal. Only when Djokovic started winning Grand Slams in big numbers did his relationship with many fans shift.

Now he might be aggravating that group even more. As one influential figure in Serbian tennis said: 'Novak's the undisputed GOAT now and that might bother some people.'

Whatever Djokovic does, however many Grand Slams he wins, he won't ever experience the kind of universal lovefest that Federer and Nadal have. 'Novak has broken all the records and yet people still criticize him and favour Federer or Nadal,' said Jelena Jankovic. 'No matter what Novak does, he still has to do much more to be accepted and appreciated. I don't know if that's because he comes from a small country. But no matter how much Novak wins, or what he does, he's still not appreciated as much as he should be. He's the greatest tennis player of all time – I can't say anything but compliment him for all he does – and he deserves more.'

Goran Ivanisevic, Djokovic's former coach, has suggested crowds' behaviour towards the Serb hasn't always been personal. When, as has happened so often, Djokovic has been crushing an opponent, spectators who have paid a lot of money for their tickets have started to cheer more loudly for the other guy in the hope that the match will be extended and they will see more tennis. While there could be some truth in that, when did that ever happen to Federer when he was in beast-mode?

It might not look it from the outside but tennis can be tribal, particularly online. For so many years, Federer's 'Fed-Heads' and Nadal's 'Rafa-Holics' had become accustomed to their favourites dominating the sport. That was just how the universe operated. Some would have felt affronted when Djokovic appeared, urged on by his 'Nole Fam'. As Djokovic's former coach Boris Becker has said, a fair few in tennis have long thought of Djokovic as a party pooper. Tennis was doing just fine, those people were thinking and saying, without Djokovic coming along and giving tennis a Big Three. Djokovic has thought about how all the iconic rivalries in sport, and all the great romantic novels, tend to be about two people rather than three. But he didn't care; he was making it a trio. The worst part for some was that Djokovic was openly saying he wanted to defeat Federer and Nadal. At the time, he knew that was divisive, and how some would admire his willingness to state his goals, while others would think: 'Look at this arrogant man.'

As the *New Yorker* magazine put it, Djokovic is the 'forever crasher'; whatever else he does, some will always see him as the guy who broke up the 'Fedal' party. That would have been hard enough for some of Federer and Nadal's supporters to take, but it would have been even trickier to process when, with his continued excellence, Djokovic turned the Big Three into the Big One. When the third man of tennis upgraded himself to the true alpha of the sport, and then – just to add to the horror – Djokovic became the GOAT.

For all the Grand Slams he has won, and the hundreds of weeks he has spent as the world number one, it sometimes feels as though Djokovic will never truly be an establishment figure in some people's eyes. There's enough in Djokovic's backstory – including having to shelter in a basement bunker during nightly bombing raids – for crowds in Melbourne, Paris, London and New York and elsewhere to have seen him as an inspirational figure. But maybe some in the West haven't been as warm and as sympathetic because of the context around those raids and NATO's reasons for striking Belgrade. That had started when Djokovic was a boy, when Serbia was a pariah nation, and when he first started travelling to tournaments: he sometimes sensed how others were uneasy when they discovered where he was from. 'When Novak was young, he learned that he wasn't going to be the most liked person because of his cultural background and many other things,' noted Gritsch. 'This is a sport dominated by Western culture and the Western media and

Novak comes from the former East. For the older generation of fans in the West, that's still something in their minds. If Novak had grown up in, say, Germany or Switzerland, it definitely would have been different.'

One of Djokovic's former coaches, Bogdan Obradovic, used to be a member of the Serbian parliament so has a unique perspective on how Djokovic's nationality has affected the athlete's image. 'Novak is a problem for this west-versus-east thing. For me, this is the most stupid part of our planet because some people hate each other. There's a Serbian flag next to his name, but he's not actually promoting our country on the court. To me, it's not Serbia on the court, it's Novak Djokovic. He's playing for tennis and he's doing great things for tennis. Everybody will come to the stadium to see tennis there, and not the promotion of a country. When you go to the cinema because you want to watch a good movie, you don't care where the actor is from or where the director is from. It's the same with Novak,' Obradovic said. 'I don't understand why people aren't admiring him and saying, "Well, Novak, we want to support you and what you're doing is fantastic". People aren't recognizing that because in the media everywhere, there is so much negativity towards him.'

Djokovic protects himself by not seeking out articles about him, good or bad (though, as he's on social media, he can't completely avoid what has been written as people post headlines and snippets). 'As an athlete you have a very defined view of yourself. If you're reading what people are saying about you, that's not going to be good for your mental balance,' said Gritsch. 'It could upset you. It could make you want to respond to what's in those articles. All that isn't necessary. That's going to take energy away from you. It's much better to stay away from that. It can also be a problem if what people are writing and saying about you is too positive. Not reading the media is how you maintain that balance within yourself.'

Traditionally, elite men's tennis has been populated by Americans and Western Europeans. Niki Pilic argued that some fans don't care for the player because they see him as an Eastern European who has got above his station. 'Politics is very much involved in our sport. People are against Novak because he comes from a small country. He's not from America. Or Britain. Or France. Or Germany. Or Italy. He's come from nowhere and he's the best of all time and some people – such as the Western mainstream media – don't like it that way. That's the truth and do you want to hear the truth or not? If you love Roger Federer more, that's OK, but I don't like extremes. If 90 per cent of a crowd is against Novak, that's also OK. But if they are applauding or clapping his double-faults, that's not good enough,' Pilic said.

'I'm not saying that Novak's profile should be on the same level as Federer and Nadal. But Novak gets one quarter of what he deserves. Novak has had to fight for exposure much more than anyone else. Novak is very colourful. There are people who love him and there are also people who hate him. Novak has the personality, he has charisma, he has a good sense of humour. And if you don't like him, that's your problem.'

Maybe those fans who think that players from small Eastern European nations shouldn't be presiding over tennis would have been OK with Djokovic winning a few Grand Slams? But winning this many, and becoming the undisputed greatest player of all time? That's just too much for them to take. Three times Djokovic turned down endorsement contracts from Nike. Would Djokovic have been a more popular figure if he had had the backing of that American company, and he had been marketed in the United States and other territories alongside Federer and Nadal? Would Western fans have been more accepting of Djokovic's greatness if Nike had slapped the Swoosh on him? What if Djokovic had been more receptive towards the overtures from Britain in the mid-2000s, and had accepted the offer of funding from the Lawn Tennis Association, which would have seen him switch his Serbian passport for a British one? If Djokovic had been a British citizen when winning all those Grand Slam titles, would the tennis establishment now be talking very differently about him?

Coming from an off-grid tennis nation is doubly hard. It's trickier to make it to the elite in the first place and then when you're there things don't come so easily. While Djokovic was able to turn down Nike as he had other options, there's no doubt that he hasn't been as commercially successful as Federer and Nadal. Djokovic has won more prize money than anyone else, but when you're operating at that level much of your wealth is going to come from off-court deals from endorsement contracts and the like. As a Serb – rather than, say, an American or a Western European – he was at a considerable disadvantage.

That's not to say that Djokovic has a loveless existence in tennis. Far from it. Djokovic has hardly played any tennis in Serbia during his career because of a lack of elite tournaments there – for a few years, his family operated an ATP tournament in Belgrade, though no more. But he's so popular there, with his approval ratings so stratospheric, that he's spoken of as a future President, should he ever want to go into politics. In Serbia, he's loved with an intensity that exceeds the love for, say, Federer in Switzerland or Nadal in Spain. The Swiss are understated in their love for Federer because that's in their national character; Serbs, being more passionate and vocal, are the opposite. Around Belgrade, it feels as though Djokovic is everywhere, on the billboards, on the covers of magazines, on the front of the 'GOAT' T-shirts on sale from street stalls along the main shopping drag. People who have always adored Djokovic tell you they love him even more because of his haters. In the Balkans and also globally, Djokovic has a loyal, lively online following, with his superfans styling themselves the 'Nole Fam' (they celebrate their support for him on 25 April, which is 'Nole Fam Day', as that was the date when he first used the term 'Nole Fam' on social media).

One Serb on the tour who speaks to Djokovic regularly said comparisons with Federer and Nadal, and particularly Federer, are misleading and unfair. Of course, Djokovic is going to look unloved and comparatively unpopular when you judge him next to the most adored players in history. Too often, this observer continued, Djokovic's standing among fans has been seen through the prism of the West. Sure, Federer and Nadal are more popular in the West, but that's not the entire world. Perhaps, as Djokovic has suggested, he is more popular than the Anglo-Saxon-dominated media would like to admit, even in countries such as Italy, as he speaks Italian and supports an Italian football team in AC Milan. All around the world, he has felt respect, which he regards as an important element of love, which is 'the ultimate energy'.

Speak to people close to Djokovic and some say that this narrative about him being unloved everywhere he goes in tennis is very tiresome. In South America and also in Asia – in huge tennis markets such as China, India and Japan – Djokovic is apparently right up there with Federer and Nadal. Gritsch suggested Djokovic was popular in Asia because he wasn't yet another champion from Western Europe, and that he was loved for coming from somewhere else, and also for not being from an upper-middle-class background like Federer and Nadal: 'They look at Novak and think, "He's one of us." '

Djokovic's friend Sascha Bajin, a German-Serbian tennis coach who has worked with Serena Williams and Naomi Osaka, has observed how some of Djokovic's fans are 'extreme' in their devotion to him. 'There are few tennis fans who are as hardcore as some of Novak's supporters,' Bajin said. 'It seems to me as though you either love the guy or you hate the guy because he's so true to himself. That's actually why I love and respect him a lot.'

Over time, some are updating and softening their views of Djokovic. After Federer's retirement in 2022 and with Nadal largely absent from the 2023 season because of injury, Djokovic was the only one of the Big Three still consistently out there on the world stage. No longer was he competing with those favourites for the public's affections. And perhaps also some have become intrigued by, and then invested in, the story of the man who just keeps on winning. Tears can also help change how a tennis crowd feels about a player and Djokovic's emotions after the 2023 Wimbledon final – he started crying when looking at his son Stefan in his box – would have altered how some perceive him. (When Stefan was asked to write a school essay under the title 'My Hero', he picked his dad.)

Friends see Djokovic as a kind and generous soul. Djokovic's former coach, Ivanisevic, calls him 'the Robin Hood of tennis' for going out of his way to support lesser players in their demands for extra prize money, even helping to set up the Professional Tennis Players Association to further that cause. Tennis players are supposed to be selfish creatures, who adhere to the principle that you eat what you kill. But Djokovic was acting against his own self-interest, urging tennis authorities to direct prize-money increases at those who lost in the early rounds of a Grand Slam, or even lower down the food chain, who didn't even qualify. Djokovic could see he had more than enough money but recognized the struggles of others who couldn't pay for a coach or to travel to tournaments and who in time would slip out of the sport, principally through a lack of cash.

Djokovic personally intervened to help a young Serbian player, Hamad Medjedovic, offering financial support over the years and in 2023 his countryman won the ATP Next Gen Finals, a tournament for the best players aged 21 and under. For a world number one who has won so many Grand Slam titles – and taken so many opportunities away from other players – Djokovic is a popular figure in the locker-room.

'I'm probably biased because we've been friends for so many years and all the Serbian players have a close relationship, but Novak is a friendly guy,' said Dusan Lajovic, a fellow Serb who has spent a lot of time with Djokovic on the tennis circuit. 'He's been very generous towards other players. You hear how Novak gives a friendly welcome to the young guys who are new on the tour. He invites them for practice and tries to give them advice. It's hard when you're young and you join the tour and you don't know anybody and everything's new, but then Novak approaches them and says: "Hey, everything's cool, you're here now." I think that helps the young guys a lot, to have someone like Novak being so welcoming. That's one of the things that people don't see on camera.'

Holger Rune, an ambitious young Dane, has spoken of how giving Djokovic has been towards the next generation, doing more for them than Federer and Nadal, even though Rune has said the Swiss and the Spaniard are often talked about as 'the good guys' of tennis. Other players tell stories that say something about Djokovic's character. Daniil Medvedev has said that Djokovic treated him exactly the same when he was ranked 400 in the world as he does now that he is also an elite player. When Jannik Sinner was still finding his way on tour, the Italian has disclosed, Djokovic gave him some advice on how he could improve his game. Sergiy Stakhovsky, a former Ukrainian tennis player who joined his country's armed forces after Putin's Russia invaded his home country, was moved by Djokovic's public support, as he was all too aware that Djokovic had been through hellish times himself during his childhood.

Djokovic has reflected on the quote from Winston Churchill that, 'we make a living by what we get, but we make a life by what we give'. Winning tennis trophies has allowed Djokovic, with the platform he has built for himself, to pursue what he regards as his other life missions. Away from the tennis bubble, his Novak Djokovic Foundation is focused on pre-school education, with the ambition of ensuring that every child in Serbia has access to an early-childhood programme. Djokovic has also been providing something else for young children and the youth in Serbia: communicating a message of hope and inspiration, that if they believe in themselves and their dreams, they can make something of their lives. But money always helps, and he has been generous with other causes, including buying ventilators during the pandemic.

'Novak is like a prince from a fairy tale,' said Obradovic. 'He's very generous. He's very stable. After he became very famous and rich, he didn't change. He stayed the same. He's helping people around him . . . He wants to help everybody. This is what everyone likes and respects about him. Whatever we as a people are doing for Novak, he is paying that back to us, to his nation. That's amazing actually. I don't see many other examples of athletes helping their countries and their people like Novak is helping Serbia.'

Some would suggest Djokovic doesn't get enough credit for the decent and noble things he does. His supporters say that while every small mistake or misdemeanour is magnified, his acts of kindness and generosity are too often overlooked, almost as if they don't fit the narrative that the media and others have created for him. 'No one talks or writes about Novak's generosity, about his humanitarian side,' said Chris Evert. 'He has been very generous towards his country, donating and raising millions of dollars, and he has been generous forming an association that gives lower ranked players more prize money. That's a sacrifice and that's a time commitment for him that takes away a little bit from his tennis or his family. No one talks about what he has been doing behind the scenes.'

*

Tennis has had villains before, of course. The 1980s was a wild time on the tennis tour when the public loved to demonize John McEnroe. Jimmy Connors was also seen as a danger to polite society. Marcelo Rios, a Chilean who rose to world number one in the 1990s, was once profiled in *Sports Illustrated* magazine with the headline 'The Most Hated Man in Tennis'. But Djokovic feels different. Connors won eight Grand Slams, McEnroe seven and Rios none. As the greatest of all generations, Djokovic is considerably more successful than those three. And while the two combative Americans seemed to mostly enjoy the opprobrium that came their way – McEnroe played up to his 'Superbrat' image and Connors called his autobiography *The Outsider* – Djokovic isn't so comfortable with his public perception.

As much as Djokovic seemed to take encouragement from Bryant's words about people only hating the greats, it seems he is still uncomfortable with how some feel about him. He regards hate as a 'horrendous emotion' and believes that if anyone feels that way about him it says more about them than it does about him. Yes, the haters confirm Djokovic's greatness, and you have to remember that tennis isn't a popularity contest; true greatness is about the number of Grand Slams you win, and other metrics like weeks spent as world number one, not how many fans blush and scream and faint at the sight of you. But – and who could possibly blame him for this? – Djokovic would like to feel some more love from the stadium. To experience a little of what Federer had everywhere he went.

But, for all the admiration and affection that Djokovic inspires among his supporters, there is no doubt that the relationship with other tennis fans has unsettled him. Though he doesn't care quite as much as he once used to, Djokovic sometimes wonders what he has done to upset the tennis universe. He can't always understand why a tennis crowd treats him the way they do, why they seem to regard him as a tennis super-villain. Some would say 'pantomime villain' or even 'cartoon villain' but that's not quite right. There's nothing cartoony about how all that hostility from the stadium – expressed as booing, whistling, jeering or applauding his double-faults and other errors – can make him feel when he's chasing history.

'Tennis players are emotional, and sensitive too, so I would assume that at times it bothered Novak when he was playing great tennis and the crowd was still against him for the most part,' said Evert. 'He's pretty honest with people and I don't think he would deny that. It must have felt to Novak as though Roger and Rafa could do no wrong while he was always being criticized.'

The way Djokovic describes it, tennis isn't quite the individual sport you imagine. If you've got the crowd on your side, you gain extra energy, strength and motivation; that's a more pleasant environment to be working in. And when you don't have the spectators cheering and screaming for you, you have to find all that from within. As much as Djokovic accepts it's his destiny – his choice of word – to usually play with the crowd against him, there are naturally times when he finds that harder to take and can't accept why the crowd are behaving as they do. If it's challenging for Djokovic when a crowd applauds his double-faults, it can also be upsetting for his family and friends; his wife Jelena has found the bad vibes around her husband on court to be truly heart-breaking. When Djokovic spoke of spending a lot of his career in 'hostile environments', he sounded more like a special forces soldier dropped behind the front lines than a tennis player on Centre Court.

They used to say about Federer that he always played at 'home' – as a tennis player, you compete all over the world, often in different cities and countries from one week to the next, but wherever he was, it sounded like he was in downtown Basel. Even when Federer was playing an opponent in front of their own people – such as Andy Murray at Wimbledon – you still always sensed the Swiss had most of the crowd with him. Unfortunately for Djokovic, he has often found himself at the other end of the tennis love spectrum; many of his matches feel as though they are 'away', played in front of a crowd favouring his opponent. Some athletes are lacking in self-awareness; Djokovic has acknowledged, to himself first and then publicly, that in 90 per cent or more of his matches he has played against the stadium as well as his opponent. That was at the most extreme when Djokovic played Federer.

The crowd were often so vocal in expressing their love for the Swiss that Djokovic developed a method of dealing with that – when the spectators screamed for 'Roger', he told himself he could hear 'Novak'. Djokovic appreciates that might sound weird or silly but when you're all alone on a tennis court that has given him some psychological comfort. There was a voice in Djokovic's head that was saying to him: 'OK, I'm not going to let that bring you down because you might lose a tennis match because of it. You're going to feel bad or angry or upset. But I'm going to help you feel better.' Djokovic repeated a positive message in his head so many times – telling himself again and again that the crowd was cheering for him – that it went beyond just saying and hearing it; he could also feel it. Only then did he believe that he had done enough mental training to cope with this. By changing the electrical frequency of his brain, he had changed the name he was hearing.

That said a lot, observed psychologist Daria Abramowicz, about what keeps Djokovic going on court, as it revealed how 'he really wants to be liked, or even loved, by the fans'. 'It seems as though Djokovic wishes to be admired as a public figure.'

Of all the elite players in recent years, Djokovic has tried harder than most to win over the crowd (though, of course, for some, public adoration came very easily). On some level, perhaps that has that been a continuation of Djokovic's experiences as a teenager new to the tennis circuit, when he saw that some people weren't sure about how to be around a Serb and that he was going to have to be doubly personable to win them over.

Yannick Noah, a former Roland Garros champion, once observed that Djokovic 'is constantly trying to seduce – it almost looks fake. He's a kid that wants . . . the attention. He sometimes does a bit much, but I am 100 per cent sure that he is a good guy.' Maybe Djokovic has even tried too hard, such as with his victory celebration of drawing 'the energy from the heavens' and then sharing that love with the crowd. That wasn't to everyone's taste, with some feeling it was overengineered; Nick Kyrgios – when he was going through his Djokovic-baiting phase – thought it was cringey and that the Serb 'had a sick obsession with being liked'. The Australian also called Djokovic a 'tool' for some of his actions during the pandemic. But – and this can be seen as an illustration of how Djokovic can win people over – by the time the two played in the 2022 Wimbledon final, it was something close to a 'bromance', and by the 2024 Australian Open, Djokovic was blowing kisses at Kyrgios, who was courtside in a commentary booth. On occasion, when Djokovic hasn't been cheered that loudly after an outrageous win or a long and entertaining point, it has looked as though he has invited the crowd to make some more noise.

Often charming and gracious in several languages – he's fluent in Serbian, English, Italian and French and can communicate in German, Spanish and Mandarin – Djokovic is capable of saying all the right things in his post-match, on-court interviews. That's particularly true in defeat when, speaking in his second, third or fourth language, and still raw from his loss, he often finds the right words in those moments. Unfortunately for Djokovic, the public relations game isn't like training or staying disciplined with nutrition and stretching; effort doesn't always get rewarded. Ultimately, as his former coach Boris Becker has noted, 'you cannot make people love you'.

Centre Court at Wimbledon, usually such a lovely place, doesn't feel like such a gentle environment when Djokovic is playing. There are supposedly few more well-mannered and benign sporting audiences than the Centre Court crowd (or at least the Centre Court crowd likes to think so). Booing is rare. But even there – inside a stadium that is spoken of as a kind of holy place for tennis, and where the crowd tends to respond when the umpire appeals for 'quiet please' – Djokovic has had some rough, wretched days. Djokovic didn't lose on Centre Court for ten years, between defeats to Andy Murray and Carlos Alcaraz in the 2013 and 2023 finals, but dominance doesn't always create affection. Djokovic and some sections of the Centre Court crowd just don't get along. Some close to Djokovic said that he seems to have more support from fans when he is away from Centre Court and around the grounds, such as when he is walking to and from practice on one of the outside courts. That might suggest that those who have access to tickets to the bigger courts and matches – probably the wealthier, better connected and more establishment types at the All England Club – have a more negative view of Djokovic than those who watch him from Henman Hill.

Some will always see Djokovic – the most successful tennis player in history – as an outsider. 'The underprivileged people, the workers, how many times did they come up to us in Novak's team and say, "We're all for Novak"? That happened so many times,' said Gebhard Gritsch.

Three times Djokovic has upset the Centre Court crowd by beating their favourite, Federer, in the final. That might explain why the crowd there is often against him. Becker wasn't alone in thinking that some spectators had disrespected Djokovic during the 2019 final. As brilliantly as Djokovic played, saving Federer's two match points to win in five sets and almost five hours, it's a contest that is also remembered for some spectators clapping his errors.

Perhaps Federer was also a factor in the crowd's treatment of Djokovic during the 2023 final as he had been attempting to equal the Swiss's record of eight Wimbledon titles. One Serbian insider invited people to imagine a universe in which Djokovic accepted the 2006 offer from the Lawn Tennis Association and played as a Briton; how differently, he said, would the British media and public treat Djokovic? Wimbledon spectators famously enjoy queuing – what they don't like is waiting for a player to serve and on several occasions, after maybe bouncing the ball a few times too many as he composed himself, Djokovic went over the limit of 25 seconds between points. The umpire gave Djokovic a time violation. Spectators voiced their displeasure. That came just two days after a semi-final that also had its fractious moments. Getting heated in his match against Jannik Sinner, Djokovic responded to a few hecklers by pretending to wipe away tears – seemingly suggesting that the spectators were cry-babies – and also with sarcastic clapping and thumbs up. That provoked boos. But Djokovic was smiling when he spoke about the crowd afterwards in the media theatre: 'All love. It's all love and acceptance.'

Djokovic's relationship with the US Open crowd is possibly even more complicated. That can be traced back to the 2008 tournament when Andy Roddick made fun of Djokovic's reputation for being a drama queen with his injuries and ailments, saying the Serbian was dealing with, among other things, 'bird flu' and 'anthrax'. When Djokovic defeated Roddick in the quarter-finals, he used his on-court interview to say it hadn't been 'nice' for the American to have suggested he was 'faking' injuries. It wasn't the smartest move to criticize Roddick inside the Arthur Ashe Stadium and inevitably Djokovic was booed by parts of the crowd. Backstage, a raging Roddick slammed Djokovic up against a locker but backed off when he saw the size of the Serb's fitness trainer and the trouble that he might have been getting himself into. While Djokovic later apologized – he had been emotional after the match, and also hadn't appreciated that Roddick had been joking – that episode seemed to set the tone for his relationship with some New Yorkers.

One of the few occasions when Djokovic felt what it was like to play a Grand Slam final in front of a supportive crowd was at the 2021 US Open final. The Serb, having won the opening three majors of the year, was just one more match away from becoming the first man since Rod Laver in 1969 to take all four in a season, which would have given him the calendar-year Grand Slam. Djokovic was so emotional in that final against Daniil Medvedev that he was in tears before the match was over – he put a towel over his head during one changeover – and he afterwards said his heart was filled with joy. He had just lost in straight sets, but he was 'the happiest man alive'.

Another rare Grand Slam final when Djokovic had the stadium on his side was the day he defeated Andy Murray to win the 2016 Roland Garros title; for the first time, he felt the love of the crowd throughout a major final (though he had been given ovations in Paris after losing in the 2014 and 2015 finals, which on both occasions brought tears to his eyes). Crowds at Roland Garros are notoriously tricky. For some Parisians, going to the tennis isn't a spectator sport; you're trying to insert yourself into the story and the drama by whistling and booing at every chance and half-chance. Some ticket-holders will even boo French players at their home Grand Slam. Rafael Nadal, the most successful clay-court player of all time, hasn't always had an easy time of it in south-west Paris. With that in mind, who really imagined that the Roland Garros crowd and Djokovic were going to have a smooth, happy relationship at all times?

Djokovic has lamented how some people come to Roland Garros looking to boo every single thing he does. While they have paid for their tickets, and he feels as though they therefore have the right to do as they please, he can't help but feel as though they are being disrespectful towards him and he's not always going to stay quiet. Even in the spring of 2023, at a tournament when Djokovic achieved true greatness by winning his 23rd Grand Slam title, an unprecedented haul for a man, he still found himself dealing with boos and jeers from some in the crowd.

Of the four Grand Slams, Djokovic arguably gets on best with the Australian Open crowd, helped by the sizeable Serbian population in Melbourne. But, as we will explore in due course, Djokovic's relationship with the Melbourne public would be severely tested in 2022.

12

DARK ENERGY

In the swirl and the chaos at the Grand Slams, when there are negative voices in the crowd, Novak Djokovic is sometimes able, he has said, to 'cocoon' himself. That depends on how he's feeling and what is happening in the match and in the stadium. Djokovic finds a way to focus on his breathing and staying in the moment. There are other occasions when he actively wants to feed off the buzz and the energy. Then there are the days when cocooning himself just isn't possible and – because he's not perfect – he can't help but react to the heckles and the boos and the negativity. And that's not necessarily a bad thing: feeling the coldness of the crowd can be enormously beneficial.

If the haters, as grotesque and absurd as they are, have helped Djokovic to understand his own greatness, they have also assisted him in matches, where he is always looking for an edge. The spectators won't have realized they are helping Djokovic by bringing out his competitive side and inspiring him to greater heights. 'If you're booing Novak and making him angry, you're doing him a favour,' said Jelena Jankovic. 'That pushes and motivates him to be even better. If the crowd is against him, he finds a way to use that to his advantage. Novak has such mental strength that he can overcome any challenge and show that he's the best.' If some tennis players are propelled by love, others can be driven by the animosity of the crowd, by having something to rail against. 'The more they cheer against me, the better for me,' Djokovic once said. 'They wake something in me that they perhaps don't want to see – a winner.'

Nick Kyrgios, another player seen as a tennis villain, has spoken of the dark energy he gets when an entire stadium is against him, and how it can feel good to be in that situation. When a crowd's down on Djokovic, his blood is up, and he has that special Serbian type of dark energy. Djokovic has an urbane side. But, underneath it all, according to Boris Becker, he has a streetfighter's mentality. Djokovic's former fitness coach, Ronen Bega, suggested the Serb has a different personality on and off the court: 'Novak's a very nice guy off the court. He's very intelligent. You can speak with him about everything. On the court, it's a different mentality. He's a fighter. When he walks on to the court, it's like he comes into the boxing ring. He's a completely different guy.'

If there have been moments in Djokovic's career when the crowd's animosity has stopped him from playing his best tennis, it has mostly helped him. 'At one stage, it may have had a negative impact on Novak's performance,' said Craig O'Shannessy. 'If you've got so many people going for the other guy, it would only have been normal if it had affected Novak and his game. But I feel as though he has thrived on that adversity from the crowd. In some ways, it has helped Novak and made him better. There have been some tough moments, but that has made him a tough competitor.' Former coach Goran Ivanisevic has observed that Djokovic has often produced stronger performances when crowds haven't been on his side. When crowds have been friendlier, Djokovic has been a calmer, happier presence, though hasn't always played better.

Mostly, Djokovic stays quiet when a crowd is against him. But he thinks that fans should expect him to occasionally respond in those moments. Some days – and 'I ask for forgiveness from the tennis universe for being who I am, because sometimes the ego controls you' – he will react. 'Misbehaving', he calls it. Maybe Djokovic's reactions have occasionally been more 'explosive' – his word – than they should have been, but his response has at least allowed him to get that emotion out of his system, as otherwise it could have started to drag him down. Naturally, another factor was Djokovic trying to show his tormentors who was actually in charge inside the stadium. To put them in their place. Such as when Djokovic told a group of British tennis fans to 'shut up' as their drumming was disturbing his post-match interview at a Davis Cup tie in Malaga in 2023 (he had earlier blown a kiss at a British supporter who had been annoying him with his loud interventions). Or the occasion at the 2024 Australian Open when Djokovic invited a tormentor in the crowd to 'come down and say it to my face', which the man declined because, as Djokovic put it, he lacked courage (as unpleasant as that situation was, it provoked Djokovic, who had been emotionally flat earlier in the match, into raising his intensity and his level). The year before in Melbourne, Djokovic had pleaded with the umpire to deal with a heckler who was 'drunk out of his mind' and was seemingly more interested in getting into Djokovic's head than watching tennis.

Djokovic can be 'uncouth' in matches, according to Andy Roddick. Telling the crowd to 'shut the fuck up', which the Serb has even done in some Grand Slam finals, would come under that description. The uncomfortable truth for those who like tennis to be U-rated is that Djokovic, the greatest of all time but not necessarily the Disney prince or Disney athlete that some would want him to be, has often performed at his best when he's not willing to play nice. Uncouth isn't the dig you think it is. Uncouth is sometimes the mood, or the mode, that Djokovic needs to be in. After all, as his friend and former footballer Zlatan Ibrahimovic has said, Djokovic is a 'Balkan head', someone who sometimes needs to explode with anger to be at the top of his game. (Ibrahimovic is a Swede with Balkan heritage).

Drama-addicted isn't quite the right way to describe Djokovic. It's just that drama follows him everywhere. Going drama-free at a Grand Slam? That just isn't possible for him, Djokovic has mused, and if a crowd is going to treat him like a villain, he's going to behave like one. As one Serbian observer said of Djokovic in those fiery, feisty moments, 'sometimes he likes to get into it with the crowd'. Spectators poke Djokovic. He pokes them back with acid stares, mockery and sarcasm. He pouts and blows kisses. He also smirks, flares his nostrils, cups his hand at his ear, puts his finger to his lips and tells them to shush or rubs pretend tears from his eyes.

Is this all instinctive? Or is there something a little calculated about the way Djokovic behaves sometimes, as if he knows it will bait the crowd and he can then feed off that? Does the man who wants to be loved also do things that he knows are going to antagonize, that will allow him to continue playing the role of villain? If he's not going to feel loved that day, is he thinking that he might as well rile the crowd and use that animosity to his advantage? Or maybe he's just, if the mood takes him, having some fun with it, such as the occasion at an indoor tournament in Paris in the autumn of 2023 when he invited fans to boo him even more. Or, at that season's ATP Finals in Turin, when he reacted to the crowd's hostility by pretending to conduct the booing. Perhaps even Djokovic can't answer that. What's certain is that he has sometimes retaliated in the most effective way possible: raising his game and taking down the crowd's darling.

'Maybe sometimes Novak is just playing his game and it's like he's in a movie. The match is just going by. Then something happens, he feels as though everyone is against him and that sparks something inside him,' said Sascha Bajin. 'He's going to want to prove a point and he's going to go all out. Where he's from, right from the beginning of his career, Novak has been dealing with so much animosity and with so many naysayers telling him why he can't do something. There's a deep motivation inside Novak to prove people wrong because he has encountered that his whole life. He's going to use that energy to push himself.'

Suddenly, it can feel as though Djokovic is more focused, more in tune with his game, that he has found a way of turning his anger into something positive. 'Sometimes it can seem as though Djokovic is using being less popular – not being loved – as fuel. You can see that on the court. He's using that to raise his energy and focus level,' said Daria Abramowicz.

There are moments when Djokovic riles the crowd not because he's goading them but because he's getting frustrated with his game. Off the court, you won't find a more controlled and disciplined tennis player. But there are times when this clean-living monk warrior, who gets up before sunrise for yoga and family hugging sessions, is red-lining on court and gets undisciplined and destructive and ends up sabotaging his own public relations game.

Confronting his 'demons', as he calls them, Djokovic can become agitated, emotional and violent. He has theatrically pulled and ripped his shirt (though he occasionally also likes to do the same after winning a big match). Djokovic once hummed a song on court when he was angry as he wanted to avoid one of his 'tantrums' and 'switch the vibration'. But often Djokovic breaks stuff, slamming his racquet into the ground with so much force that it crumples or splinters. Instantly, Djokovic will feel remorse for being so destructive. In that moment, he will ask himself why he did it, and he will remind himself that he is a father of two and think about the thousands of children who will be watching his every move. There had been a small voice in Djokovic's head whispering softly: 'OK, try to do what you do best, but do it with dignity, do it with style.' But then, because he can't stop himself, Djokovic went ahead and broke the racquet anyway and felt – and this seems like a strong word – that he had *betrayed* himself as he hadn't behaved as he wanted to. He feels shame.

But only for a moment or two. Djokovic doesn't stay ashamed for long as he has learned not to be. He has found that there's nothing to be gained from putting himself down. It's far better for Djokovic to forgive himself and to accept that he is a flawed human being and that these things can happen when he's out there on his own under enormous amounts of stress. He allows himself to move on. The old racquet is a mangled mess. Djokovic takes a new one from his bag; he's making a fresh start, practically and emotionally. 'Novak likes to let out the raw emotion. He's releasing stress and tension and letting go of the anger. He plays better after that,' said Bajin. 'I like how Novak handles it.'

Igor Cetojevic has told Djokovic he doesn't like it when he breaks racquets, but he understands why he does it. 'If you're at a certain level, you must be aware that you have some good days and you have some bad days, and on bad days sometimes Novak explodes and he breaks racquets. The pressure on Novak is enormous and this is his way of controlling that pressure. Some people control the pressure in a different, less aggressive way, but that's his release. Novak knows I don't like him breaking racquets, as I've told him, but it's OK and he knows that he can forgive himself afterwards for his mistakes.'

Releasing anger on the court allows Djokovic to touch the heights of his talent. 'If an athlete is showing they are mad, angry or frustrated or fired-up, that's really healthy,' Abramowicz said. 'One of the fundamental rules of life is don't keep those emotions inside. You need to find a healthy way to release them. It's simple biology that if you keep those tough emotions inside, and you internalise all the time, it just starts to eat you up. That could affect your body and cause injuries and will definitely decrease your performance. It's important to be able to channel and release your anger, frustration and other emotions.'

Even when Djokovic is in a hot rage on the court – breaking racquets and decorum – he never gets so angry that he can't remember the gameplan and what he's trying to do. There's little downside when getting angry. 'When Novak got mad, he still had the gameplan at the forefront of his mind,' O'Shannessy said. 'I never felt as though when he got angry, that was the end of it. I never felt that at all. He would try to get his head right as much as possible. I don't think he ever completely lost the plot and lost the gameplan. Novak was unbelievably good at absorbing and then retaining a gameplan. Some players I've worked with, they remember a gameplan for a set and then they kind of forget it. They can get lost on court. I don't remember that ever happening with Novak. He would never get lost in a match.'

While clearing his head, Djokovic is also riling the crowd. Centre Court didn't like it when he turned into the All England Club axeman during the 2023 final and whacked his racquet against the net post, leaving a dent in the wood. 'Novak's not always politically correct on court,' said Ronen Bega. 'He's acting in a way that Federer or Nadal wouldn't. He's really emotional and a lot of the time people don't like what they are seeing.'

Most damaging and disastrous of all was the moment at the 2020 US Open when Djokovic – raging at dropping his serve in a fourth-round match against Spaniard Pablo Carreno Busta – took a spare ball from his pocket and angrily swiped it away, accidently striking a female line judge in the throat. The official fell to the ground at the back of the court, choking and clutching at her throat. Djokovic, who had been the favourite to win the title that summer, was disqualified. For Djokovic's sake, it was just as well that he was playing in an empty Arthur Ashe Stadium – this was during the pandemic and before the vaccines were ready – as if there had been 23,000 New Yorkers all around him, it could have got ugly. But, as quiet and as still as it was on court, it was an afternoon of drama and chaos. While New York tennis fans weren't there in person, they would have been judging him from afar.

Djokovic's expulsion didn't just deprive him of the chance to win another Grand Slam title. It also damaged his relations with the New

York tennis public. No wonder Djokovic left the city feeling 'sad and empty'; he was sorry to have caused the line judge 'such stress'. 'So unintended, so wrong,' Djokovic wrote in an apology posted on Instagram, though he hoped it would be 'a lesson for my growth and evolution as a player and human being'. 'There are certain incidents and moments that affect your life and form you as a human being and getting disqualified from the US Open for hitting a line judge was one of those for Novak,' said Chris Evert. 'That was a big thing for Novak as he would have gone back and thought about it and he would have said to himself: "OK, I was a little reckless there. I've got to be more aware of other people. I need to be careful." He would have thought about how, as a tennis player, you can't be slamming balls around.'

On that occasion, Djokovic was unlucky; he didn't hit the ball with full force, and he clearly hadn't intended to take down a line judge. But there had been previous occasions when he had been fortunate when venting his frustrations and could have hit an official or a spectator. In an angry moment in his quarter-final against Czech Tomas Berdych at Roland Garros in 2016, Djokovic appeared to be about to whack his racquet against the clay when it slipped from his hand and went flying towards the back of the court. The line judge moved out of the way. Djokovic recognized he was 'lucky' that he didn't hit the official, as if he had he would have missed out on his 'Nole Slam'. Later that season, Djokovic thrashed a ball away in anger at the ATP Finals at The O2 Arena in London, which could have struck a spectator. Though, as Djokovic said afterwards, it could have been serious but it wasn't. It also could have snowed inside The O2 Arena, Djokovic went on to say, but it didn't. Why focus on what didn't happen? Djokovic also felt the media were acting as though he was the only player ever to have got frustrated on court.

For several years before his expulsion from the US Open, Djokovic had been living dangerously. Competing at the Monte Carlo Country Club in the spring of 2019, the Serb threw his racquet in the direction of the ball and it ended up in the crowd. Thankfully, he didn't hit anyone, but it was another episode that could have been worse. When Djokovic was defaulted in New York, it felt as though his previous actions were catching up with him.

*

For almost all of 2023, Djokovic was the only one of the Big Three still out there on the tour. Federer retired in 2022 while Nadal was mostly absent with injury. Djokovic was no longer in a popularity contest with the two most popular tennis players in history and that showed: he was more relaxed. He looked free. This was a new, 'chilled' Djokovic, observed Evert. 'For years, they always came as a threesome. Novak has always been stuck with two of the most beloved guys around. And he was always the bad guy. The biggest change I've seen recently in Novak was when Roger and Rafa were no longer in the picture and Novak became more relaxed and free to be who he is and to say what he wants. Novak's the leader now and this is his stage,' Evert said.

'Being in a popularity contest with Roger and Rafa didn't always bring out the best in Novak. I felt like he tried too hard at times to win the crowd over or he got too controversial. Now he's chilled about it and I think people are starting to change their minds about Novak.'

Maria Sharapova, an expert on the tennis-celebrity-marketing crossover, once said to Djokovic that she's not so keen on the word 'brand'.

But how else but brand-building would you describe Djokovic's activities in the autumn of 2023, in the months after winning a 24th Grand Slam title at the US Open? Djokovic, who ended his business relationship with his long-time agent Edoardo Artaldi after his New York City victory, played in a celebrity golf match in Rome in the build-up to the Ryder Cup match between Europe and the United States. It felt as though Djokovic was everywhere that autumn, as he also made appearances in Paris at the Rugby World Cup final and at the Ballon d'Or ceremony, where he presented the prize to the best female footballer. Djokovic's profile was growing outside tennis. This felt new but, as ever, Djokovic was doing things differently, asking Carlos Gomez-Herrera, previously his hitting partner and assistant coach, to also be his team manager, to work alongside his other manager, Mark Madden.

While he was at one time more impulsive, it seems as though Djokovic is now more measured when speaking in public. The new, evolved Djokovic – 'a deep thinker and a gentleman', according to Evert – is unlikely to repeat the controversy of 2016 when he suggested that female tennis players didn't deserve to be paid the same as their male colleagues as they weren't generating the same amount of attention or selling as many tickets. 'Billie Jean King and I accosted him at Miami and said: "We'd like to talk to you." We spoke and he was great. We all say things in the moment that maybe we don't really mean,' Evert said. 'Novak's now a little more thoughtful in what he says. In times before, his words were sometimes impulsively said, but he's more measured now in the way he speaks and he knows that it's going to have an impact, no matter what he says.'

If Djokovic is now more measured, that's not to say that he has been self-censoring or holding back. He's still going to say what he wants, and the words that come out of his mouth are more likely to be an accurate reflection of what he thinks. If others don't like that, so be it. 'Novak is saying what he feels and he's saying it with confidence, not worrying about the fallout, or how it's going to seem or sound, or the criticism,' said Evert.

Djokovic has, for the most part, made peace with how, in his eyes, the media sometimes doesn't portray him fairly and doesn't move on from his mistakes as quickly as they do when others get it wrong. He won't let the media drag him down or slow him down. Media attacks aren't going to change how he thinks about himself or what he's doing. 'Novak isn't afraid to speak out and to show himself,' Evert said. 'He's not afraid to be criticized. That's the difference between him and Roger and Rafa. I don't think Roger and Rafa ever wanted to be controversial or to be criticized, and by the way I'm not saying that's a good thing or a bad thing, that's just their nature, they're more introverted than Novak.'

One reading of Djokovic's relationship with the public is that, as much as he wants to be more universally loved, he isn't willing to compromise his values in pursuit of that adoration. That he will keep 'going against the mainstream', even if it costs him fans' affection. 'Does it bother Novak that he's not more loved by the crowd? For sure it does. He wouldn't be human if that didn't bother him,' Sascha Bajin said. 'Everyone wants to be loved and appreciated by the crowd. Everyone cares about this. But does Novak care more about the acceptance and appreciation of the crowd than his own values? That, I don't think so. That's why I like the guy so much as he won't jeopardize his own values and views to get the fans to like him. Being loved more by the crowd isn't one of his priorities as you can see with his behaviour and I respect him tremendously for that.'

When you're at Djokovic's level, there are times when you have to play the game and say all the right things. But he has been more daring than most would have been in his position. For Djokovic's supporters and friends, that has given him authenticity – they like how he doesn't pander to the tennis establishment for an easy life. That he no longer seems to chase public approval, as he might have done in the past. Djokovic was going to be himself, whether people liked that or not. 'I have a feeling that in the past Novak was trying a little bit too much to be proper – I'm talking here about outside the tennis court – and sometimes I was even forcing him not to be so proper,' said Janko Tipsarevic. 'But he's now way better at speaking his mind.'

One Serbian insider close to Djokovic agreed: 'What makes Novak Novak is that he's authentic. He has taken stances that people didn't like. If he was so eager for people to love him, he wouldn't have done so many of the things he did.' The days leading up to the 2022 Australian Open – quite possibly the most chaotic days in the history of the sport – would appear to support that analysis. By then, Djokovic was used to occasionally being seen as a tennis villain. He was going to stay true to his values, whatever the public relations hit. But events before that year's Australian Open went way beyond that; this was when Djokovic transcended tennis and attained a new career high of public opprobrium, becoming, he felt, a villain of the world.

13

PRISON LIFE

If you're looking for Peak Djokovic – for a moment that illustrated, more than any other, his true Novak-ness, when he was doing, saying and thinking things that were surely beyond all other tennis players – it wasn't one of his seemingly impossible feats in a Grand Slam final; or even a moment of off-court wonder, flexibility and human origami when he stretched and folded himself into a new position. Peak Djokovic was when he was inside an Australian immigration centre and – with a friend's encouragement – he reimagined his detention as a learning opportunity. Djokovic was in a 'prison' in all but name, at the centre of a rolling, all-consuming, global controversy, but this was also, as his friend was reminding him, an occasion for spiritual growth.

Inside the converted Park Hotel – which was where Djokovic ended up after believing he had a medical exemption to enter the country and play the 2022 Australian Open without being vaccinated against Covid – he was filling his lungs with the stale, scuzzy air, which must have taken away some of the joy of his daily breathwork. The tinted window in his room was screwed shut. As were all the other windows in all the other rooms in this immigration detention centre – just a few miles from Melbourne Park – that the other detainees were calling the 'Park Prison'. 'Just like the rest of us, Novak wouldn't have had any fresh air in his room,' said Hossein Latifi, an Iranian asylum seeker who had already been in the Park Hotel for months, and inside the system for nine years, when Djokovic checked in. The only access to fresh air in the five-storey building was a tiny balcony off one of the rooms where some of the men went to smoke but, as the guards were trying to keep their celebrity guest apart from the other detainees, that wasn't an option during the Serb's stay. Djokovic would have to do his conscious breathing with what must have been some of Melbourne's stalest air, recycled a thousand times by the failing – and potentially Covid-spreading – air-conditioning system.

Endlessly going around and around the building, the thick, dirty air added to the oppressive atmosphere inside this nightmarish 'prison' in Carlton, a university suburb north of the city centre. A place where, for most, the horror was, like the air-conditioning, on a loop. Djokovic was sharing the facility with around 30 men, many of them traumatized; most had been in the system for years when the tennis player entered their subworld and, in Latifi's words, almost every one of them was already 'broken' or 'destroyed'. Some men were forever in tears or on the edge of tears. Others were non-responsive. Many were heavily medicated, taking pills to help them sleep or to smooth out their depression and anxiety. 'Every single person in that building, me included, was depressed. The system destroys you, mentally and physically,' said Latifi. 'I think Novak would have felt that atmosphere. I think he understood the situation and what we were going through.'

Just for a few days, Djokovic was experiencing what it was like to be treated like a 'sub-human', according to Alison Battisson, a human rights lawyer who had several clients in this 'crappy', no-star hotel. In tennis, Djokovic had attained true alpha-maledom. But not in the Australian immigration system, where – after his visa had been cancelled ahead of the 2022 Australian Open – he had been reduced to 'unlawful non-citizen', which is about as low status as you could be in Australia.

As the doctor who taught Djokovic how to think as well as how to eat, Igor Cetojevic is one of the most influential figures in his life. When Cetojevic heard Djokovic was inside the Park Hotel, he contacted the athlete to encourage him to learn more about how the other men, all trapped inside the system, were suffering. While Cetojevic was no longer working with Djokovic by this time, he was talking to him as a friend and had some advice for how he could make the most of the time in the facility: 'Novak, observe these guys who had been staying there for years. Just be aware of how blessed you are. You've never previously had exposure to people who had suffered at that level so take the opportunity to learn from them and from this experience. This is a learning experience – being inside that jail, and being around those guys, is a very good time for you to collect information.'

To borrow a phrase from Djokovic's friend Maria Sharapova, he wasn't about to throw himself a pity party in the Park Hotel. If he felt sorry for himself, it was only very briefly. As Cetojevic said to Djokovic, being in the Park Hotel would be an inconvenience for him, getting in the way of his plans to win that year's Australian Open for a tenth time, but others in that building had it much worse than he did. 'There was a guy in there from Iran, Mehdi Ali, whose childhood had been stolen, who had come to Australia when he was 15 years old and who was by then a big man in his twenties as he had spent almost ten years stuck in a room,' Cetojevic said. 'I said to Novak: "The best game ever in life is to see life in real time. Your top game is to understand life. See this boy and see yourself. See how he suffers and then ask yourself what your suffering is. A few days in there? He has suffered almost ten years. You're there just a few days, which is a little bit inconvenient." Novak was showing compassion to his fellow humans. I also suggested to Novak that, if possible, he could show the other men a good time as they had never had a chance before to see a big star. I said: "Just talk to them. Be in a position to help them when they are in that prison."'

Djokovic was 'deeply touched' by the other detainees, telling the BBC how 'my hardship was nothing close to what those people are going through'. 'Definitely it wasn't pleasant but I don't want to sit here complaining about conditions in the detention centre because I stayed [for a few] days and some people there have stayed for years,' he said. While Djokovic didn't have a chance to speak to Mehdi inside the Park Hotel, he feels as though he has a connection with him and would welcome the chance to meet some day. It was a period, according to Craig Tiley, the CEO of Tennis Australia, that highlighted Djokovic's compassionate side. 'There's a side to Novak that sometimes gets missed and that's how he has empathy for people who don't have the same advantages as him,' said Tiley, who was in regular contact with Djokovic during that period. 'I've been around Novak and I've seen him care about others and talk about others, and particularly those that are disadvantaged. A good example was his view on those that were in [the Park Hotel] and his befriending of people there. He sided with the minority, with people who weren't getting a fair shake. That's where he naturally goes.'

Imprisoned inside the Park Hotel and inside your own head, it was possible not to see or have any meaningful conversation with anyone else all day, aside from the guards. Even if you left your single room and shuffled along the corridors, there was a good chance you would still be alone; most of the other men tended to stay in their own spaces. They often didn't want to talk to anyone else, whether face to face with their fellow detainees or video-calling their families (what was there to say in those calls, aside from how there was still no news on when they might get out, or even the prospect of getting out?). For 24 hours a day, or thereabouts, detainees would be in their rooms, which were each around 9 square metres (97 square feet). His room would soon have felt like a cage, Latifi said of Djokovic, who was accustomed to the vastness and the comforts of his family property in Marbella in southern Spain. Every day got to you and brought you down, Latifi observed; he felt himself becoming increasingly more anxious, leading to his panic attacks inside the Park Hotel.

If everyone in there felt a sense of isolation, Djokovic was even more alone, as he had been put on his own floor of the building, away from the others. The guards were careful that Djokovic stayed on his own floor, and the others were on theirs. Battisson suspected – she couldn't say for sure – that was because the Australian government didn't want Djokovic to have the chance to witness how horrific it was for the other men's physical and mental health. But any claims that it was done for Djokovic's safety were untrue, according to Battisson, who said the other detainees were 'distressed, peaceful and intelligent men' with no past record of violence (though if anything did occur, the guards could have called in their equivalent of the riot squad or chemically restrained the men).

There also would have been some concern, Battisson said, about 'communicable diseases', such as Covid-19, which had previously spread in the hotel, which had resulted in at least one man being hospitalized, and in the facility becoming known, aside from 'Park Prison', as the 'Outbreak Hotel'. Detainees who were unvaccinated against Covid – such as Djokovic – should have been worried about the building's air-conditioning system, which was moving the same air in and out of the rooms and up and down the corridors: you were getting everyone else's stale, potentially Covid-infected, air.

As a non-lawful citizen, Djokovic didn't have any rights in the Park Hotel; he certainly didn't have any privacy. He would have been searched before entering the facility – more likely a pat-down search than a cavity search, according to those familiar with the process – and officers would also have been through his belongings. Just as invasively, Djokovic would have been asked for his full medical history, with questions about vaccinations all the way through to whether he had ever had any sexually transmitted diseases. That document was not confidential, as it could have been requested by government ministers and agencies. The same was true of his detention dossier, which included a record of his behaviour and demeanour inside the system.

There was no lock on his door and the guards could have entered at any time of the day or night, shone a light in his face and turned over his room. Djokovic, a man who for many years had been living a life seemingly without limits, was experiencing something new and shocking and dehumanizing: he felt powerless. No wonder he was struggling to sleep. Having seen for herself how feeling powerless can degrade men's mental health, Battisson imagined that a loss of control, even for just a few days, would have been deeply disturbing for Djokovic: 'He's someone who likes to be very in control of his body and mind and diet. I wouldn't be surprised if being out of control would have had some impact on his mental health.' The month before Djokovic entered the Park Hotel, there had been a fire in the building, and Battisson said that the detainees were kept in the basement while it was put out: 'Can you imagine Djokovic being prevented from leaving a burning building?'

The TripAdvisor reviews of the Park Hotel wouldn't have been kind; the food was so grisly that it twice made Latifi vomit. While not completely inedible, it seemed to have very limited nutritional value and there wasn't much variety: the joke inside the Park Hotel was whether you fancied the chicken and rice today or the rice and chicken. Typically, according to someone who has sampled the food, that would have been served with several sad pieces of lettuce that had seen better days and a three-day-old apple. Eating the regular 'prison' food would have created 'disturbances' in Djokovic's body, according to Cetojevic. Djokovic's body, which hadn't processed any gluten in years, might have been inflamed and lethargic, and could have potentially rejected the food. In time, the Serbian government would arrange for gluten-free packages to be delivered to Djokovic.

In this cruel and sub-human place, you were prevented from interacting with passers-by outside. If not quite blacked-out, the glass in Djokovic's window was tinted. As Latifi said, Djokovic would have been able to look out of his window at the people of Melbourne on the streets below going about their lives: walking places, drinking cups of takeaway coffee, laughing. But, on the other side of those sealed windows, the public could barely see Djokovic, Latifi and the rest, hidden away in the city centre. All Latifi and others could do was wait and hope, holding on to some faint possibility of future freedom. If the air inside their rooms was stale, so was their daily routine and the narrative. 'The system is designed to break you mentally,' said Latifi.

Some of the refugees, Latifi included, have mixed feelings about Djokovic's cameo in their lives. On the face of it, Djokovic being detained in the Park Hotel was the best thing that had happened to them in years. Latifi was grateful that Djokovic's presence brought attention to the Park Hotel and, in his words, 'shone a light' on what was happening to them and what he regards as the inhuman cruelty of the Australian asylum system.

Until Djokovic, some had said this had been a prison hiding in plain sight close to the centre of Melbourne (there might not have been bars on the windows but in nearly every other aspect it was very prison-like). When news broke that Djokovic was inside, his supporters gathered outside the Park Hotel, as did television crews and journalists; one of Melbourne's secrets had become global news. A few months afterwards, the hotel was closed down; the attention that Djokovic had brought to the facility is thought to have been a factor in that decision (some close to Djokovic like to think that at least some good came out of what was generally a distressing episode for him). Djokovic's time in the Park Hotel also could have helped some of the detainees get legal resolution. Latifi, whose nine-year ordeal began in 2013 when he arrived by boat at Australia's Christmas Island, would eventually be released in spring 2022.

And yet, at the same time, there was also some bitterness and hostility among Djokovic's Park Hotel cohort that it had taken the athlete spending a few nights there for Australia, and the world, to care. There was also resentment that Djokovic, as a celebrated athlete, found a fast resolution, while others festered. The detainees were probably asking themselves: 'Do we have to pick up a tennis racquet for people to start listening to us?'

Many of the men heard that Djokovic was getting special treatment. Battisson couldn't comprehend how Djokovic was given permission to leave the Park Hotel for a meeting at his lawyers' office in the city. That's not something that the average detainee ever got to do. In another break from the norm, Djokovic was provided with exercise equipment, as well as a laptop. However, Djokovic apparently didn't get everything he would have wanted, such as a personal chef or access to a tennis court. Djokovic was still an unlawful non-citizen, but he was, without doubt, the most privileged non-citizen that this place had ever seen. Sub-human? Maybe the category just above that. For all that, Latifi wouldn't have wanted Djokovic to have spent even another day in the 'Park Prison'.

Many of the men who were detained in the facility with Djokovic, and who have since got out, have continued to suffer. 'I might look happy on the outside sometimes but, on the inside, I'm still broken,' said Latifi. 'We are depressed now and I hope we get something from the courts [from taking legal action] as otherwise we will be depressed forever. I'm an unhappy person. They destroy your life for years, and also your family's lives, and nobody cares about it.' Another asylum seeker, Don Khan, spoke of how his time in the Park Hotel has left him mentally disturbed: 'I would hear voices all the time. And when I turned to see who was talking to me, there was no one there. When I was asleep, I had dreams of fire, of people being killed. I saw all their blood and I was always nervous.'

Being inside the Park Hotel has also changed Djokovic. While Djokovic was already a tennis 'Godzilla' – according to his former coach Bogdan Obradovic – the experience made him even stronger.

They're too young now, but in time Djokovic would like to tell his children the story of when he ended up in a detention centre in Melbourne, and an experience that changed him. From the outside, the Park Hotel is beige and faceless, grey and instantly forgettable. But if you have been inside, it's not somewhere that's going to fade from your memory. Djokovic has said that the time he spent there – while infinitesimal compared to what the other men endured – will always stay with him. 'The mental torture and the physical effects of spending 24 hours a day in a 9 square metres space would change anyone,' said Latifi. 'I don't think Novak is going to forget those days. But I'm laughing sometimes at this. That was just a few days. Compared to spending years in the system, that's nothing.' Djokovic is sensitive to that, which is why he has been careful about what he has said about the conditions he experienced there; whatever he went through for a few days, he has recognized that others experienced much worse for much longer.

Djokovic had flown into Melbourne to play what Roger Federer had once dreamily called 'The Happy Slam', the Swiss riffing on Australia's image as a laidback, sun-bleached, beachy place; what Djokovic ended up doing was becoming a prisoner in one of the darkest corners of Australia. 'It seems that Novak's heart is in the right place. I would like to think that he had a taste of what it's like to be treated as sub-human and that he took that experience and realized, as I'm sure he already knew, that he leads an incredibly privileged life,' Battisson said. 'Novak worked hard for that, but the fact is he is very privileged, and other people, through no fault of their own, are in these horrific situations that are almost impossible to get out of for years. I think that that has given him an understanding of these issues, and how a supposedly first-world country like Australia treats these vulnerable people. Hopefully that has left Novak with a sense of outrage.'

This might sound absurd, even offensive, to some of the other detainees, but those few days inside the Park Hotel helped Djokovic to reach a higher level as an athlete. 'This experience has made him a better tennis player, with greater persistence and determination,' Cetojevic said.

Staying at the Park Hotel was life-enhancing. 'In the short term, there was disappointment for Novak but in the long term it was good. It's only when we go through hard times in our lives that we can grow up,' Cetojevic said. 'Often in our life we have really bad times and then very good times soon afterwards as we have learned from that experience and applied that new knowledge. One of the big questions we discussed together a long time ago was how to cope with life. Novak needed maturity. It's like with wine, it needs time to mature and settle, and a human is the same. You need to settle in life and to have experiences and learn from those experiences. Bad experiences are there for a reason, to help you grow up. If you can survive a hard time – if you're suffering and then you pass it – you will be stronger than before. That's the reason why Novak's a great player.'

Cetojevic has sometimes pondered why younger generations of players, while technically sound, have struggled to match Djokovic.

He has concluded it must have been because of a difference in maturity. Much of that has come from Djokovic's experiences on the court, but also from off it, such as inside the 'Park Prison'. 'All of Novak's experiences are helping Novak to be the best. Novak has a readiness to learn. You learn from bad days and you move on, that is his philosophy. He doesn't walk around thinking he knows everything. He's continuously learning, even in prison.'

14

'THE VILLAIN OF THE WORLD'

Instagram was Novak Djokovic's undoing (a sentence which makes this sound like a modern fable about the perils of social media, and maybe that's exactly what this is). If he hadn't posted a picture of himself in Spain before starting his journey to Melbourne via Dubai, announcing he was 'heading Down Under with an exemption permission, let's go 2022', he might never have had his visa cancelled or seen the inside of the Park Hotel. What if posting that image – which was taken at an airport and showed him smiling and leaning on a trolley heaped with his racquet bag and other luggage – was the greatest blooper of Djokovic's career?

Some in Australian legal circles would suggest that was possibly the moment when the Australian Border Force decided they were going to move on him. 'If Djokovic hadn't posted on Instagram, I think he would have been fine,' said Alison Battisson, the human rights lawyer who had clients inside the Park Hotel with Djokovic. 'Without that post, I believe he would have just sailed through [immigration].'

Djokovic's post had ended the speculation about how he would manage to compete at the 2022 Australian Open, because players either had to be vaccinated against Covid-19 or have a medical exemption, which were approved by independent medical panels. But it also started plenty else. Djokovic was flying into one of the world's most locked-down cities and many people in Melbourne, after all their sacrifices, were never going to love the idea of a visiting athlete getting an exemption to play tennis. But Djokovic couldn't possibly have imagined that a single post on a platform he loves would enrage some of the Australian public, put the Australian Border Force on alert, sabotage his tennis plans, start a diplomatic firefight and make him feel as though he was, in his own words, 'the villain of the world'.

To Battisson's mind, there were two possible scenarios. One was the over-zealous Border Force official who happened to be following Djokovic's Instagram account, who spotted that post and thought to themselves: 'Aha, I've got him.' 'It literally could have come down to one individual,' Battisson suggested. The second scenario – and this one is a touch darker – is that someone in government had seen Djokovic's post and had sent a directive to the Border Force to interview him when he arrived to see whether his story stood up. Djokovic was unfortunate that the Australian Open fell when it did, according to Craig Tiley, who noted how that was a particularly difficult time for Australia, with the country trying to figure out how to deal with new variants of the virus. 'In many ways, it was a timing thing with Novak,' said the CEO of Tennis Australia. 'If the Australian Open [hadn't been at the time when emotions were so high], it would have been a very different outcome for Novak.'

Others might suggest that Djokovic's Instagram post was ill-judged or even inflammatory. He would counter that that missed the point, which was that, in his understanding, he had permission to travel to Australia. Minutes after landing at Melbourne's Tullamarine Airport from Dubai, Djokovic and the three members of the team he had travelled with were asked to leave the plane before other passengers disembarked and were then, according to the Serb, 'escorted' to passport control; the Australia Border Force had been waiting for him.

It was just before midnight on 5 January 2022, by which point Djokovic had been travelling, if you also included layovers, for 25 hours. The passport control officer asked Djokovic whether he was vaccinated against Covid. Djokovic said he wasn't but that he had a medical exemption and he produced some printed paperwork which he believed supported that. In a brief conversation, it was clear that the officer wasn't satisfied with Djokovic's answers. The officer called over an official from the Australian Border Force, who would lead the interrogation of Djokovic, which took place in a small, anonymous room with a table, two chairs and a video camera that was recording the conversation (there was also a small handheld voice recorder on the table that was capturing what was said).

That interrogation went through the night, stretching over eight hours, though it was paused several times, allowing Djokovic the chance to rest on a sofa in a corridor. In the middle of the night, a bed was found for Djokovic in another room and he lay down, put his headphones in and tried to sleep. But he was woken soon afterwards. Increasingly exhausted, both mentally and physically, it was no wonder that he became, as he would later write in a signed affidavit, 'confused' and 'upset' about how the night was unfolding. It was just before 8am when

Djokovic's interviewer informed the athlete that his visa had been cancelled. Minutes later, a female officer said these alarming words to Djokovic: 'My name is Beck, I'm an officer of the Australian Border Force. It has come to my attention that you are an unlawful non-citizen in Australia. Therefore, I am detaining you.'

Ordinarily, someone in Djokovic's legal situation – an unlawful non-citizen – would have been handcuffed while being escorted through the airport and out the back to a waiting van with blacked-out windows. But no photographs of Djokovic in handcuffs have ever been published. There is, however, an image of Djokovic standing at passport control. Possibly, officials didn't put the cuffs on Djokovic to spare him the embarrassment, but they might have handcuffed him when he was in the van on the way to the Melbourne Immigration Transit Accommodation Centre, where he would have been processed. From there, he would have been taken to the Park Hotel, which could have been chosen because it was easier to isolate him there than in other detention centres. The suspicion has been that security would have been enhanced at the Park Hotel for Djokovic's stay with more guards on duty.

The hardest part of the whole episode for Djokovic, according to his friend Igor Cetojevic, wouldn't have been the loss of privacy or agency but 'when he realized that they were using him', and by 'they' he meant Australian politicians. 'Novak would have seen how they were using his name and his career and creating this idea that he was a bad guy when actually he's a person with exceptionally high ethics, a good human being,' Cetojevic said.

The growing consensus in Serbia was that powerful people were conspiring against Djokovic because they didn't like how a man from a small Eastern European nation was dominating tennis, and they had found another way of stopping him. There was something quasi-religious about the support for Djokovic during that time, with his own father Srdjan likening what was happening to the crucifixion. With protest rallies and press conferences in Belgrade fuelling the outrage, Srdjan also compared Djokovic to Spartacus, a leader of a slave revolt against the Romans. In Srdjan's view, 'they [were] stomping all over Novak to stomp all over Serbia and Serbian people', with Australia 'trying to bring Serbia to its knees'. Djokovic had sent a message to his family, which his brother Djordje read out in Belgrade: 'God sees everything. Moral and ethics as the greatest ideals are the shining stars towards spiritual ascension. My grace is spiritual and theirs is material wealth.'

The situation fast became a diplomatic flare-up, which inevitably meant that the language was undiplomatic, with Serbian President Aleksandar Vucic accusing Australia of 'maltreatment' and 'harassment' of Djokovic. Some of the strongest words came in a statement from the Serbian foreign ministry, claiming that Djokovic was being treated like 'a criminal, terrorist or illegal immigrant' and that the Serbian public 'has a strong impression that Djokovic is a victim of a political game against his will, and that he was lured to travel to Australia in order to be humiliated'.

Some would say that what happened was a fiasco caused by Australian government agencies and Tennis Australia, with Djokovic unlucky to have become caught up in that. But some people close to Djokovic were saying it had been a plot. 'Yes, of course it was planned. Everything was in place, all ready for him,' said Cetojevic. 'It's like a Venus Flytrap. It was just waiting for the fly to come in and it was going to be a huge media story. In Novak, they had a recognizable person, a star, and even better someone from a small country who was good to play with. We are pro-Novak in Serbia and that's normal. He's a special hero. We are a small nation and we're looking for some big guys to be the leaders and to give us something to be proud of. We see this injustice and as a nation we got upset that he was trapped like this. We got emotional.'

Many in Serbia suspected that Australian politicians, and the Western world, had it in for Djokovic because he's Serbian. Djokovic would be inside the Park Hotel for Serbian Orthodox Christmas, which only made the situation more emotive. 'It was a political thing with Novak – politicians showing how much power they had,' said Bogdan Obradovic, also speaking from his perspective as a former member of the Serbian parliament. 'You remember in the 1990s the relationship between America and the European Union and Serbia. They pushed us to the limit, with the bombing campaign and then destroying the economy until it was crushed. Then they pushed Novak too much in that moment – it really was too much. Novak didn't say anything negative to the Australian people or about the country. He just didn't understand why they were doing that, especially in that moment when he was looking for his tenth title. I don't see how one tennis player without the vaccine can change anything. I don't see why people were making such a problem that Novak hadn't had the vaccine. He never got a proper answer to the question: what was that all about?'

Here's a question that's easier to answer: how could you possibly have taken your eyes off this story? You couldn't, of course. It felt as though everyone was invested. The situation in Melbourne was already volatile, with a hint of menace. Tension was high between the police and Djokovic's supporters on the streets, with officers using pepper spray on fans who had been chanting 'Nole' and who had surrounded his car as it left his lawyers' office.

Adding to the air of anxiety in the city and around Djokovic, Craig Tiley needed security for himself and his family after receiving death threats. Tiley was being criticized from all sides – from those who said he was somehow responsible for Djokovic entering Australia in the first place, and then from others who said he had somehow helped to get Djokovic removed from the country. 'Anytime you're in an environment where there's uncertainty, it's unnerving. In my case, you're protecting the people you're close to. For me, it was about taking care of family and friends, as well as taking care of our team, our staff,' Tiley recalled. 'There was a lot of pressure at the time. There was anxiety about what was going on, but that was more about protecting family, friends and staff.' Tiley was in regular contact with Djokovic at the time; it was hugely important to him – both personally and as the leader of Tennis Australia – that the athlete was 'alright'.

Djokovic has never been vanilla. Tennis fans expressing strong opinions on him wasn't new. That had been happening for years and he was accustomed to it. But now, for the first time, people outside tennis – seemingly the whole world – had views on him too. Djokovic was a 'non-citizen' stuck in a small room, and yet at the same time he was everywhere: on the news, getting monstered online, and the subject of endless offline conversations. For a few days, it felt as though the world was talking about nothing else. 'The attention of the world was on Novak. It was global news,' Tiley said. 'I don't think he had previously had that attention, or pressure, on him. It was intense. Other athletes have had personal tragedies, which have been traumatic, but I don't think any other tennis player or athlete has been through something as extreme and as public as what we saw with Novak.'

Djokovic would have had some dark moments during that episode in Australia. But he was able to get through that time, Obradovic suggested, because he's an extraordinarily positive person. 'You can see on Novak's face that he's a happy person. Novak's extremely positive. You start to feel that energy when you spend time with [him] and then you like to be in his company, whether it's talking or watching a movie together. Novak is just having fun in life. It's so simple – you don't have to analyse that too much. He's positive and that's it. Novak's positive first thing in the morning and he's positive at midnight. He's positive 24 hours a day and I can tell you that because many times I spent the whole day with him. He's pushing that positivity all the time and in every way. Novak loves life. He likes to have fun. He wants to talk, he wants to listen, he wants to do something every single piece of the day and he wants to have a plan,' Obradovic said.

'When something negative happens to him, like in Australia, he packs that negativity away somewhere – in his mind or in his soul – and he keeps it there and then he carries on. That would have allowed him to get through that time.'

At such a dangerous time, Djokovic was careful about the language he used in public; he didn't want to aggravate matters. 'It wasn't easy but Novak acted like a gentleman,' said his friend Sam Osmanagic, the 'Bosnian Indiana Jones'. 'In every public statement – even while in detention, in the court and then leaving Australia – Novak always showed the utmost respect for Australia, the Australian people, the tournament organizers and his fans.'

While Djokovic doesn't read newspapers, he was on social media, and couldn't avoid snippets and links to articles. His reputation was getting scorched. Djokovic was uncomfortable reading what others were saying about him, as he sensed that people, including his fellow tennis players, were reaching the wrong conclusions about him. Djokovic had been prepared not to travel to Australia, and then he got Covid and applied for a medical exemption, which he received. He was aware that people were saying it seemed very convenient that he got Covid in the middle of December, as that allowed him to gain a medical exemption. But, as Djokovic later reflected in an interview with the BBC, there was nothing lucky or convenient about getting Covid (the first time he had it, in June 2020, he had more symptoms). One of the most damning things said about Djokovic was that he was acting as though he was above the rules, when most people in Australia had stuck to some of the world's strictest regulations. But he didn't feel as though he used his elevated status to gain access to Australia. Djokovic's application for a medical exemption, which had been signed off by two separate independent medical panels, had been anonymous.

For some, he was 'No-vax Djokovic'. A reprehensible anti-vaxxer and a menace to society and public health. Never mind that Djokovic had never once said he was part of any anti-vaccination movement, even though he had said in a Facebook live chat in April 2020 that he 'wouldn't want to be forced by someone to take a vaccine' to be able to travel around the tennis map to compete. Believing in freedom of choice and an individual's right to decide what to put in their body, which he saw as a fundamental human right, Djokovic would never tell others whether to have the vaccine or not.

Also, Djokovic wasn't ideologically opposed to vaccines. He had had vaccines as a child, and he wasn't saying that the Covid vaccine was ineffective; he just felt as though he didn't have enough information about how it might affect his athlete's body. 'Very mindful' of what he put into his body, which he felt had been central to his longevity as a top sportsperson, Djokovic was used to carefully reviewing and evaluating any supplements or sports drinks he was taking. There was a precision and an attention to detail which he felt had allowed him to remain in the tennis elite for so long; he didn't want to take the risk that the vaccine could have had a negative impact on his body. This didn't emerge until January 2022, but early in the pandemic, in 2020, Djokovic had become the controlling stakeholder in a Copenhagen-based biotech firm, QuantBioRes, that had been working to develop a treatment, not a vaccine, for Covid.

For others, Djokovic was a freedom fighter and a defender of human rights, pushing back against the medical mainstream and the media orthodoxy. Some cared deeply; for others, it felt as though this was just entertainment, an amusing celebrity takedown. Being at the centre of that, having every aspect of your life picked over, would have been overwhelming. Djokovic was going to get deported; he was also getting his reputation trashed. A photograph went around the world showing Djokovic maskless at a tennis event with children in December when he would have had Covid – but while he had done a test that morning, that was before he got his positive result back. That wasn't an excuse that he could have used for why he went ahead with a pre-arranged interview and photoshoot with *L'Equipe*, a French sports newspaper, as by then he knew that he had the virus. Djokovic would later acknowledge that meeting the journalist had been an error of judgement. But, in the moment, he hadn't wanted to let the writer down.

Even before he had been detained in Melbourne, Djokovic hadn't had a quiet pandemic: he had already taken some public relations hits. At a time when many around the world wouldn't leave home without a mask and a bottle of hand sanitizer, the images from Djokovic's Adria Tour exhibition series in June 2020 – which showed the players hugging and dancing topless in a Belgrade cabaret club – were always going to be provocative. In the public relations game, perception counts for a lot and, for some, it looked like a superspreading event. Djokovic's supporters would suggest that any criticism of the tour – which even came from Wimbledon's 'disappointed' chief executive – was unfair as he and the other players had followed the protocols that were in place in the Balkans. The players hadn't been required to wear masks at that time. Djokovic thought he had been the victim of a 'witch hunt'. 'Novak was trying to do something positive and everyone was accusing him, saying: "Why did you organize that tour?" That was a tough period for Novak,' said Obradovic. 'Novak was having so many problems and it felt as though everyone was against him.'

When several of the players, including Djokovic, caught Covid, the tour was abandoned. But, for the Serb, that was hardly the end of it as those images would resurface a year and a half later when he was being characterized as a subversive, or even a threat to society. In this global pile-on, another story was brought out for a few more airings – how Djokovic's wife Jelena had shared a video by Dr Thomas Cowan on her social media account which suggested a link between 5G technology and Covid. The video was given a 'false information' label, which was awkward, though it should be noted that she later said in a statement that she hadn't endorsed the video and hadn't claimed that the claims were 'true or not'.

Everything that had happened over the previous two years was building to what you might describe as Djokovic's pandemic series finale in Melbourne. 'There was this big buzz around Novak,' said Cetojevic. 'Maybe it's not the best comparison but look at Jesus. He was also exposed and punished by officials at the time. He was also against the mainstream of politics and ideas. And time would also tell that he was on the right path.' Cetojevic, who knows the inside of Djokovic's mind about as well as anyone, said the athlete needed 'acceptance' to get through that time. 'Novak had to accept the world for how it was, and not how he wanted it to be. It was also important, and Novak understood this, to accept himself and his choices. In life, you must accept yourself and keep your light, and not try to imitate others. When you try to imitate other people that doesn't work and that's when we lose our path.'

When the buzz was at its peak, Cetojevic messaged Djokovic to tell him he was 'a light for human rights'. 'I like people who have their own unique personalities and Novak is a unique creature. The pandemic was a challenge for the whole of civilization. Some people are lights. They don't give in to media pressure. Novak is someone who doesn't give in to media pressure, who's not a blind follower. He's a knowledgeable guy and an aware guy. He knows there's a big scam there [Covid vaccines, in his opinion] and he doesn't like to be trapped. Generally, Serbians don't like to be put under pressure from anybody. We fight. We're very peaceful people generally but don't push us into a position to fight,' Cetojevic said.

'Novak is a guy who has invested all his life – certainly since I've known him – in health and nourishment. And he fully believed that the vaccination wouldn't help him. Novak believed in freedom of choice, and that people could do whatever they wanted to do. Some people have information and some people don't. Some people are influenced by the media, some are not. He decided to be unvaccinated. Novak didn't want to be part of an experiment. Some people are still trapped by the media but we can now see the medical consequences of the vaccine. Novak chose with good intentions and he chose properly.'

Others in Djokovic's situation – knowing that all the other leading players were vaccinated – would have wavered and would have rolled up his sleeve to have the jab. Some would call Djokovic stubborn or obstinate, saying that he denied himself the chance to add to his greatness – but others, including those close to him, say it was a principled decision. Some weeks after returning to Europe from Australia, Djokovic reflected on how he had been able to 'hold my ground' under such immense pressure and scrutiny and he wondered whether it could be traced to his background. From a young age, when he often travelled to tournaments on his own, Djokovic had become more self-reliant and independent thinking that most players of his age. As a child, it must have often felt to Djokovic as though he was out there on his own in the world, fending for himself, and now, as an adult, he was having to do the same again.

A number of people in Djokovic's life were sceptical of how the medical mainstream was responding to Covid-19, with his friend Osmanagic describing the vaccine as an 'experimental genetical pharmaceutical product'. Osmanagic had spoken to Djokovic about how the high levels of negative ions in the tunnels beneath the Bosnian pyramids would have boosted his and any other visitor's immunity against Covid and other viruses. Osmanagic wanted to give Djokovic some scientific 'proof', so showed him the instruments that were used to measure the tunnel's energy properties. 'I had a conversation with Novak about the measurable properties of the tunnels. I even got our instruments to show him the concentration of negative ions so he was very aware of that. Covid was a virus and negative ions enable our bodies to fight viruses,' said Osmanagic. 'As far as the vaccine is concerned, or the experimental genetical pharmaceutical product, we really don't know the content of this product. But I do know the content of what's happening in the tunnels.'

Time passed slowly inside the Park Hotel. But, unlike the other 'guests', Djokovic had a hearing within days. In the eyes of the law, Djokovic was comparable to a cargo ship with perishable goods needing to dock in the port, which was why his case was heard much faster than others. While a judge overruled the cancellation of Djokovic's visa, on the grounds that the tennis player hadn't been treated fairly by the Australian Border Force officials, and Djokovic was released from the Park Hotel and allowed to train at Melbourne Park, nothing was normal. In some cities and on some courts, Djokovic feels more comfortable than in other spots on the tennis map – one of those is Melbourne's Rod Laver Arena. Ordinarily, Djokovic arrived in the city each January feeling energized and motivated, wanting to start his season in the best possible way, and drawing on his memories of past successes.

'This is my terrain, this my court, this is where I rule and I feel my best,' he had said the year before of playing in the Rod Laver Arena, but did he still feel the same, now there were news helicopters in the sky when he practised?

Even more unsettling for Djokovic was his sense that some of the other players were upset with him, based on a perception that he had used a loophole to sneak into Australia. And for hijacking the news agenda before the opening Grand Slam of the year, at a time of the season when everyone should have been talking about the possible tennis storylines at Melbourne Park. But no one was discussing the actual tennis – and who might go deep into the Australian Open and win the title – only about whether Djokovic should or would be deported. He was hurt by the way some of the players were looking at him and also by their energy around him, which was making him uncomfortable. These were people he saw more than his family and he cared what they thought about him.

Far from being aloof, Djokovic had previously tried to use his star-power to help his colleagues in the locker-room, co-founding the Professional Tennis Players Association, which was agitating for lower-ranked players to receive a greater portion of the prize money. But, in that moment, it felt as though that had been forgotten. Lost in all the arguments about visas and vaccinations. Djokovic felt as though his reputation was being lost in a swirl of 'continuing misinformation' (his words). One thing he wanted to address was the story about his travel declaration form, which stated – incorrectly – that he hadn't travelled anywhere else in the 14 days before he landed in Melbourne. Djokovic had spent some time in Serbia in that period before flying from Spain to Australia, via Dubai. But he hadn't been trying to deceive; he said it had been a 'human error' by a member of his team who had filled in the form for him and ticked the wrong box. Surprisingly, one of the few players who was openly supportive of Djokovic was Nick Kyrgios, as the two hadn't been very friendly with each other until that point (the Australian's intervention started the process of turning their animosity into a full-on bromance).

One of the most bizarre cameos was from Nigel Farage, a contentious British politician who was one of the forces behind Great Britain's lamentable exit from the European Union. When Farage popped up in Belgrade, Andy Murray wasn't going to let that pass. Murray posted a video of Farage in the Djokovic family's trophy room and then commented on social media: 'Please record the awkward moment when you tell them you've spent most of your career campaigning to have people from Eastern Europe deported.' In 2023, when Farage was wrongly 'de-banked' by Coutts private bank, who closed his account – although Farage was later reinstated and in receipt of an apology – an internal document mentioned his links with the Djokovic family, the implication being that an association with Djokovic wasn't good for his reputation.

Djokovic had been miscast as the front man for the anti-vaxxers. That's not a position he ever sought. When, in the aftermath of the court ruling that overturned the original decision, Djokovic had his visa cancelled again, it was after an intervention by Alex Hawke, the Australian immigration minister, on 'health and good order grounds'. In a document submitted to the court, Hawke argued Djokovic was 'perceived by some as a talisman of a community of anti-vaccine sentiment', and as such could incite 'civil unrest' and encourage Australians not to have the vaccine. That saddened Djokovic, who appealed unsuccessfully against the decision. 'I completely disagree with that perception. I'm really sad and disappointed that I was deported on that basis,' he would later say in an interview with the BBC. 'I do inspire people but I don't inspire them to go out on to the streets and protest and be part of the anti-vax.'

Throughout the 'whole Australia saga', as Djokovic called it, no one ever asked him for his opinion on vaccination so he never had the opportunity to articulate his thoughts. 'It's unfortunate that there's been a misconception and a wrong conclusion around the world based on something I completely disagree with.'

*

Any regrets? Yes, Djokovic has a few of those. But those regrets have mostly been about the smaller aspects of his career, such as when he has broken racquets in a hot rage and then moments later, when his head has been a little cooler, he has looked at the twisted, broken remains and felt remorse. Djokovic accepted he didn't get everything right during the pandemic; he shouldn't have gone ahead with the *L'Equipe* interview when he had Covid. What Djokovic doesn't regret, according to Obradovic, is being unvaccinated against Covid, even though that decision took away opportunities to win more Grand Slams and came with a reputational cost. Djokovic has said as much in public. But, whether in private or public, the message is the same: no regrets.

As much as Djokovic has dedicated his life to tennis, and to winning as many Grand Slams as possible, he was clear in his head that the possibility of winning any one title wasn't as important to him as continuing to take care of his body. Djokovic understood the consequences: he knew that not having the vaccine would reduce the number of opportunities he had to win majors, and he could live with that. But he still felt a sadness that he couldn't play in Melbourne. Watching the 2022 Australian Open final was a trying experience for Djokovic as he so desperately wanted to be on court, but that didn't mean he regretted being unvaccinated and everything that came with that. The only lightness that day was his son Stefan who, whenever Rafael Nadal won a point on his way to beating Daniil Medvedev, was bouncing around and pumping his fist, much like the Majorcan.

The 2022 Australian Open wasn't the only Grand Slam that Djokovic couldn't play because of his stance on the vaccine. Later that season, with the United States government requiring non-citizens to be fully vaccinated against Covid if they wished to enter the country, he also couldn't compete at the US Open.

Someone once said that any year you win a Wimbledon title is a good year – and Djokovic did just that, beating Nick Kyrgios in the final, having been able to enter the United Kingdom without the vaccine – but he had missed two of the season's four majors. Two more chances to have had added to his collection of Grand Slam titles. But let others concern themselves with what might have been; that wasn't eating up Djokovic. 'Novak will never regret the decision he made about the vaccine. For sure, he's not thinking how he could have won more Grand Slams if only he had had the vaccine,' said Obradovic. 'Novak takes his time when making a decision. He thinks and he talks and then he makes his mind up. He's not making decisions in the moment; he's very tactical and strategic. That's going to help you to avoid big mistakes. Novak would have understood what happened and why. In his head, he had maybe been predicting that they would do some bad things to him. But he didn't care. He was always going to be strong and stick to his beliefs.'

For all the surface civility and Djokovic's inherently positive nature, was there not some inner anger at what had happened in Melbourne? If Djokovic hadn't been deported before the 2022 Australian Open and had been released from the detention centre to compete at Melbourne Park, he would have been an angry and 'dangerous motherfucker', according to Kyrgios. While that didn't happen in 2022, was Djokovic energized by anger a year later when – with overseas travellers no longer needing to be vaccinated to enter Australia – he landed in Melbourne attempting to win the title for a tenth occasion and to go level with Rafael Nadal on a record 22 Grand Slams? The Novak Djokovic Revenge Tour, some were calling it, and if that sounded a little strong, there's no doubt he would be extremely motivated in 2023. Some close to Djokovic questioned whether he should be going back to Australia, to the country that had caused him so much discomfort and hardship. But there was no chance he was going to skip the 2023 Australian Open; he had something to prove.

'They had poked the bear,' said Todd Martin. 'Novak was steadfast. Regardless of what anybody believes about vaccines, mandates and policies during pandemics, Novak was resolute. The greatest characters in our world's history have learned how to be inspired by failure. I'm not going to label Novak's deportation from Australia as his failure. I think it was a collective failure of systems and organizations and humans. But the world's greatest characters, they resist failure, but when it occurs, they use it, one way or the other. They take what doesn't go right and use it. They make things better, one way or another. This became additional motivation for him.'

Tiley spoke of Djokovic's 'unbelievable resilience', both in 2022 and then at the 2023 Australian Open. 'For Novak to respond in the way he did, coming through that time and then in 2023 coming back to the event which had caused all that emotion, was truly remarkable,' he said. 'Novak was able to get through that time with the realization that the tough period he was in would pass.'

Djokovic wasn't going anywhere. 'The small politicians in Australia had prodded Novak and he wanted to show that he was the best,' Cetojevic said. 'Those politicians, they're nowhere now. But Novak, he's still on top.'

15

OBSESSION

'I'm telling you that Novak has a very deep secret inside his mind.' So deep, said Bogdan Obradovic – speaking from the perspective of someone who mentored a young Novak Djokovic and later captained him to Serbia's Davis Cup success – that the player himself possibly doesn't even know what it is. If you're looking to understand Djokovic's greatness, and how he has won so many Grand Slams, Obradovic doesn't imagine you will find any answers by looking at something as basic and as obvious as forehands and backhands and the mechanics of how his strings hit the ball. You must consider Djokovic on a supernatural or paranormal level. Obradovic has never told Djokovic this but he believes that this champion, someone he has known since he was a ten-year-old boy, has a source of mental energy that comes directly from a higher being: 'I think Novak goes somewhere over the line which belongs to the god, to the creator.'

If Obradovic isn't quite calling Djokovic a tennis deity, he's saying that the Serb is the only one who has this source of energy – this energy that is both godly and exclusive – which apparently means he can heal himself and go again and again. The first time they met, when Djokovic was just a child, Obradovic felt as though the young boy brought such strong 'cosmic energy' to the tennis court that he had thought he might have been in the presence of 'an alien from outer space'. But, over the years, Obradovic started to sense something else about Djokovic. How Djokovic suffered so much and was often empty and alone – as that's elite tennis for you – and yet, while others would have 'crashed' in those circumstances, he was able to keep on pushing.

'I'm not someone who is going to say something like this just because Novak's the best of all time. That would be stupid for me. I'm just telling you what I saw. In some moments, you can see that he's healing himself. He's a magic guy, believe me,' Obradovic said. 'Other great athletes – and I'm talking about people like Michael Jordan and Michael Phelps – they had so much help from the external world. That's how they recharged their batteries. Lots of tennis players recharge their batteries through the external world. But Novak is the only one, I believe, who charges his battery from his internal world. And that's why he is so special. He has some antenna or some connection with the supreme guy. He's picking up some energy. I don't know what he's doing. Maybe even he doesn't know what he's doing but he's capable of doing it.'

Some will be sceptical, but Obradovic can't see how there can be another explanation for Djokovic's extraordinary powers. 'It has to be like that. If he was a normal guy, he would have crashed after all these moments in his career. The reason that Novak has won so many Grand Slams, it's not about forehands and backhands, it's about this, this energy resource he's using and this ability to recharge his batteries inside him.

There's no cable. It's inside him. There's something really big and huge in his mind. Maybe he will tell us one day or maybe he will need to discover what it is first and someone will do some tests on him and after that we will see. We get energy from the sun and from water and food. We also get energy from love, from loving someone and from them loving you back. But what happens when something's crushing you and you're not getting energy from the normal things like the sun, the moon, and your family. That's when you go much deeper and use another source of energy, and that's what Novak has been doing.'

If only Nikola Tesla, the celebrated Serbian scientist and inventor, was still alive today, Obradovic has mused, as maybe he would be able to explain Djokovic's energy. Wherever the source of this energy, Obradovic said it has kept Djokovic looking and feeling youthful. 'This is why he looks so much younger and why he hasn't had that many injures and the problems that athletes of that age usually have with their bodies.'

*

There's a question that keeps pinballing around Djokovic's head. As he has told his close friend Janko Tipsarevic, he is constantly asking himself this question. Before making any decision – and that could be something monumental or a small and seemingly inconsequential choice – he thinks: 'How will this help my tennis?' That's the prism through which he sees his life. Everything he does is for the greater goal of becoming a better tennis player. It's not enough to make good decisions on the practice court and when he's playing matches; he also needs to ensure that every aspect of his life is geared towards helping him win more Slams. If Djokovic believes that doing something would harm his tennis, or possibly slow him down in any way, he won't do it.

As Djokovic once told Tipsarevic: 'When you set yourself a goal, and you're determined to do it, from the beginning it has to be that every decision you make ultimately has to help you reach that goal.'

Tipsarevic's favourite athlete is Kobe Bryant, the late basketball player and Djokovic's former mentor. Tipsarevic sees a lot of Bryant in Djokovic, who has a ferociously competitive attitude that propels and guides him through his daily decision-making. Over the last 20 years or so, Tipsarevic has observed from up close how Djokovic has 'the sheer willpower to achieve whatever he wants to do'. 'If Novak decides to do something, he has this ability to essentially put his life on hold for the greater goal. That means that nothing else is important. We make hundreds, if not thousands, of decisions every day. Every single small decision that Novak makes on a daily basis, he asks himself whether doing this is ultimately going to help him achieve his goal or not. People might see that as being very difficult, which it is, but he is like this. He lives his life in that way.'

As one of Djokovic's former coaches, Dusan Vemic has also had a front-row view of Djokovic's dedication. 'There are no gaps – he's so meticulous with his lifestyle and his daily routines. It's not a case of Novak saying: "Today I feel like it and I'll do it, and tomorrow when I don't feel like it, I won't do it." He lives it every day. The work that he puts in, on and off the court, it really reflects who he is as a champion. Novak keeps it simple and to the point. He's not wasting time on things that don't matter to him. In his life, he values his family first, his friends and then his sport. He lives every single day to fuel his engine to the best of his abilities, such as with the purest food, grown from the most natural sources. All of us know that's the right path, but Novak is the only one who has been living it. And there are always new goals, always more Grand Slams he wants to win.'

As Tipsarevic said of Djokovic: 'It's never enough.' Others might have been satisfied a long time ago. But Djokovic has what Tipsarevic calls 'a continuity of obsession'. Djokovic's greatness is 'incessant', his former coach Todd Martin observed, and that comes from how he approaches his tennis. 'Many of us have things in our lives that are incessant but they're mostly tedious. When I see Novak, I tell him how much I marvel at his level of play, and his success and maturity,' Martin said.

Djokovic has been asking himself, 'How will this help my tennis?' since he was a teenager. People around Djokovic still talk about the time when he was 15 years old and had just completed a pre-season training block with a number of players – some of them already competing on the ATP Tour – in Germany and Austria. A party was planned to mark the end of the bootcamp and Djokovic approached his then coach Dirk Hordorff with an urgent question: 'I need to ask you something. Is it good for my tennis if I go and have a beer or a glass of wine?' Hordorff replied: 'Listen, you can do it if you feel like it. You've worked very hard for weeks and you need to relax. There's no problem.' Djokovic's response was astonishing for a teenager who was new to that elite world: 'I don't mean any disrespect, but I didn't ask for your permission. I asked if this was good for my tennis.'

Years later, Djokovic is still scoping out every decision. Even in the thin top slice of tennis society, that approach is rare. In fact, Djokovic might be the only athlete that committed to his game. Knowing that goes some way to understanding how he has stayed at the top of the sport for so long, and how he has won so many majors. As Obradovic noted, NBA basketball players might want to drink and smoke 'big cigars' at the end of the season, but you won't see Djokovic doing something like that. 'Novak stretches his career because he is very smart and knows what to do for his body. He's doing everything that's necessary for his tennis and to be the best possible player he can be.'

Far too many tennis players make the mistake of believing that if they're performing well on the court, they will be able to think clearly, they will feel good about themselves and they will have a good, happy life (the unfortunate result: a fair few unhappy and under-performing athletes). But, according to psychologist Daria Abramowicz, who has worked with Iga Swiatek, it's the other way around – almost every aspect of your life away from tennis will impact on how you play. If you have a good, happy life, you're more likely to be a great tennis player. Djokovic understands that. Get good at living and you will become a better tennis player; that's the Djokovic model. As Abramowicz noted, it appears as though everything in Djokovic's life is arranged so that he can be the best possible player he can be. It's an unfortunate truth that no tennis player will ever achieve 100 per cent of their potential. But, according to Abramowicz, Djokovic is 'as close as possible to 100 per cent and that's one of his biggest qualities'.

One of his superpowers is optimizing his life – including through his routines and with the people he has around him – to ensure he's producing the best possible tennis he can. 'Somehow people still seem to think that recovery is just about the physicality, but it's not. There are four levels of recovery – there's cognitive, emotional, social and physical. My take is that Djokovic is able to understand, differentiate and take care of these four levels,' Abramowicz said. 'He's creating a platform that enables him to perform at his absolute best.'

*

Obsession brings creative tension. If there has often been an intense – and highly stressful – atmosphere on the practice court, that has been because that's how Djokovic has wanted it. He's not an entitled tennis diva. He's not being difficult and demanding for the sake of it. But Djokovic asks a lot of his team when preparing for competition as he feels it has to be that way if he is to upgrade his game; that's more productive for him than a working environment that's smooth and benign. Working with Djokovic, his former coach Goran Ivanisevic once said, he can make you 'nervous 24 hours a day, nothing is ever alright'.

'Novak always demands absolute focus from anyone he works with,' said Gebhard Gritsch, his trainer. 'Maybe you have seen *The Last Dance* with Michael Jordan? It's like that with Novak. If you're at that level, you need to optimize every single training session and to do that you must optimize the situation. You need to have some kind of intensity, some kind of pressure, that is related to the performance on the court. You need to push everyone around you, even the hitting partner, to give their best and to analyse the situation to improve. If things aren't happening, you need to find solutions.' There have been times when Djokovic has left the practice court feeling 'pissed off' and 'bursting with anger'. Times when, as Djokovic told his friend Chervin Jafarieh, he has been 'discontented' with himself, with his coaching team and with 'the whole world'. He's been angry because every day he feels the desire – or even more pressing than that, the psychological need – to improve. 'Novak approaches every day wanting to get better and this is necessary. He knows that he must make these changes and to get better,' Gritsch said. 'The focus he has, that's just incredible. I think that's the big difference between him and other athletes.'

Djokovic is forever reinventing himself: he must be on about the 20th upgrade by now. What worked for him last year isn't going to cut it this season because he knows his rivals are also continuing to develop their games. They're moving on so Djokovic must find a way of developing his tennis that puts him beyond them. As his friend Dusan Lajovic observed, Djokovic isn't going to make changes that will make him 20 per cent better; he's looking to refine his tennis. Small changes – so small that many might not even notice them – that could bring about big moments. 'Novak is constantly trying to become a better player. It's constant effort from him,' said Lajovic. 'If there's a way of improving his game by 1 per cent, he's going to find that. He's constantly searching for things that are going to diversify his game, and will improve his overall characteristics as a player, and that's amazing to see, especially at his age.'

The first time Ivanisevic met Djokovic – when the Serb was just 13 years old – he got a sense of what an extraordinary talent he was. It was the end of 2000 and Ivanisevic had had a rough year on the ATP Tour, losing in the first round of more tournaments than he would possibly care to remember. When Ivanisevic came to Niki Pilic's academy to train, Pilic was brutal in his assessment of the Croat's conditioning: 'Goran, you're fat. You need to lose some kilos.' One Sunday, after they had practised for a couple of hours, Pilic said to Ivanisevic: 'Go play with that kid with the black hair over there for a few minutes.' In the end, Ivanisevic hit with Djokovic for 23 minutes. 'It was like Novak was hypnotized on the court,' Pilic recalled. 'He didn't hit one ball in the net in those 23 minutes.'

In the five years that Djokovic and Ivanisevic worked together – an historic, often dramatic, player-coach partnership that ended in March 2024 – the Serb brought new levels of focus and commitment to the practice court, far beyond what he had shown as a boy. Ivanisevic often believed that Djokovic's game was working beautifully only for his player to strongly disagree, and to say he wanted to fix his serve, backhand or another aspect of his game that he didn't think was quite right. Ivanisevic considers Djokovic a tennis genius. He also recognizes that Djokovic wasn't an easy guy to work with. Those two observations are, of course, connected: Djokovic's greatness has come from a willingness to never be happy on the practice court, to always push for more. And Djokovic didn't want Ivanisevic to offer up gentle, honeyed, encouraging words; he wanted to be challenged, to hear critical analysis of his game that was going to compel him to get better.

For an insight into the creative tension that existed between Djokovic and Ivanisevic in practice and away from the cameras, consider how Djokovic spoke to – or yelled at – his coach during matches. Cranky is a word Ivanisevic has used to describe Djokovic when he was competing. Sweary is another adjective that might capture how Djokovic communicated with his then coach in those heated moments. On occasion, because he doesn't appreciate being shouted at for no reason, Ivanisevic bit – and swore – back. One difficulty for the pair was that umpires knew all the Serbian and Croatian swearwords – a consequence of Balkan players' success in recent years – so they had to use slang and even make words up. But, in the moment, when Djokovic was angry, he often didn't stop to consider whether officials and others might have understood his obscenities: his feelings were going to spill out of him, without the asterisks. It wasn't all directed at Ivanisevic – some of the colourful words from Djokovic were for others in the box, including assistant coach, hitting partner and agent Carlos Gomez-Herrera, physiotherapist Miljan Amanovic and trainer Marco Panichi.

Watching a Djokovic match from his player's box was never going to be a relaxing experience. But Ivanisevic could be forgiving towards Djokovic as the Croat understood, perhaps more than almost anyone else in the sport, what he called 'the mayhem' of professional tennis. He appreciated how playing tennis can provoke strong emotions – once he broke all his racquets at a tournament in Brighton in England and so was unable to continue, and when he won Wimbledon in 2001 as a wild card, he had three warring voices in his head: Good Goran, Bad Goran and Emergency Goran. No doubt it also helped that in a noisy stadium, Ivanisevic could only hear about half of what Djokovic was screaming at him. Djokovic and Ivanisevic were friends as well as work colleagues; their relationship was about more than tennis, which must have allowed Djokovic to be even more open in how he spoke to his employee (after the split, Ivanisevic disclosed in an interview with Sport Klub how there had been a time when he would have been ready to die for Djokovic if that had ever been necessary). Ultimately, Djokovic was grateful that his team could tolerate how his tongue can sometimes be as vicious as his groundstrokes.

Hard work, and the burn in the lungs and the muscles, can be psychologically comforting for Djokovic – all those hours on the practice court make him feel as though he has done everything in his powers to prepare. But there's been a subtle shift in Djokovic's mindset. In the past, he would berate himself if he felt as though he hadn't completed his routine in full, saying: 'You're not good enough now, you're going to lose now.' But Djokovic has come to appreciate there are moments when he can break his routine, though that can be a challenge for his brain. Less is sometimes more, such as during the 2023 Australian Open when he had a 3cm (1in) tear in his hamstring and he thought he was better served by not training on the days between matches, and also at Roland Garros that same season where he also didn't practise on some of his 'off' days. But don't interpret this as softness on Djokovic's part – it's wisdom and greater awareness of what's best for him. If he had thought that going even harder on the practice court would have increased his chances of winning, that's what he would have done. It goes back to that question that Djokovic keeps asking himself: 'How will this help my tennis?'

Speak to anyone who has ever worked with Djokovic and they will tell you he's a perfectionist. 'The level of detail when Novak gets ready for matches, the level of detail to get his body prepared, to make sure his game is there, to make sure the strokes are where they need to be – it's as high a level of perfectionism as I've ever seen in any sport,' said Craig O'Shannessy, his former strategy coach. 'Being backstage with Novak, I saw he wanted things to be as perfect as they could possibly be and to control what was around him as much as he possibly could. He's going to push himself further and harder to improve and to make sure that he's staying ahead of his rivals. He's not going to be taking any shortcuts anywhere with anything. He's going to be taking everything to the max to try to improve and to find the perfect representation of himself on the tennis court.'

Others in tennis can't help but notice how Djokovic is more meticulous than anyone else on the tour. 'If you've got Novak on the other side of the court, you know there's a guy who is absolutely focused on what he eats, who is absolutely focused on how he prepares and trains, and who doesn't leave one stone unturned,' said Craig Tiley. 'As Novak's opponent, you're going to be thinking: "Oh boy, this isn't going to be easy – he's doing everything I wish I could have done." Over the years, I've seen Novak become even more focused on taking care of the things he needs to take care of to become as great as he is. That's what is so difficult for Novak's competition – they see and they hear about the lengths that Novak goes to with his preparations.' Marketa Vondrousova, the 2023 women's Wimbledon champion, suggested Djokovic's dedication is unmatched in tennis: 'For me, it's incredible the motivation he has. I mean, it's amazing. I feel as though Novak is the one – out of all of us in tennis, men and women – who is the most professional. If you see him practising, he's doing everything at 100 per cent.'

O'Shannessy recalled one morning at the Monte Carlo Country Club in December 2017, where Djokovic was doing his pre-season training. 'Novak stretched and warmed up for an hour and a half. I had never seen somebody prepare to practise how he did, going through so many exercises. I thought that nobody in their right mind is going to work that hard and then still practise. And then he practised for two hours. What impresses me so much is his off-court dedication to making his body right and getting it ready for competition.'

There are few other athletes who have Djokovic's relentless approach; he's sometimes had to look outside tennis for kinship, information and insights. Djokovic's friendships with NFL star quarterback Tom Brady and footballer Zlatan Ibrahimovic have helped him to understand what else he could have been doing to better himself. Brady's dedication meant he was winning Super Bowls in his forties while Ibrahimovic was still playing when he was the wrong side of 40. Being able to talk openly with the few who understand the suffering and the sacrifice that are required – and downloading all their expertise – has helped Djokovic to go to new, previously unimaginable places. Other tennis players will look at Djokovic and accept they simply can't match him. 'If you're, say, number five or ten in the world, and you want to get to number one, you basically have to outwork whoever is at the top,' said O'Shannessy. 'So you go and have a look at Novak and see what he does on a daily basis – what he does in matches, how he prepares, his nutrition and what he does with his body – and you'll be like, "I don't know how to beat that." Novak sets the bar so high in terms of his professionalism. Just look at the temple that is his body. It's perfect for tennis. You're trying to outwork Novak? Good luck with that.'

No athlete is ageless. But Djokovic has been doing a fine job at repelling Father Time, with ex-coach Ivanisevic marvelling at how the player was moving around the court like a ninja. Astonishingly, Djokovic's physical conditioning in 2023 – the year he turned 36 – was almost as good as it was in his twenties. This isn't how it's meant to be. While Djokovic would have lost some explosive power and some of his maximum speed, that decline has been small, according to Gritsch. 'Novak seemed to still be in very good physical shape, still very close to his top level, and that's quite amazing,' Gritsch said. But it was possible he was playing at a higher level than ever before in 2023: an athlete known for his precision tennis has become even more precise, which made him more of a force. 'Over the years, Novak understood more about how to control his precision game and he became even more precise. What he might have lost physically was at least compensated by getting even more precise with his movement.'

Precision matters deeply to Djokovic. His serve now has extra precision. In Gritsch's view, the rhythm and the motion are perfectly suited to Djokovic's game, his personality and the way his body naturally moves. To understand Djokovic as an athlete, you have to know a little about biomechanic principles. 'It's about basic human movement principles,' Gritsch said. 'If the principles are right, you can play your own natural game, so it suits your own body. If you keep on working, and have the perfect set-up, and you have the rhythm, the balance and the stability, you will continue to increase your precision. And that's what happened.'

Djokovic was a remarkable tennis player in his twenties. He's even better in his thirties. Djokovic won 12 majors in his twenties, the rest in his thirties. 'One special thing with Novak is that I don't think anyone has really played at this level into their thirties and accomplished so much,' said Chris Evert. 'Half of his majors have come in his thirties, if I'm not mistaken, and you can attribute that to the physical as well as the mental side.'

Other coaches have admired how Ivanisevic enhanced Djokovic's game. Djokovic's abilities at the net are much improved – he's harder to pass now than he was a few years ago. Ivanisevic, one of the greatest servers in the history of the sport, helped Djokovic to improve that shot. Ivanisevic did what Djokovic asked of him: he brought 'some serve magic' to the team. 'Novak's serve is very effective. It wasn't 15 years ago but it is now,' Martin said. 'His forehand continues to improve and his backhand is awesome, as reliable as it comes. As the years have gone on, Novak has understood more about the front court and has become better and better at volleying. Goran has been super-helpful in that part of Novak's game.'

Gael Monfils, a Frenchman who is a few months older than Djokovic, noted the Serb has made game-changing improvements: 'Novak's doing stuff better. You can see he's serving much better now than he was at the beginning of his career. It's hard to imagine now but his forehand used to be [the part of his game] that would crack a little bit. And now, not at all. He's got stronger year after year.'

*

He's the future billionaire who hardly cares for money. No one in tennis history has won more prize money than Djokovic has – he's approaching $200 million, and that's before we even get to endorsement deals, bonuses and appearance fees – but it's not cash that excites him, that motivates him to keep on suffering on the practice and match courts. Djokovic has been at both extremes: as a boy, his family of five had next to nothing (just ten Deutschmarks at one point in the 1990s), and now he has what *Forbes* magazine might call generational wealth. While money has allowed him to live a more comfortable life, it hasn't in itself brought him joy. Rather than being motivated by money, Djokovic's obsession is purely how many Grand Slams he can win, and on being happy and fulfilled. 'I've never met someone who has achieved so much in his life and who has all the possibilities, and basically the world in the palm of his hand, and who is so modest and down to earth,' said Tipsarevic. 'Novak's the least materialistic person you could meet who is in his position.'

Money can warp athletes' mind and soften their will to win. That's never been a concern with Djokovic. 'Novak's not doing it for the money, for the big houses, the yachts and the private planes,' Obradovic said. 'He understands all that and the money that comes from tennis, of course, but it means nothing to him, believe me. Nothing. He's free like an eagle.

He's part of nature and he doesn't care. If you said to him, "What's your motivation? Do you need more money?", he would say, "No". You could ask: "Do you need this or that?" And he would say: "No, I need happiness." What he wants is to be a happy person. And where is he happy? On the tennis court. Not to be a recreational player. He still wants to compete at the highest level. He wants to fight. I talked with him so many times about all these subjects and all these things. Let's be honest, he's a superstar. And he's been like that all his life. But he's not counting on that. He still has his first love and that's tennis. Man, how has he managed that?'

Djokovic's attitude towards money is in keeping with his unpretentious approach to life. 'There's a humility and a modesty to Novak,' said Tipsarevic. That's not to say that Djokovic wouldn't like it if Tipsarevic called him the greatest tennis player of all time to his face. 'If I told Novak that I thought he was the GOAT, he wouldn't be embarrassed. He would like it very much. He knows my opinion. He's very, very quietly confident. This is not a person who is lacking in confidence. You have to be confident. There's no way you can be that good and that dominant, and become the greatest of all time, if you don't have that quiet confidence. He's just not being all Conor McGregor [the boastful, bombastic mixed martial arts fighter] about it, if you know what I mean?'

Fame and success haven't changed Djokovic, according to Cosmin Georgescu, his old roommate from Niki Pilic's academy in Germany. 'When I was coaching Ernests Gulbis, I arranged a practice with Novak at Wimbledon and it was the first time I had seen him in years. Novak was still the same guy. He was joking around a bit and he was interested in me, asking me how I was and how everything was going.' While Pilic himself said he was thrilled that Djokovic has become the greatest tennis player in history, he felt as though it was even more important that he had shown himself to be 'a really good human being'. 'Novak has won everything but he's relaxed and his feet are on the ground.'

Many athletes in Djokovic's position would be braggy and insufferable. He's a long way from that. Wherever you go in Belgrade, people have stories about a small act of kindness from Djokovic that hadn't made the news, or a moment that demonstrated his humanity and humility. Obradovic spoke of Djokovic as a superstar but as the simplest of superstars. There was the time a few years ago – Djokovic was a young man then – when Obradovic walked into the locker-room after practice and found him having a 'lazy massage': Obradovic called it that because a masseur was manipulating Djokovic's body and doing the stretching for him. He 'cursed so much' at Djokovic. About the only clean part of Obradovic's emotional reaction was when he said to Djokovic: 'Man, you're so lazy. I hate this.' Obradovic suggested to Djokovic that if you're capable of doing something for yourself, then that's what you should do, rather than asking someone else. Obradovic said to Djokovic: 'People will bring you what you need if they think you're the big guy. No, no, don't do that. Don't be like that. Do it yourself. You have to stay normal.'

That was about the last time that Obradovic ever felt as though he had to speak to Djokovic about not getting above himself. Over the years, he has seen how Djokovic is polite and respectful towards those around him, including staff cleaning and maintaining practice courts. Obradovic said that the way Djokovic eats is another indication of the player's humility – he doesn't put any food on his plate that he's going to leave and then throw away. He is careful about how much he takes and he eats it all. If he still wants a little more, he will take it. Obradovic said

Djokovic is that rare thing: the superstar who doesn't act like a superstar. 'All of us around him, who have been in his team, we don't think that he fully understands who he is. He's such a simple person.'

And yet – and Djokovic has been open about this – he has a big ego. And how his ego can play with him. For some time, Djokovic felt as though his ego was the enemy. But he has found that befriending his ego has allowed him to disarm and control it. 'Hey,' he has said to his ego, 'you're inside me, let's team up.' Djokovic has seen how his father 'likes to show off' about having a successful son; he laughed at how his dad obtained permission to hang giant banners of him from the building in Belgrade where the family have a restaurant, which were big enough for people to see from the highway as they drove into the city. But Djokovic himself isn't so interested in fame and celebrity or in acting like a star; he doesn't particularly like seeing himself on billboards, and that's not what fuels him, though he has come to accept that's part of being an elite tennis player with a portfolio of endorsements.

Keeping it simple has allowed Djokovic to stay true to himself and to achieve greatness, Obradovic said. 'That's why Novak is such a big champion – he's simple. From the age of ten until now, he's doing the same things but they are getting bigger and bigger. He's so patient. He goes step by step, making the small steps,' Obradovic said. 'Because of the stupid internet, everyone today feels as though they have to change everything the whole time but they are making a big mistake. Why? Think of your grandmother's soup. She is preparing some soup. You know the flavour. It's going to be the same every single day. Are you going to eat it? Yes, you will because you like it so much. We start to change things that are good. Novak knows not to do that.'

From a young age, Obradovic spoke to Djokovic about how genius is often simple, how the Beatles used two or three chords in many of their songs and how Nikola Tesla thought about his work in a simple way. 'When I was working with Novak, we did simple things. We didn't do anything special. People asked me why I was doing something with him and it was often because he was making so many mistakes. How are we going to clean up that part of his game? With repetition. Repeat, repeat and repeat and then you start to do the good things. Some days he was like a small lion trying to climb up a tree and always falling down. But then one day he got to the top of the tree. That came from repetition,' Obradovic said.

'I watch him when he's practising now and I have this feeling that every day he's still doing the same things that he has always done on court. He's watching the ball and expressing his energy every single time and that's something which is going to bring him back to the court tomorrow and the next day. The positive things that he's doing are very simple. He loves tennis, he's very dedicated to tennis and he's doing everything in his life – restricting whatever he needs to restrict – because of tennis. He still has the challenge. Whatever else happens in his life, he's still out there on the tennis court.'

16

GOAT

Going out naked in public once again. Not, as it turns out, one of Novak Djokovic's anxiety dreams but what it feels like, when he's awake, to speak openly and honestly, knowing he's probably going to get slammed for being so candid. Sharing your ambitions – verbalizing how you wish to win more Grand Slam titles than anyone else in the history of tennis – only invites accusations of arrogance and creates more pressure. And that's precisely why Djokovic, who seeks an uncomfortable life, has been so explicit about his goals.

He needs to feel that extra pressure, scrutiny and expectation because that energizes him and provokes him into elevating himself and his game. Most other players, who feel as though they're already living a high-pressure, high-stress existence, would rather not discuss their aspirations in full and in public. They'll deflect, they'll underplay, they'll call the other guy the favourite, even if that stretches credulity and insults people's intelligence. They'll leave plenty unsaid about what they're hoping to accomplish on the court because they think that will give them a quieter, easier life and, they're hoping, a smoother ride to a title. Djokovic, meanwhile, would rather put it all out there because he wishes to raise the stakes. By being so open, he's not just creating a mood and an environment in which others will demand more from him; he will be expecting more from himself. He's said it now; there's no backing down.

Djokovic's expressive nature – his willingness to be so open about how he is feeling and what he wants – is, to some degree, thanks to his father. A young Novak heard how Srdjan would always vocalize how he was feeling. Srdjan didn't hold anything in; he let it all out. This is the family that Djokovic's soul chose for him, he believes, giving him an upbringing that allowed him to learn life lessons such as those. It would appear Djokovic is inherently more open and transparent – more authentic – than many others in tennis. But there's also something calculated about talking so freely about his ambitions; he goes looking for more pressure, he's trying to feel uncomfortable. Only then does he feel the 'fire', as Dusan Vemic put it, and continue giving his all.

'The question with Novak has been, "Will he find enough reasons to keep going?" The last couple of years, he realized that even if it risked him sounding arrogant or something – which he isn't – he needed to put pressure on his own back,' said Vemic. 'Novak needs to have expectations for himself and from anybody and everybody as then he can have that fire and keep pushing and keep finding a reason why he should keep living the life of a world-class athlete. Why does Novak want more pressure? Because he thrives on it. That gives him that spark and fire. When the pressure is on him, that's when he plays his best tennis. You rarely see him underperform in those moments.'

After all these years on the tennis circuit, Djokovic is still connected with his inner child. He can still feel some of the love for tennis that he first felt as a four-year-old picking up a racquet for the first time in the Serbian mountains. That pure, simple joy is compatible with the sometimes messy, often complicated, always fraught business of setting and then chasing the grand goals of winning a record number of Grand Slam titles and spending more weeks at number one in the rankings than anyone else. In Djokovic's mind, any top-tier tennis player who doesn't articulate that they're chasing those same ambitions isn't being entirely honest. Since he was a child, Djokovic had two goals that propelled him through every practice and match: to win Wimbledon and to become the number one. In 2011, he achieved everything he had ever wanted and very quickly after that he realized it was time to dream new dreams. Greatness, in short. Nothing less than becoming the most successful tennis player of all time – the best in his golden generation with Roger Federer and Rafael Nadal, and also all generations. And for years, he backed himself to get there.

It's for others to say whether Djokovic is the GOAT; his focus has been on generating the big numbers to settle that debate and create that rare thing among tennis's chattering classes: consensus. Or – this being tennis, where fandom is more tribal than the sport's sometimes genteel sensibilities might suggest – about as close to it as you're ever going to get.

When you're making so much history, it's almost inevitable that you also become a tennis historian, and that's what happened with Djokovic, according to Boris Becker. You're in search of some context, some deeper understanding, of what you're achieving. For some time, Djokovic has been very aware of what legends of the sport did in years past and what he had to do to put himself above all those names. When Djokovic arrived on the tour, his childhood idol Pete Sampras was at the top of the men's leaderboard with 14 majors and people were openly wondering whether anyone would ever get close to that number. But then came the golden generation, with Federer, Nadal and Djokovic all passing the American, all getting into the twenties, the kind of numbers that were once considered impossible. For many years, Federer was considered the greatest of all time, with 20 Slams. But then he too was eclipsed by Nadal and Djokovic. The thought would have occurred to the Serb: if you want to be sure of remaining at the top of the tree for a good while yet, you must keep on winning as many majors as you can. Otherwise, who knows who might come along in the future and bump you down the list?

As you go deeper into your thirties, playing the Grand Slams takes more out of you – mentally, emotionally and physically. Scheduling becomes an art form, and Djokovic has embraced that. To some degree, he has been guided by how Federer did it, how you can play enough to keep your game at a high level, but not so much that you're ruined for the Grand Slams.

At 11 months, the tennis season is punishingly long and you can't possibly bring your best level to every event you play. The majors are the ultimate test for any tennis player but even more so when you're operating at Djokovic's level and you know that those are the titles that will define you. 'Novak tailors his seasons for his priorities, starting with the Grand Slams,' said Janko Tipsarevic. 'I don't think he necessarily prioritizes being number one but he's so good it happens anyway.' If Djokovic's head isn't quite right at the ATP tournaments, his team won't be fretting – they'll just waiting for the moment, because they know it's coming, when the Serb switches into Grand Slam mode. It's almost as if Djokovic is playing two different sports – regular tennis, that happens away from the majors, and then Grand Slam tennis, which makes his brain fizz.

'Novak's mind is as hard as a rock. You can see that by how he stayed at the top for so long by playing fewer tournaments,' said Dusan Lajovic. 'Usually players need matches, they need to be in the tournament rhythm, especially going into a Grand Slam, but for him that's not the case. After the results he has had, he has built the confidence that he doesn't have to play as much, not even just before a Grand Slam. Novak knows he can start slowly. He gets his rhythm by the fourth round and then he's almost unbeatable. It's not like he was born with the mentality like this. He's been working on this.'

It was many years ago that Djokovic accomplished everything that his father had ever wanted for him. But Djokovic still wants more. While he is happier in his mid-to-late thirties than he was earlier in his career, he's not so content or satisfied that he doesn't want to keep pushing, striving, seeking. Fatherhood hasn't dulled his ambition either. While it can be painful to leave his children for weeks at a time, that means that when he does travel to tournaments, he's even more motivated to make the trip worthwhile, which means nothing less than making the winner's speech on the Sunday afternoon. Being a dad can also be a motivation, with Djokovic driven by wanting to win Grand Slams in front of his children, on the occasions they travel with him and they're watching in the stadium. 'When you have achieved so many things, you mentally settle down. At some stage, you have to be content with what you achieved. That gives you more happiness in life,' said Gebhard Gritsch. 'But when I watch Novak playing, I can see he still thrives on competition in really tough matches. He just enjoys that so much. That keeps him going.'

It's incredible, said Daria Abramowicz, how Djokovic has stayed 'so hungry for more in tennis'. 'Even after all the years, Djokovic still has this will to compete. Is it about breaking records and being the GOAT? Or is it about the love for competition? Or maybe it's about the winning feeling, or about being acknowledged as the best, despite having less support and love from tennis fans than Roger Federer and Rafael Nadal? My take is that it's probably a little bit of everything. His motivation is constant. He also has determination and grit and that's very important for his mental performance.'

Clearly, each of tennis's Big Three wanted to be the best. But, in Abramowicz's view, each has been motivated in slightly different ways. Federer wished to be the maestro. Nadal is wired differently, said Abramowicz, saying that the Spaniard combines an off-court softness with a ferociously competitive nature on the court: 'Rafa has always fought for every point, bringing a huge level of energy.' Djokovic, meanwhile, wants to feel as though he's the best. 'Novak sometimes appears calm and collected and it looks like he's locked in. Sometimes it looks as though he's fighting something inside himself. Other times, he fights with his player's box or with the crowd. But he's always trying to find a solution to be the best,' Abramowicz said. 'Even if it doesn't go well on court for him today, he is looking for a way to ultimately prevail, to always become better and to go towards winning. My sense is that Novak wants a feeling of satisfaction and confirmation that he's the best.'

*

It's too simplistic, Todd Martin suggested, to say that Djokovic is driven to succeed. Actually, his former coach has observed, Djokovic's greatness has come from resisting failure. 'Novak has figured out how to resist failure. There's such a palpable willpower. He has a willpower that's hard to come by. Other people will say it's a determination to succeed. I don't know. I love positivity but that might be too simple. To me, there's both a persistence towards success but there's a high level of resistance to failure. For me, that will always resonate the most when observing Novak's remarkable success. There's something in Novak's mind that refuses to lose,' Martin said.

'I would say Novak and Rafa are the two best players at resisting failure. But that willpower is impossible to sustain. Literally impossible. Rafa has often had moments throughout the course of a season when he has struggled with it, perhaps because he lost some confidence in his movement or in the way he was hitting the ball so he has had these blips. But Novak can go three years without those blips. Now granted, he might then lose that willpower for a few months. At least that's the history. But he can sustain that willpower, which maybe can be dumbed down to saying that he has a remarkably high level of focus.' It's that 'incomparable resistance to failure' which has made Djokovic unbeatable for long stretches, Martin said. 'That willpower comes from his head and also from his heart. That willpower is within him. It's among him. It's also demanded of those around him.'

Mentally and emotionally, Djokovic is stronger than anyone else in tennis and, just as importantly, he is aware of that. That is a significant advantage, said Chris Evert, who in her playing days was known as the 'Ice Maiden' on account of her ability to stay cool and composed. 'When

Novak walks out on the court, he knows he's mentally and emotionally superior to any opponent. He knows his opponent might be more powerful and might show flashes of brilliance, but he accepts that and he also knows that his opponent might have let-downs, as well as nerves and unforced errors. Novak just knows himself and his strengths and weaknesses better than anyone else knows themselves,' Evert said. 'He's disciplined and very intentional with everything he does on and off the court, whether that's sleep or diet or training or practice. That carries over into his matches, where he's focused and totally in control. I've never seen anyone so intentional in everything he does. I love the way Novak values each point, playing each one as if it's a match point. There are very few unforced errors from him, very few dips in his concentration and play. He's the epitome of consistency. Over five sets, it's hard to beat him because of that mental focus.'

Dealing with the pressure is one of Djokovic's most important qualities. 'If you're going to win so many Grand Slams and become the best player in history, you need to be able to handle the pressure because that's not going to go down. All the time, that's only going up,' said Ronen Bega, Djokovic's former fitness trainer. 'When the tension is high, he functions very well. Sometimes players don't know how to control their emotions and the tension on court. But Novak is able to control his emotions and to direct his emotional energy in the right places.'

Can a Wimbledon final that lasted for almost five hours be described as an instant classic? Perhaps it can. And if ever there was an illustration of Djokovic's mental fortitude it was his victory over Roger Federer in the 2019 Wimbledon final, in which he saved two championship points before taking the fifth set 13-12 in a tiebreak. It was the longest ever

Wimbledon final and for the most part, Djokovic has acknowledged, Federer was the sharper that day. And yet Djokovic found a way of producing his highest level in the crucial moments, and that was enough. It helped, of course, that Djokovic was comfortable with winning or losing that match; as much as he wanted to win, and he was doing everything in his powers to lift that golden, pineapple-topped trophy again, he also accepted that it might not go his way, and there was something calming and freeing about that.

Even when Djokovic becomes emotional on court, you never get the sense he's panicking. 'It's amazing how Novak copes with difficult situations during matches,' Jelena Jankovic observed. 'Other players would panic or get really nervous. Like other players, he has ups and downs but what he's able to do better than other players is find a way to get himself up and stay calm and focused and really strong mentally in the important moments. At the crucial times of the match, he's the strongest one of all.'

But what if Djokovic's head isn't as still and calm as it might appear to his opponent or to those watching? What if, internally and externally, tennis feels to him like an endless firefight? While Djokovic has occasionally made winning Grand Slam titles look easy, that's not how it has ever felt inside his head – while you've been snacking on your strawberries, he's had years of inner turmoil. And it's not as if these jitters, insecurities and negative voices are only an occasional concern for Djokovic – they're there, in his head, every single time he plays a match. As Djokovic once told Maria Sharapova, he feels as though tennis is both a battlefield and a school of life: he's triggered more on court than he is anywhere else in life. In those high-pressure moments, all kinds of emotional issues – Djokovic has gone so far as to call them traumas – can surface.

Athletes tend to be presented as 'fearless warriors', Djokovic once told Chervin Jafarieh. In Djokovic's world, you're generally supposed to be robust, macho and emotionally cold and hard. If you open up, and admit to having any doubts, you risk being thought of as weak. But, as Djokovic once said, vulnerability is a beautiful thing. Just as he has been open about his ambitions, he has also been honest about the mental battles he has had to overcome in pursuit of those goals. He has flaws and weaknesses. Djokovic doesn't mind you knowing – other athletes will try to hide this about themselves – that he's an imperfect human being.

Everyone feels fear on a tennis court, Djokovic believes, and anyone who says otherwise is fibbing. It doesn't help, he thinks, when people are saying things such as 'fear doesn't exist'. He doesn't like it, he told *60 Minutes*, when he hears people in sport telling athletes: 'Just think positive thoughts – be optimistic.' That's not an approach that's ever going to work. If Djokovic is like everyone else in tennis – in that he also feels fear on court – what sets him apart? It's his ability not to stay in that emotional state for too long. When Djokovic was younger, he tried to ignore the doubts in his mind, but that was futile; they weren't going away anytime soon. Now when he's feeling negative, he acknowledges that feeling. That helps him to reset and then he's ready to go again.

Getting to a place where he's able to reset his head has taken a lot of practice. People talk about Djokovic as a born winner and how he was gifted a strong mind. No, not true, he has said. Discussing mental strength in that way is to miss or downplay how much time and energy he has put into the mental and emotional sides of tennis, to the extent that he has placed as much emphasis on training his mind as he has on his muscles and refining his technique. 'Novak has a beast mode on court but his mental strength isn't something he was born with,' said Viktor Troicki, Djokovic's old friend and former Davis Cup teammate. 'When he was younger, he had a lot of trouble in some moments with his focus, with the energy, with everything. But he has worked very hard on his mind and his focus and now he's almost perfected that part. Mentally, Novak's been growing and growing, and believing in himself more and more, and that's why he's the biggest right now, why he has become the best ever.'

Other players are aware of how much work Djokovic has put into developing his mind for tennis. 'Novak's got so much experience, he's been doing it for so long and he takes his mental game real serious,' said American Frances Tiafoe, a former US Open semi-finalist. 'He's got the desire that nobody else has. It's pretty much that simple. Novak's got stronger over the years. He's able to raise his level when it counts. Mentally, he goes to a different place and he's super calm.'

The mental training has included working for a while with the performance psychologist Jim Loehr, who considers Djokovic to be 'an exceedingly bright man' fascinated by abstract concepts, details and how the body and mind work together. Djokovic has also consulted with his spiritual guides, along with his team and family, to find a way of being in the best possible emotional state. But ultimately, Djokovic knows it's up to him as you shouldn't expect others to fix your problems. He also appreciates he's never going to fix his mind for good – he's never going to reach a moment where he has everything figured out because that's not how it works. That's why he's always looking for fresh ways to get back to his optimal state.

As Loehr has reflected, one of the trickiest things about tennis is the amount of time between points – with even longer gaps between games when changing ends – as your mind is always looking to go time-travelling. It's dragging you back to what went wrong or it's fast-forwarding to some moment in the future. There's a voice in Djokovic's head that keeps asking him on court: 'What's going to happen – am I going to win or not?' What's best for you is being more in the moment, thinking only of the point you're about to play. It's all too easy to become distracted, to be consumed by what-ifs and negative emotions, and to be down on your game and yourself. To be telling yourself that you're just not good today. Someone in Djokovic's orbit who understands the power of the mind to change how you experience the environment you're in is Wim Hof, the ice bath evangelist. As Djokovic once told Hof, there are environmental factors that can distract a tennis player, such as having a blinding sun in your eyes. Add that to the other insecurities in your mind and the danger is that all that negativity can flood your brain.

That's when Djokovic must try to shift the conversation in his head, to get back to the positive messages of telling himself that he is good enough, that he's going to try to perform to the best of his abilities and that however the match plays out, he will accept the result. It helps, Djokovic has found, to know that whatever has happened in the past, the next time he appears on court he will be disturbed and distracted in some fresh way. He's prepared for that.

Conscious breathing – being aware of his breathing – is the simplest and the most effective way for Djokovic to practise mindfulness in the white heat of a Grand Slam final or wherever else he finds himself feeling under stress or emotional duress. On occasion, Djokovic has felt a kind of choking sensation, with a shortness of breath, and that drains him of energy. It's in moments like that, or any kind of stressful stage of the match, that Djokovic focuses on his breathing, even if it's just for one or two breaths, though if he has time, he will do so for ten or more. He might even close his eyes for a few seconds as he does that as then he can truly feel himself being centred again.

Think of it as a kind of emotional and mental recovery process, with Djokovic trying to stop being so down on himself, regaining control and putting himself back into an optimal state. It's unrealistic for anyone, even someone who has trained his mind as much as Djokovic has, to stay in the present for an entire match, particularly one that lasts for hours. Where Djokovic elevates himself from other players is accepting he has lost his focus and then quickly recovering in his mind.

Tennis is a complex sport – with so many different dimensions, which challenges Djokovic on every level – and yet when he's truly in the moment, he finds he doesn't have to think. On the very best days, he's in a flow state – the ultimate for any tennis player, athlete or human being – when everything comes easily and automatically and he's just doing, rather than thinking then doing.

Can you put a percentage on how much of elite tennis is in the mind? Djokovic's father thinks you can – he says tennis at the highest level is 95 per cent in the mind. Everyone can serve and hit forehands and backhands – but what separates the champions from the solid professional, Srdjan has indicated, is what's going on in your head. His son is doing what he can to ensure that his self-belief always out-hits the fears and insecurities in his head. Ideally, Djokovic wants to reach a state where he doesn't just think he's going to win but he feels it in every single cell in his body because, as he once told Jay Shetty, 'that's when the magic happens'.

What does it say about Djokovic that he's able to be so open about those fears and doubts? 'Novak's very transparent about a lot of things,' said Craig O'Shannessy. 'When things are going well, he'll let you know, and when things aren't going well, quite often he will explain that. He tries to be as open as he possibly can.' But O'Shannessy said there are limits to Djokovic's openness: 'Like all players, Novak doesn't want to give away secrets. There's definitely a level of secrecy that goes on with being an elite tennis player.'

If there's mayhem in Djokovic's head whenever he plays a tournament, his mind was contending with even more fears and concerns at the 2023 Australian Open. He was back in the country that, just a year earlier, had housed him in an immigration detention centre and then cast him out for being a potential menace to society. Others were calling this Djokovic's revenge tour but living in the past, resentful and vengeful, wasn't his style. Of greater concern: how would the Australian public treat him on his return? Another complication was a tear in his hamstring – other players might not have even played, but he had the help of 'placenta doctor' Marijana Kovacevic, a Serb who has been known to use a horse placenta treatment. Even more unsettling was how some in Melbourne seemed to be suggesting that Djokovic was faking that injury. Why was it, Djokovic wondered, that people seemed to doubt him more than others? Why couldn't they accept what he was saying? Some around Djokovic were starting to feel as though dark forces were conspiring against him to disrupt his efforts to win the Australian Open for a tenth time and to share the men's Grand Slam record with Rafael Nadal with 22 titles.

Adding to the uncertainty in Djokovic's head was the outrage over a video taken at Melbourne Park that showed his father Srdjan standing next to a man holding a flag with Vladimir Putin's face on it and who was also wearing a T-shirt with the pro-war 'Z' symbol. Less than a year after Russia's invasion of Ukraine, the video was a big, ugly story in the second week of the Grand Slam – which is just when a player doesn't want to have anything else to think about – with Ukraine's ambassador to Australia urging Tennis Australia to remove Srdjan's accreditation. Srdjan, who said his family had experienced the horror of war and wished only for peace, suggested he had been unintentionally caught up in controversy; when posing for pictures with tennis supporters, he had been unaware of what the man had been holding and wearing. Djokovic said his father had been 'misused'.

To avoid being a distraction, Srdjan left an empty seat for Djokovic's next match, his semi-final. It was empty again for the final, which saw Djokovic beat Greek Stefanos Tsitsipas in straight sets. For years, Srdjan had put all his energy and money into helping his son realize his seemingly impossible dream of tennis greatness, dealing with the loan sharks and the naysayers. But when Djokovic had this moment – with his level at the Australian Open about as high as it's ever been – his father thought it was for the best if he was elsewhere, not at Melbourne Park but in front of a television. That hurt Djokovic. In the moments after beating Tsitsipas, Djokovic pointed first at his head and then at his heart. Soon he was as emotional as he had ever been after winning a Grand Slam title.

After climbing up into his player's box to celebrate with his team and his family, Djokovic became so overwhelmed that he could no longer stand up: he lay down on the floor and sobbed. On returning to the court, the tears kept on coming.

He sat down on his bench, head down, weeping into a towel.

*

You don't get to the top of tennis – or near the top – without experiencing a few psychodramas, both your own and those of your opponents. But, for all their practice competing against others on the tour, elite players often find reading Djokovic's mind difficult, as hard to decipher as Cyrillic script. 'Before a match, Rafa will be jumping up and down and intimidating you a bit with his intensity, whereas Novak is calmer before and during a match. It's a little trickier to read his mind,' said Casper Ruud, a Norwegian who was on the other side of the net at Roland Garros in 2023 when Djokovic won his 23rd Grand Slam title. Djokovic is, after all these years, still a mystery to some of his peers. Gael Monfils, who lost the first 19 tour-level matches he played against Djokovic, the most lopsided series in the history of the ATP Tour, is still trying to figure out how the Serb thinks. 'What makes Novak's mind so strong? I really don't know how to give you a rational answer. That's a tough one. I wish I knew why, to be honest, as I would try to use that for myself. He's a legend. He has something special. And I feel as though even if Novak explained his mind to us, it would be tough for [anyone else] to replicate.' And if you don't know what Djokovic is feeling and thinking, what chance do you possibly have of getting into his head?

Djokovic, though, is generally more successful at first peering into an opponent's head – and then getting inside it. Tennis players are forever looking to leave mini psychological bruises on their opponents. When changing ends, or when sitting down on his bench between games, Djokovic is looking to make eye contact with his opponent: that's one way of seeing how his rival is feeling on court. There's no physical contact in tennis, as Djokovic noted in an interview with *60 Minutes*, but there's plenty of eye contact; you can jab away at each other with your eyeballs. Djokovic is aware of what's on the big screen in case it shows his opponent hydrating. Then Djokovic will be very interested: how's his opponent drinking his water today? Curious to understand how his adversary is feeling and what he's thinking, Djokovic is gathering as much information as he can. Is his rival's shirt clingy with sweat? How's his opponent breathing? There's more: Djokovic is also scrutinizing how his opponent is talking to his coaching staff.

It helps that Djokovic has been in these situations so many times before. More often than not, that allows the Serb to get a good read of how his opponent is handling the occasion.

What's clear to Ruud, and so many others, is how Djokovic has been able to play his finest tennis on the biggest points, which is an indication of a player's mental strength and ability to deal with the pressure of the occasion. 'When it matters the most, Novak plays some of his best tennis almost all the time,' said Ruud. 'He has stepped it up in the most clutch moments of his career. Of course, you're going to lose some matches and titles but it feels as though 95 per cent of the time in tough matches he finds some kind of inner drive or motivation to play his best. He's been very open about the mental part of the game. Anyone can play a forehand or a backhand but can they do it when they are under pressure or when they're playing the most important points? Novak's been able to do that, which is why he has pretty much on top of every record. Novak has taken his mental game to the highest level. He's a tough warrior. He never backs down, never gives up. Novak has been incredible. The last three or four years, it's been ridiculous what he has been able to do.'

Twenty-three Grand Slam singles titles was an unprecedented number in men's tennis: with his victory in Paris, Djokovic became the most successful male player in history (as well as the first man to win each of the four majors at least three times each, which was either the treble quadruple or the quadruple treble). This wasn't Djokovic's first opportunity to move above Federer and Nadal on the Grand Slam leaderboard. That had come in the 2021 US Open final when Djokovic had been swinging for a calendar-year Grand Slam – having already won that year's Australian Open, fought back from two sets down to beat Stefanos Tsitsipas in the Roland Garros final and also been victorious at Wimbledon – only to lose meekly to Daniil Medvedev. That occasion in New York City in 2021 was a reminder of how even the greatest athletes have off days, that a GOAT can also be human. On the Roland Garros clay in 2023, Djokovic found a way of countering Ruud's forehand, the gathering pressure and expectation and all his stormy thoughts.

For most observers, that was the moment when Djokovic settled the debate about who should be considered the greatest, though naturally there were some dissenters, including the most hardcore of Fed-heads. Djokovic has spent more than 400 weeks as the world number one, and over 100 more than the next on the list, Federer. Janko Tipsarevic suggested that the 'head-to-head battles' were further confirmation of the Serb's greatness. Djokovic won 27 matches against

Federer with 23 defeats and, at the time of writing, he was also ahead in his series with Nadal.

Almost from the beginning, since Djokovic was a boy, his father was telling everyone in Belgrade how his son would be the greatest tennis player of all time. There were a few eyerolls at the time. It was when Djokovic was in his thirties that most in tennis caught up with how Srdjan had been right all along. For a few years, people in tennis debated which of the Big Three should be regarded as the GOAT (though 'debated' might give the impression that this conversation was always cordial and well-mannered, which it wasn't).

The purists, the traditionalists, the style-conscious and all the Fed-heads articulated the case for Federer when he had won more majors than anyone else, and they gave him extra points for artistic merit. Others made the case for Rafael Nadal, for also winning an absurd number of Grand Slams and for the uncompromising way he went about it. But the more Djokovic kept winning majors – the more he spoke openly about his ambitions, and then used the resulting pressure to elevate himself and his game – the clearer it became that he was the greatest. Some things in tennis are undoubtedly subjective – who has the prettiest backhand? – but others aren't, and when determining who the GOAT is, you have to go with the hard data on who has won the most majors, which is now Djokovic. That might upset those who don't think it's fair to compare the generations but that seems like the most sensible way to judge true greatness.

Djokovic's mentor, Niki Pilic, said the data is compelling. 'In tennis, there is evidence for how good a player is. That evidence is the numbers, and those numbers tell you that Novak is the best player of all time.

Do people want to hear that or not? That's another story. But Novak has won more Grand Slams than anyone else,' he said. 'I mean, Federer played some fantastic tennis, there's no doubt about that. And Nadal won Roland Garros so many times. But when you look at the numbers, it's clear. If you share a generation with Federer and Nadal, and Murray too, and you still spend more than 400 weeks as the world number one, that's incredible.'

Djokovic plays every match twice. The first time is in the cinema in his head before he walks out on court. Naturally, he's picturing himself winning that match as he believes there's power in that. Visualization has been one of Djokovic's mental practices since he was a small child, imagining what it would look and feel like to be the Wimbledon champion, and he has continued doing so throughout every stage of his tennis life. Djokovic had pictured becoming the most successful male tennis player in history, with a win in Paris in 2023, and so that's what he did.

*

Defeats don't chew on Djokovic's soul. When he loses a match – even a Grand Slam final he could or even should have won – he learns from the experience and then, almost instantaneously, he moves on. Regrets are only going to slow him down. Far better to look forward than to live in the past. 'Novak's got this amazing ability to bounce back and to move forward. He's relentless,' said Dusan Vemic. 'All the losses, as soon as they happen, they're already in the past, and he has the ability to look forward. Someone else who had the same experiences might be haunted by them for days, weeks, months, years or forever. But Novak has this ability to grow from each and every experience. His mind is brilliant – he finds a way, whether the experience was good or bad, to use that to make a better version of himself. There aren't many athletes like Novak Djokovic.'

For Dusan Lajovic, the most impressive part of Djokovic's mind is how his friend and countryman is able to 'leave things in the past'. 'Novak loses a tough match somewhere, and then at the next tournament, you don't see that bothering him. He's able to forget things,' said Lajovic, who has been ranked inside the world's top 25. 'Novak has a way of processing defeats in the right way.'

In the moment, losing can be devastating. Djokovic appreciates that this might sound weird, but he adores that painful feeling, as it's a reminder of how much he still cares. But that's not to say that a defeat is going to put him into a spiral. Usually, it's the opposite; defeats can make him soar. In Djokovic's mind, losing a match isn't the end of the world or even close. His late mentor Kobe Bryant used to say that failure was part of success because of everything you take from those experiences. And maybe failure is the wrong word here. There's a quote from Sadhguru, an Indian mystic and yoga practitioner, which has resonated with Djokovic: 'For a committed person, there's no such thing as failure.' When someone's committed to doing something – such as trying to win an unprecedented number of majors – you're going to be focused before and after any setback. That's not going to change how you feel about your goal, and that's why there's no failure. You're better for the experience – you've forgiven yourself for not raising your game at the decisive moments, and you have considered where you need to improve – and now you move on.

Athletes aren't the 'almighty' superbeings or 'demi-gods' that people make them out to be, Djokovic said in a conversation with Chervin

Jafarieh. He's noticed how some fans can recall all his best moments, all the occasions when he demonstrated a strong mind. Is that because they like to draw parallels between what's happening in their own lives and any adversity Djokovic is facing on a tennis court, and so when he does well, they feel as though they're somehow part of that success? But there have also been times when Djokovic wasn't able to play the right shots at the right moments. The pressure was on and yet he didn't surge to victory, as you might have expected him to. At decisive moments, Djokovic served double-faults or he missed easy shots. A tennis player competing at Djokovic's level is going to win a bunch of titles but is also going to have some matches when things don't go their way, and he wishes people would talk about that a bit more. That would give the tennis public a more nuanced view of tennis players. As much as Djokovic is a perfectionist in the way he prepares for matches, he's also accepting of how he isn't going to play flawless tennis every day.

One of Djokovic's superpowers – the ability to avoid marinating himself in regret and self-pity after a defeat, and instead become a stronger athlete as a result of any setbacks – was evident after the 2023 Wimbledon final. If Djokovic hadn't put a drive volley into the net when he had a break point in the second game of the fifth set, it's very likely he would have gone on to defeat Carlos Alcaraz. It was an awkward shot as the wind inside Centre Court had caught the ball and he wasn't able to hit an overhead and instead found himself playing a drive volley while falling backwards. There's a parallel universe in which Djokovic hit a winner with that volley and went on to be Wimbledon champion once again, which meant he would have arrived at the US Open later that summer with a chance to complete the calendar-year Grand Slam. But he didn't spend the rest of the summer thinking about what might have been on Centre Court or contemplating how he had lost to a 20-year-old opponent who was closer in age to his son Stefan than to himself.

Playing against the younger generation can 'awaken a beast in me', Djokovic told *60 Minutes*. He was so 'pissed off' by that defeat he felt as though he needed to win every match he played during that summer's North American hard-court swing. That Wimbledon defeat stung; it also helped him. Djokovic responded by asking more of himself, pushing even harder and becoming a better tennis player. To some degree, Djokovic was happy to have lost that Wimbledon final, he would tell the *Sunday Times* six months later, because it was a defeat that 'got me going'. It was an animated Djokovic who saved Alcaraz's championship point in the Cincinnati heat, eventually winning the three-set final after almost four hours and celebrating, Incredible Hulk-style, by shredding his shirt with his hands. That felt like a significant moment, a big, emotional response to anyone in tennis who had been wondering whether, with one narrow Wimbledon defeat, Djokovic was somehow finished as a Grand Slam-winning force.

Too ancient to win majors? Hardly. Later that summer in New York City, Djokovic would shake with emotion after becoming the oldest US Open men's singles champion. Even more significantly, of course, Djokovic's 24th Grand Slam made him the most successful player – male or female – since the professional era began in 1968. When you're playing for history, it's even more important for Djokovic to stay in the moment, and not to spend too much time thinking about the record you're chasing, which was why he had asked his team and family not to talk about history before he played Medvedev. Serena Williams had won 23 major singles titles. But with his win over Medvedev – one of the most hard-fought straight-sets victories of his tennis life, with the second set alone lasting an hour and three quarters, and with the Serb needing to draw on what he called the 'innocent child energy' of his daughter Tara, who was smiling courtside – Djokovic had one more.

For all the customized items of clothing that Djokovic wore in 2023 to celebrate making history – we're talking here about the jackets with the numbers on them that were produced in Melbourne, Paris and New York – the most meaningful was the T-shirt he put on in the moments after winning the US Open. Twenty-four was the number that Kobe Bryant had worn for the Los Angeles Lakers, and Djokovic wanted to use the moment to remember his friend with a T-shirt with both their pictures on it and the words 'Mamba Forever'.

It was the fourth year – after 2011, 2015 and 2021 – that Djokovic had won three Grand Slams. And the third season, having done the same in 2015 and 2021, that he had appeared in the maximum number of matches at the majors – 28 – and won 27 of them, coming just one victory short of calendar-year perfection (in 2015, his only defeat had been to Stan Wawrinka in the Roland Garros final). Of those seasons, 2023 was the most astonishing of all as that was the year he turned 36. Closer to 40 than 30 and he was producing some of his finest tennis against opponents who, in some cases, were 10 or even 15 years younger than him.

By winning the 2023 US Open, Djokovic tied Margaret Court, but there are a couple of asterisks against the Australian's body of work, one being that she won 13 of those titles when tennis was still amateur. Another is that 11 of Court's majors came at the Australian Open during a period – spanning both the amateur and professional eras – when many top players didn't bother travelling to that event, resulting in a weaker field. Court was another reason for Djokovic to keep on pushing in 2024. There would be much to play for, driven by a desire to create as much history as humanly possible at the Slams.

Everyone has an occasional off day, even Djokovic, who wasn't quite himself at the 2024 Australian Open, where he lost in the semi-finals to Jannik Sinner, for what was his first defeat at Melbourne Park since 2018. Striving to reach 25 majors, and to put himself out there on his own ahead of Court, Djokovic was astounded by his level: just how inexplicably low it was on a stage, the Rod Laver Arena, where he had previously experienced so many soaring highs. In the first two sets of a four-set loss, Djokovic felt as though he wasn't doing much right at all. In his analysis, it was one of the worst matches he had ever played at the Grand Slams. This wasn't a familiar feeling for Djokovic. Ten times he had had the best possible start to a season, winning the Australian Open just a month into the new year, setting him up for the rest of the tennis calendar. Not this time, though. But, as surprising as that performance had been, it was also a reminder of how Djokovic's tennis had been so exceptional in Melbourne for so many years, to the point that his excellence had long been taken for granted by most. The expectation, absurd as it was, was that Djokovic would never have an off day.

Have a rough day in Indian Wells and it's going to seem as though all the billboards in the desert about the tournament being 'Tennis Paradise' are mocking you. Returning to competition at the Indian Wells Tennis Garden in California in March, Djokovic lost in the third round to Luca Nardi, a 20-year-old Italian ranked outside the world's top 100 and a 'lucky loser' (meaning he had been beaten in the qualifying rounds but was given a spot in the main draw after someone else withdrew). A few days later, Djokovic announced he wouldn't be playing in Miami, the second half of America's Sunshine Swing, because 'at this stage of my career, I'm balancing my private and professional schedule'. Something very surprising happened: Djokovic went into the European clay-court swing without a title to his name that season.

In another unexpected development, he also arrived on the blood-orange courts of Monte Carlo – for his opening tournament of the European clay-court season – without Goran Ivanisevic, after their five year-collaboration, which had brought no little drama and tennis history, came to an end. In Djokovic's view, their 'on-court chemistry had its ups and downs, but our friendship was always rock-solid', while Ivanisevic was saying they had grown tired of each other and he felt as though he could no longer help. A few weeks later, there was more change in Djokovic's team; he split with fitness trainer Marco Panichi and rehired Gebhard Gritsch. But while some in tennis catastrophized, speculating wildly about what this all meant for Djokovic's future, his supporters were resolute: this was no time for panic. There had been uncertain times, even downturns, before, and remember how he had recovered from those to add another layer of greatness? Going into the Australian Open, the objective had been to win all four majors and a first Olympic gold medal, which would have been an unprecedented season in men's tennis. While that golden season was no longer possible, Djokovic wasn't discouraged: he was going to keep on swinging, sliding, seeking.

*

Why constrain discussions of Djokovic's greatness to tennis?

In recent years, it has increasingly felt as though it goes beyond that, and he should be compared with athletes across all sports. 'It's not only about tennis now. [Novak] is in the conversation about the greatest athletes of our time,' said Chris Evert. 'That's the recognition he's getting now.' Viktor Troicki is another who believes that Djokovic is among the greatest athletes in the world and you suspect he's not just saying that because they're friends and countrymen. 'For sure, with his records, Novak is one of the best athletes in the world,' Troicki said. 'Can you say he's the greatest athlete of all? Comparing athletes from different sports is tough, and there are so many great athletes around the world and across sports, but what you can say is that Novak is up there, that he's on that list.' It felt as though Gael Monfils spoke for many of the current players on the tennis tour when he said: 'Is Novak the greatest athlete in the world today? That's really subjective. It's a personal opinion, I guess, and it depends on how you rate tennis. But if you're looking at the top ten greatest athletes globally, Novak's one of those ten.'

Djokovic's midnight-black hair is now flecked with grey but his mind is as fierce and energetic as ever, particularly in the most intense moments – how else to explain how, of the 18 tiebreaks he played at the majors in 2023, he won 16? Tennis players aren't supposed to be this good in their mid-to-late thirties. But Djokovic doesn't care much for what he is supposed to be doing; here is someone who when he sees the word 'impossible' notes that the same letters can spell out, 'I'm possible'. Djokovic doesn't believe in limits. They're only an illusion of your mind, he has reflected, and why would he want that? And, anyway, there are so many more interesting things going on inside Djokovic's head.

INDEX

Imaz, Pepe
'Amor y Paz' 117–21
hugging 118–19
'love and peace' 117–22
impersonations of others 45, 60–5
inat 14. *see also* anger
Indian Wells 2024: 275–6
injuries 80–1, 82, 128, 134, 264–5
inner child work 51, 143–4, 253
Instagram 125, 126, 211
Ivanisevic, Goran 237, 238–9, 244, 276
Ivanovic, Ana 10, 13, 62

Jafarieh, Chervin 33, 53, 126–7
Jankovic, Jelena 8, 13–14, 42
Jolovic, Milan 43
journaling 125–6

Khan, Don 207–8
King, Billie Jean 195
Kopaonik 17–18
Kosovo 43
Kovacevic, Marijana 264
Kyrgios, Nick 116, 179, 186, 225, 228

Lajovic, Dusan 173
Latifi, Hossein 200, 203, 205–6, 207
Laver, Rod 182
Lawn Tennis Association 42
and Novak's British citizenship 37–41
Loehr, Jim 261, 262
'love and peace' 117–21

Madden, Mark 195
Markovic, Neven 5
Martin, Todd 45–7, 52
McEnroe, John 64–5, 100, 120, 150, 175
Medjedovic, Hamad 173
Medvedev, Daniil 174, 182, 228, 273–4
Melbourne 212, 216–17
Melzer, Jurgen 50, 52, 83
mental approaches
focus at a young age 21–2, 33–4
psychological aspects of tennis 47–8
visualization 20–1, 270
mental strength 28, 31, 257–63, 267–8, 270–2
Miami Open 101, 134, 276
mindfulness. *see* breathwork
mindset changes 45–9, 52–6, 58, 65, 97–8
Monfils, Gael 80, 266
movement around the court 24–5, 135–6, 138–9, 158, 160
Murray, Andy 41, 61, 66, 75, 101, 115, 131, 141, 143, 226

Nadal, Rafael 45, 47–9, 63, 64, 100, 101, 126, 140–1, 157–8, 182–3, 228, 256
and failure 257
before matches 155–6, 266
rivalry with Novak 46–8, 53–4, 100, 164–7, 194, 254, 256, 268–70
Wimbledon 2018: 155

unconventionality 109–15
US Open 181–2
  2007: 60
  2011: 100
  2018: 161–2
  2020: 192
  2021: 182, 268
  2023: 273–4

vaccine controversy 199–210, 219–20,
  222–4, 226–8
Vajda, Marian 46, 50, 54–6, 122
  dropped by Novak 135
  returns to team 138
'Valley of the Pyramids' 104–7
Vemic, Dusan 8, 21–2, 52–3
Visoko 104

visualization 20–1, 270
volleying 161, 244–5, 272
Vucic, Aleksandar 215

Wawrinka, Stan 145
Williams, Serena 60, 273–4
Wimbledon Lawn Tennis
  Championships 108, 113,
  180–1
  2011: 99
  2016: 144–5
  2018: 155, 156
  2019: 180–1, 258–9
  2022: 228
  2023: 172, 272–3
wolves, importance to Novak 123–4
Wozniacki, Caroline 60

ACKNOWLEDGEMENTS

One of the joys of writing this book was a long weekend in Belgrade. The people I met in the city – including in Novak Djokovic's old neighbourhood, Banjica, and at his old tennis club, Partizan – were, almost without exception, warm and open. As I quickly discovered, it seems as though pretty much everyone in Belgrade speaks impeccable English and almost everyone has a Djokovic story they want to tell, often about a small act of kindness. Reflecting the global nature of tennis and Djokovic's life, my research took me far beyond Belgrade: I'm grateful to all who have shared their insights (most of them on the record, but some, while very happy to provide background information, didn't want their names to appear in these pages).

Special thanks to Slobodan Maricic of BBC Serbia for kindly helping me find some of the voices in this book and for patiently translating articles in the Serbian media, and to Tom Hiddleston for his perceptive, thought-provoking WhatsApp messages about this project. As ever, I'm thankful for the support and encouragement of my agents at David Luxton Associates: Nick Walters, David Luxton and Rebecca Winfield. It's been a pleasure working with Trevor Davies at Octopus, along with Leanne Bryan, Matthew Grindon, Ailie Springall, Lucy Carter, Nic Jones, Giulia Hetherington and the rest of their fabulous team.

PICTURE CREDITS